TRAINING FOR YOUNG DISTANCE RUNNERS

Laurence S. Greene, PhD
University of Colorado at Boulder

Russell R. Pate, PhD
University of South Carolina

Human Kinetics

Library of Congress Cataloging-in-Publication Data

Greene, Laurence S., 1960-
    Training for young distance runners / Laurence S. Greene, Russell
R. Pate.
        p.   cm.
    Includes bibliographical references and index.
    ISBN 0-87322-406-X
    1. Running for children.   2. Marathon running--Training.
I. Pate, Russell R.   II. Title.
GV1061.18.C45G74   1997
796.4'2'083--dc20

96-26110
CIP

ISBN: 0-87322-406-X

Human Kinetics would like to express their thanks to Mahomet-Seymour High School and St. Joseph-Ogden High School and their coaches and athletes for their assistance in obtaining many of the photos in *Training for Young Distance Runners*.

Acquisitions Editor: Martin Barnard; **Developmental Editor:** Ann Brodsky; **Assistant Editors:** Julie Marx Ohnemus, Andrew Smith, and Jim Burns; **Editorial Assistant:** Coree Schutter; **Copyeditor:** Bonnie Pettifor; **Indexer:** Theresa Schaefer; **Graphic Designer:** Stuart Cartwright; **Graphic Artist:** Francine Hamerski; **Photo Editor:** Boyd LaFoon; **Cover Designer:** Jack Davis; **Cover Photographer:** © Photo Network/ Mary Messenger; **Interior Photographer:** Chris Brown unless otherwise indicated; **Illustrator:** Keith Blomberg; **Mac Artist:** Jennifer Delmotte; **Printer:** Versa Press

Human Kinetics books are available at special discounts for bulk purchase. Special editions or book excerpts can also be created to specification. For details, contact the Special Sales Manager at Human Kinetics.

Printed in the United States of America   10 9 8 7 6 5 4

Human Kinetics
Web site: http://www.humankinetics.com/

United States: Human Kinetics, P.O. Box 5076, Champaign, IL 61825-5076
1-800-747-4457
e-mail: humank@hkusa.com

Canada: Human Kinetics, 475 Devonshire Road, Unit 100, Windsor, ON N8Y 2L5
1-800-465-7301 (in Canada only)
e-mail: humank@hkcanada.com

Europe: Human Kinetics, P.O. Box IW14, Leeds LS16 6TR, United Kingdom
+44 (0)113-278 1708
e-mail: humank@hkeurope.com

Australia: Human Kinetics, 57A Price Avenue, Lower Mitcham, South Australia 5062
(08) 82771555
e-mail: liahka@senet.com.au

New Zealand: Human Kinetics, P.O. Box 105-231, Auckland Central
09-523-3462
e-mail: humank@hknewz.com

Contents

Foreword

I've been coaching high school age runners for more than 42 years now, and have been a runner for even longer. Running has been a big part of my life, and has provided me many great experiences, including 19 state x-country championships, 18 national x-country championships, and coaching on the U.S. Olympic staff in 1988.

Much more satisfying to me than the titles and honors is to be a part of the development of young runners, and seeing them enjoy the sport is some of the special ways I have. As teenagers, runners' improvement can be dramatic. A demanding training schedule combined with the proper motivation will often produce results far exceeding the athlete's or coach's expectations. At York High School we've had 160 runners achieve all-state honors, and another 9 go on to be collegiate all-Americans, with many of them reaching performance levels no one would predict when they entered the program as freshmen.

The benefits of distance running at an early age are similar, in many respects, to the benefits of running at any age. Running requires discipline. Rolling out of bed each morning before 6 a.m. to get three to ten miles in before school or work takes dedication. It also keeps you away from bad habits and promotes positive ones. Instead of staying out late and partying, then sleeping in and being late for school, the disciplined runner is getting a good night's sleep and feeling refreshed for the start of the day.

The fitness benefits of running are obvious. Show me a fat runner and I'll show you a slow runner who fatigues quickly. But besides promoting leanness, running develops an individual's cardiovascular system and provides many other health benefits.

Discipline and fitness aside, perhaps the biggest payoff of running as a teenager is the opportunity for self-development. A coach can help, but in the end the athlete is the one who determines how much he or she can accomplish in running. Some runners learn how to set and meet goals, others learn how to measure themselves against and exceed personal standards of performance, and still others learn and survive the ups and downs of competition. Most high school runners should and do experience all of these things.

In *Training for Young Distance Runners*, Larry Greene and Russ Pate help ensure that aspiring runners and their coaches will share in the many benefits of running. This book will help you check your approach to training, and make sure that it's built upon the right principles. Once you know it's sound, you can tailor the information to meet your specific running program's needs.

Smart runners are typically the best runners, so read the book, then put it to use. And keep running—to make the most of your potential as a person and an athlete.

Joe Newton
Head X-Country and Track & Field Coach
Elmhurst (IL) York High School

Preface

Training for Young Distance Runners seeks to provide runners 12 to 18, their coaches and parents, sport scientists, and sports medicine professionals with the information, techniques, and programs that will produce the best possible outcomes for young competitive runners. Two major themes convey our philosophy in the book. First, positive outcomes require a developmental approach to planning training and competition. This means that all of the young runner's experiences should promote a gradual progression toward his ultimate potential—whether it is to make the varsity team or to compete in the Olympic games. In this developmental approach, the most important goal of all is self-improvement.

The second major theme of this book is that training young runners involves the art of applying science. This philosophy, made popular by Frank Dick (former director of coaching for the British Athletics Federation), means that planning successful programs requires both an understanding of the scientific foundations of distance running and a creativity in designing training and competitive experiences.

We'll provide the scientific principles and guidelines you'll need to make good decisions about the types and amounts of training that will bring out the best results for each individual. Because each runner is unique and has specific training needs, we don't offer a "paint-by-numbers" approach with lists of daily training sessions. Instead, we present principles and procedures to help you apply the science of running to the art of designing and implementing training. With this scientific background as your canvas, you can become the artist by using your creativity to develop a masterpiece: an endurance athlete who gradually acquires the fitness and skill to perform at her greatest potential.

Training for Young Distance Runners is divided into three parts. After we present a brief introduction about youth distance running, part I (chapters 1-5) covers topics on the science of distance running: developmental factors, nutrition, physiology, psychology, and biomechanics. In part II (chapters 6-8), we present information about training principles and methods. You'll learn about all of the key training methods for developing runners, including technique training, circuit and weight training, hill running, and specialized interval training. Finally, in part III (chapters 9-12), we guide you through the step-by-step process in designing an effective training program. This process is like a journey that begins with goal setting and planning, then uses selective training methods to help runners progress to their final destination: their fullest potential as endurance athletes.

Acknowledgments

I am very grateful to a good friend, Ed Prytherch, for helping to create several of the figures and for sharing his excellent strategies for training young distance runners. Thanks also to Catherine Lempesis, a superior coach, who kindly invited me to be a part of the 1993 South Carolina state champion Spring Valley Girls' track and field team.

Thanks to those who offered their expertise in sport science and training: Dr. Jeff Simons, Cyndi Long, Don Kardong, and my coauthor and former professor, Dr. Russ Pate. And to two former coaches, John Brogle and Al Schmidt—I am grateful for your guidance.

Special thanks to Malcolm Coomber, my friend and former coach, who guided me to my best performances and showed me that with proper preparation, athletes can reach levels beyond their dreams. Malcolm's influence and ideas about training are present throughout this book. Here's to 15 years of inspiring and insightful collaboration about a passion that, more than anything else, has shaped both of our lives: the pursuit of excellence in athletics!

—Larry Greene

I would like to extend sincerest thanks to my colleagues on the faculty in the Department of Exercise Science at the University of South Carolina and to the graduate students with whom we are honored to work. It is the personal support and intellectual stimulation provided by these people that have enabled me to pursue professional projects such as this book.

In addition, I wish to acknowledge the coaches who are responsible for developing in me a lifelong love of running. They are my father, Robert Pate, who guided me into track and field and who helped me survive the inevitable losses that come to young athletes; John Chew, who showed me how to enjoy distance running and who introduced me to the sport's wonderful culture; and the late Vern Cox of Springfield College, who brought to his coaching a remarkable ability to make each athlete feel like the most important one on the planet.

—Russ Pate

Introduction: The Young Runner

One of the most important lessons for those involved in training young athletes is that they are not simply "little adults." When you consider differences between youth and adults in size, physical abilities, and psychological characteristics, you realize that we must organize sport experiences for youth differently from those of adults. So for sports such as youth baseball, softball, basketball, and football, coaches adjust the size of the playing field, equipment, and rules of the game to account for the young athlete's developmental level. For example, in children's first experience with organized baseball or softball, they hit the ball off a tee. With growth, maturation, fitness, and experience, young athletes advance to higher levels of participation that are more like the adult sport. The tee in baseball, for example, is replaced by an adult pitcher and then by a youth pitcher.

Have you considered how youth distance running differs from the adult version? What about the proper developmental progression of training and racing for young runners? These are critical questions for coaches, parents, and sports medicine professionals to consider when designing training and competitive experiences specifically for young distance runners. Many special physical and psychological demands make youth distance running different from adult running and other youth sports.

WHAT MAKES YOUTH DISTANCE RUNNING SPECIAL?

Success in all youth sports requires high levels of physical fitness, technical skill, and motivation. For all young athletes, training to develop these qualities can be very demanding. But distance running can place extraordinary requirements on the young athlete's body and mind. Let's address the physical, psychological, and skill-related demands for individual success in distance running and consider ways to meet these demands safely.

Physical and Psychological Demands

A general aim of competitive running is to endure, to persevere through fatigue. Yet, the whole notion of endurance is unfamiliar to most beginners. For instance, in their earliest experiences with running, children *stop* when they get tired. They don't run to endure; they run because it feels good and it's fun. So what happens when 12-year-olds first come out for the cross-country or track team and are encouraged to train and race through fatigue and discomfort? Their initial responses may be, "Why am I doing this? Running isn't fun anymore. It's boring and it hurts."

Most beginners simply lack the fitness and skill needed to experience the true pleasure of running fast over long distances. They know that running can be fun, but they may not yet appreciate the strong feelings of accomplishment and satisfaction that can come from challenging your physical limits. Such positive outcomes depend on a sound training program that is based on scientific principles of development and endurance performance. Yet, above all, young runners will benefit if their training and competitive experiences are fun. Throughout the book, we'll provide suggestions for making training fun and interesting. For starters, we encourage coaches and parents to act on the philosophy that running is fun. An authoritarian style, where the coach orders athletes around like soldiers in boot camp, simply will not work with young runners. Moreover, parents who place pressure on their children to train and compete will likely drive them away from running.

Along these lines, we challenge adults to teach young runners that, although running will sometimes cause discomfort, it should never be painful! Coaches should never use running as a form of punishment by saying things such as, "If you don't run this 400 in under 80, you'll have to do two more." No one should view training as a way to inflict pain. Instead, training is for conditioning the body so that it's easier to run fast in races.

Parents and coaches should encourage young runners to watch elite adult runners on television to see that, when done properly, distance running is not as hard as most people think. Contrary to popular opinion, you hardly ever see well-conditioned runners collapsing from fatigue, gasping for air, or struggling to finish in agony. In fact, the leaders in big races (such as the New York City Marathon) usually come across the finish line in good form with smiles on their faces!

Goals in Distance Running

Performance goals in distance running, and the cognitive, or knowledge-based, abilities needed to achieve them are different from other youth sports. Consider the example of a beginning baseball player. He may need time to master the physical skills such as batting and throwing but will quickly pick up on the objectives of the game. He knows that success means making contact with a pitched ball or fielding a grounder and making the throw to first base. He clearly understands that hitting a home run is a great feat, but more modest goals, such as getting on base, can help the team and bring the individual a special sense of accomplishment.

Of course, in distance running, no one hits, catches, or throws anything! As a consequence, young runners may not know what goals to shoot for or what a good performance means. While it may be pretty easy for young runners to understand the objective of "winning a race," it is much harder for them to conceive what it takes to run a six-minute mile or to finish in the top 25 in a cross-country race.

Runners who do not have clear-cut goals and tactics for achieving them may come to think that finishing first is the only measure of success. This would be unfortunate because only a few runners, usually the fittest and most experienced, have a realistic chance of winning a race. Begin-

ners and less-talented athletes who view winning as "the only thing" will likely suffer disappointment, loss of motivation, and perhaps injury in striving to reach unrealistic goals. Worse yet, they may simply not strive for any goals at all.

We challenge coaches to convey what success means in distance running. Young athletes rely on their coaches to help them set goals and strategies. "What's a good 800-meter time for me? About what place should I shoot for in next weekend's race? What plan should I use to set a new PR (personal record)?" Coaches who help their athletes answer these kinds of questions play an essential role in building motivation, dedication, and goal-oriented focuses. Particularly for young runners, these qualities of "mental fitness" are just as important as physical abilities such as endurance or speed.

Technique and Cognitive Skill Demands

One of the great misconceptions about competitive distance running is that runners do not require skill, or a high degree of precision in movement and in strategy. Skill-related demands are easy to overlook when you consider the great physical demands of distance running. In fact, most books on coaching runners are about conditioning the body to withstand physiological stress. In contrast, much less information exists on how to improve running technique or tactics.

We believe that technical and cognitive skills are just as important in cross-country and track as in any sport. A good example is running technique. Sport scientists have shown that improved form and efficiency can lead to better performance and reduced risk of injury. Many coaches, however, do not prescribe technique work as a regular part of training (probably because a myth has persisted that running is a natural skill that no one can improve upon). As you will learn in chapters 5 and 6, technique training is a valuable part of the young runner's program.

One cognitive skill that is fundamental to success in distance running is pacing. It involves judging how fast to run by the "feel" of the movement and by feedback in the form of split times and instructions from the coach. Many young runners lack this skill. In fact, we have watched hundreds of races in which young runners sprint like mad at the start and then struggle to finish. Sometimes youth races look more like tests of survival than the controlled, well-paced efforts that characterize elite adult races. As we'll discuss in chapter 4, teaching pacing skill is a real challenge. But it is one that will pay high dividends by improving the athlete's performance and enjoyment of running.

SPECIAL DEMANDS OF YOUTH CROSS-COUNTRY, TRACK, AND ROAD RACING

Distance running isn't one sport—it's three sports! As you know, the competitive forms are cross-country, track and field, and road racing. All three involve the same movement and share the basic aim of getting from start to finish as fast as possible. Each running sport, however, requires somewhat different physical abilities and strategies. The combination of the three sports raises key problems and presents special challenges for coaches in designing training programs.

To help illustrate one such challenge, table 1 presents an overview of the competitive seasons for young runners in the United States. Note that they have opportunities for training and racing on a year-round basis. In fact, this is one of the key differences between youth distance running and other youth sports that feature regular off-seasons for rest and participation in other activities. For motivated young runners, year-round participation may be appealing because they can enjoy running, continuously working to improve their

skills and performances. Unfortunately, however, extensive training and racing can place young runners at risk for injuries and psychological burnout, or loss of interest. Therefore, we challenge coaches to design training programs that help young runners develop progressively, while still enjoying participating without overdoing it. Ironically, one of the most important features of an effective program is "down time" during which the runner takes a break from the stress of endurance training and enjoys other activities. In chapter 10, we'll discuss incorporating these breaks into the program.

Let's consider other special challenges for young runners and their coaches, focusing on specific physical, psychological and strategic demands of youth cross-country, track, and road racing. As you read, think about how you would design training and competitive experiences to meet these demands.

Cross-Country Challenges

Cross-country racing brings to mind images of rolling hills, rugged terrain, and wooded trails on cool Saturday mornings in autumn. The bright colors of falling leaves are matched by the uniforms of runners from different teams. Camaraderie and spirit abound as teammates encourage one another to stay in the pack. These are just a few of the features that make cross-country running especially appealing for young runners. The most obvious challenge of cross-country racing is the distance over which races are held. Youth events are typically as long as three miles or 5,000

Table 1 Overview of Competitive Seasons for Young Distance Runners in the U.S.			
Fall **September-November**	**Winter** **December-February**	**Spring** **March-May**	**Summer** **June-August**
• Cross-country training and racing	• Rest	• Outdoor track training and racing	• Rest
	• Indoor track training and racing[a]		• Road racing
	• Road racing		• Cross-country training and racing

[a]Athletes in many states, especially in the South, do not have indoor track and field seasons.

meters, making a high level of endurance fitness a key requirement for successful performance. To conquer demanding courses, cross-country runners need good strength and technique as well.

RACING DISTANCES VARY

Around the world, racing distances for youths vary according to the rules of state and national federations. In the United States, for example, boys' and girls' cross-country races are contested over different distances, depending on the state. Youths in most states race metric distances such as 3,000 and 5,000 meters. In some states, they race imperial distances such as two and three miles. Track racing distances also vary state by state. In most states, youths race 800, 1,600, and 3,200 meters. Only a few states feature 1,500- and 3,000-meter track races. In contrast, these latter two events are standard for youths in countries such as Australia, England, and Canada. Throughout this book, we will refer to racing distances interchangeably to try to cover different parts of the United States and the world.

Many young runners favor cross-country because of its emphasis on team scoring. As in all sports, it's fun and inspiring to work toward a team goal such as winning a big dual meet or qualifying for the state championship. Although it's desirable to have camaraderie and a tight pack of runners, it's also important to realize that cross-country is still basically an individual sport. The team will benefit if each runner performs up to potential. Thus, coaches must keep the team together but not overlook individual needs. A "herd" approach, where everyone does the same training session with the same objective every day, is not a good idea for distance runners— especially in cross-country. For example, it would be risky for a 14-year-old who has just joined the team to attempt the same demanding workouts as an experienced and highly fit 18-year-old. On days when training plans call for intense and challenging work, the coach should separate these runners so that they are with teammates of common ability and experience. Then, on easier days that are intended for rest and recovery, the whole team can work out together. Throughout the book, we'll offer guidelines for individualizing training.

One of the greatest challenges in cross-country is developing a good racing strategy. Since all courses are different, "running for time" won't be an optimal plan, unless athletes are trying to better their times from previous races on the same course. In addition, a course may be inconsistent in terrain from mile to mile or kilometer to kilometer. So a race strategy to run certain split times, such as 6:00 miles or 3:45 kilometers, may not be useful. Instead, "running for place" is often the best strategy for cross-country runners. This strategy demands pacing skill, a good "feel" for how much effort and energy can be spent over the long distance without excessive fatigue. As we'll stress throughout the book, young runners need plenty of training and experience to develop pacing skill.

Track and Field Challenges

Track and field has all the excitement of a three-ring circus. During competitions, track athletes share the performance stage, so to speak. It's always fun to see runners, jumpers, and throwers displaying their different abilities and skills. Even though track runners no longer have center stage as they did in cross-country, track racing is still like being in the spotlight. After all, there are no trees or hills to hide behind on the track!

The key challenges for coaches during track season are planning and overseeing training in a number of different event areas. They often need to prepare special workouts for middle-distance athletes (800 to 1,500/1,600 meters) as well as long-distance athletes (3,000/3,200 to 5,000 meters). For example, an 800-meter runner will work more on developing speed than a 3,200-meter specialist whose training will be geared more toward building endurance. It takes considerable coaching skill (and several stopwatches!) to organize training where groups of runners are doing different workouts.

Some distance runners prefer track over cross-country because it gives them a chance to display their individual talents. An athlete with good speed may have greater success and more fun competing in 800-meter races than in cross-country. One who lacks natural speed but is gifted with endurance may be drawn to the longer races of 3,000 to 5,000 meters. Placing an athlete in the right event is another coaching challenge. Coaches must consider the young runner's ability, level of fitness and experience, preference, and potential for future success.

Track can be very different from cross-country in terms of strategy. In track races, time goals, such as 2:20 for 800 meters or 5:00 for the mile, make it easier to set an objective plan. The best track runners know how to use split times during a race to judge whether their paces are on target for achieving their goals. On the track, runners can also shoot for place goals using a number of different racing strategies. In chapter 4, we will discuss various tactics such as even pacing, front running, and kicking.

Road Racing

Over the last two decades, road racing has become a popular and exciting form of competitive distance running. For the most part, however, this sport is geared toward adult runners. In the United States, for example, high school associations and governing bodies such as USA Track and Field do not sponsor youth events on the roads. Even so, most road races include nonsanctioned age divisions and awards for children and adolescents. These incentives, along with large crowds and a festival-like atmosphere, make road racing fun for young runners. One problem exists, however. Although some races are as short as one mile, most are between eight kilometers (4.97 miles) and the marathon (26.2 miles). As we

will discuss in chapter 1, these longer racing distances are unsuitable for beginners.

Does that mean young runners should forget about road racing? No, but we recommend limited involvement. An occasional 10K can serve as a good workout for building endurance fitness. But young runners should learn their formative lessons in cross-country and track before graduating to road racing. Still, the excitement of road racing can boost young runners' motivation levels during preparation for the upcoming cross-country or track season. It's especially exciting for beginners to be in the same race as elite adult runners who are heroes and role models. Instead of competing for a time or place like the adults do, however, young runners should run road races for fitness and fun. A good developmental program will inspire young endurance athletes to keep running into adulthood when they can pursue road racing seriously if they choose.

The special demands of youth cross-country and track present unique challenges for runners, their parents and coaches, and sports medicine professionals who work with young athletes. For the adults who supervise training and competitive experiences, the key to meeting these challenges is a developmental philosophy marked by a commitment to keeping running fun and helping athletes progress gradually. In the following chapters, we'll help you cultivate this developmental outlook, beginning with key developmental factors such as growth, maturation, fitness, and experience.

PART I

THE SCIENCE OF DISTANCE RUNNING

Training for distance running is about making the body work better—more effectively and more efficiently. To make the runner's body work better, you have to know how it works in the first place! How do the muscles get energy? How do they use the energy to move the body over long distances? What causes fatigue and how can a runner overcome it? What role does the mind play in endurance performance and how can you develop mental fitness? Does technique, or the runner's form, make a difference? What effect do growth and maturation have on the physical and psychological factors that contribute to performance success?

Here in part I, we'll answer these questions using knowledge we've gained from reading about and conducting studies on the physical and psychological capacities of children and adolescents. We'll present the science of distance running as it relates specifically to 12- to 18-year-old runners. We'll focus on developmental factors (chapter 1), nutrition (chapter 2), physiology (chapter 3), psychology (chapter 4), and biomechanics (chapter 5). You will learn how the runner's body and mind work and how their functioning can improve with training. As you read, keep in mind that the real challenge of designing an effective training program is to *apply* scientific knowledge and principles. So, after we discuss the science of running, we'll help you with this application in parts II and III.

CHAPTER I

Development of a Runner

Perhaps the greatest challenge in planning effective training for young runners involves accounting for the influence of development, or changes that occur over time. Adults who supervise young runners need to know much about the physical and psychological changes that occur during adolescence. They must adapt training programs to help runners stay healthy and progress during periods of rapid physical and maturational development. In addition, young runners should be informed about the natural, genetically determined changes that will occur in their bodies because these changes can result in either gains or, unfortunately, setbacks in performance.

Think of development as the product of growth, maturation, fitness, and experience:

**Development =
Growth × Maturation × Fitness × Experience**

In this chapter we'll examine the four parts of the "development equation" and show how each influences the developing runner's ability to train and race. We'll focus on developmental changes in the growing and maturing body, its capacity to adapt to training, and potential risks of injury from excessive training. In addition, we'll present developmental guidelines to help you make decisions about the appropriate types and amounts of training for young distance runners.

GROWTH AND BODY SIZE: IMPACT ON RUNNING ABILITY

Growth refers to increases in height and weight and other changes in physique that occur during childhood and adolescence. Many growth-related changes lead to improved ability in distance running. In fact, even without training, young runners can better their performances just by growing! For example, increases in leg length may result in a longer and more efficient stride. As the heart and lungs get bigger, their capacity to pump oxygen-rich blood to the muscles improves. Furthermore, growth of muscle mass enhances speed and power.

While growth results in many favorable outcomes for young runners, you should be aware that disadvantages may also occur. Take the example of a 13-year-old boy who grows six inches taller over a single summer. Coming out for cross-country in the fall, he may encounter difficulty controlling and coordinating his longer legs. He may be at greater risk for injury as well. During pubertal growth spurts (periods of accelerated increases in bone length), the joints weaken temporarily because muscle mass and strength develop at a slower rate than bone. Because the bones are lengthening without a compensating increase in muscle mass and strength, the joints are susceptible to injury. Recent studies provide alarming evidence of very high rates of knee injuries in high school cross-country and track runners. It is likely that a combination of growth and improper training is responsible for these injuries.

Growing bones are susceptible to injury as well. Bones lengthen at their two ends in soft tissue, called *epiphyseal growth plates*. Until they *ossify*, or harden, the growth plates are very weak; thus, stress fractures of the epiphyseal regions can occur in young runners who train excessively during periods of rapid growth. Later in the chapter you will see developmental guidelines for beginners undertaking regular, demanding training only after completing the growth spurt.

Coaches should assess each athlete's growth status before planning training and competition. To help coaches plan, tables 1.1a and 1.1b show height and weight values (by percentile) for a large sample of girls and boys, respectively, between the ages 12 and 18. Let's look at how coaches might use this information. Consider the case of two 12-year-old boys: Brad is four feet, seven inches tall and weighs 72 pounds, and Bill is five feet, three inches tall and weighs 114 pounds. Looking at table 1.1b, you'll see that Brad's height and weight are about at the 10th percentile for boys his age. That is, 90 percent of 12-year-old boys are taller and heavier than Brad. Bill is about at the 90th percentile—only 10 percent of 12-year-olds are taller and heavier than he is.

Using these data and a record of Brad's height and weight over the last few years, you might conclude that he has not yet experienced his growth spurt and that he may be at a competitive disadvantage compared with Bill, due to his smaller size and strength. The coach might consider curbing Brad's training load until *after* he goes through his growth spurt. Then his bones

Table 1.1a   Height and Weight (by percentile) for 12- to 18-Year-Old Girls

Age	Percentiles						
	5th	**10th**	**25th**	**50th**	**75th**	**90th**	**95th**
12	4'7"/67[a] 140/31	4'8"/71 142/33	4'10"/81 147/37	5'0"/92 152/42	5'1"/106 156/48	5'3"/124 160/56	5'4"/134 163/61
13	4'9"/75 145/34	4'10"/80 148/36	5'0"/89 153/41	5'2"/102 157/46	5'3"/117 161/53	5'5"/136 165/61	5'6"/148 168/67
14	4'10"/83 149/38	4'11"/89 152/40	5'2"/98 156/45	5'3"/111 160/50	5'5"/126 165/57	5'7"/146 169/66	5'8"/161 171/73
15	4'11"/90 151/41	5'0"/96 153/43	5'2"/106 157/48	5'4"/118 162/54	5'5"/133 166/60	5'7"/153 171/70	5'8"/171 173/78
16	5'0"/96 152/43	5'1"/101 154/46	5'2"/110 158/50	5'4"/123 162/56	5'6"/137 167/62	5'7"/158 171/72	5'8"/179 173/81
17	5'0"/99 153/45	5'1"/104 155/47	5'3"/113 159/51	5'4"/125 163/57	5'6"/139 167/63	5'7"/160 171/72	5'8"/182 174/82
18	5'1"/100 154/45	5'2"/105 156/47	5'3"/113 159/51	5'5"/125 164/57	5'6"/139 168/63	5'7"/160 171/72	5'8"/182 174/82

[a]Top row shows values for height/weight in feet and inches, and pounds. Bottom row shows values for height/weight in centimeters and kilograms.

Adapted from NCHS growth tables, National Center for Health Statistics (1976, U.S. Department of Health, Education, and Welfare, Rockville, MD).

Table 1.1b   Height and Weight (by percentile) for 12- to 18-Year-Old Boys

Age	Percentiles						
	5th	**10th**	**25th**	**50th**	**75th**	**90th**	**95th**
12	4'6"/66[a] 138/30	4'7"/69 140/31	4'9"/77 144/35	4'11"/88 150/40	5'1"/101 155/46	5'3"/116 159/53	5'4"/128 162/58
13	4'8"/74 143/34	4'9"/79 146/36	4'11"/88 151/40	5'2"/99 157/45	5'4"/114 162/52	5'6"/130 167/59	5'7"/143 170/65
14	4'11"/84 149/38	5'0"/90 152/41	5'2"/100 157/45	5'4"/112 163/51	5'6"/129 169/58	5'9"/145 174/66	5'10"/159 176/72
15	5'1"/95 155/43	5'2"/102 158/46	5'4"/112 163/51	5'7"/125 169/57	5'9"/143 174/65	5'10"/159 179/72	5'11"/175 182/79
16	5'4"/105 161/48	5'5"/113 164/51	5'7"/124 169/56	5'8"/137 174/62	5'10"/155 178/70	6'0"/172 182/78	6'1"/189 185/86
17	5'5"/113 165/52	5'6"/122 168/55	5'8"/133 172/60	5'9"/146 176/66	5'11"/163 181/74	6'1"/184 184/84	6'2"/201 187/91
18	5'5"/119 166/54	5'7"/128 169/58	5'8"/138 172/63	5'10"/152 177/69	5'11"/168 181/76	6'1"/185 185/88	6'2"/211 188/96

[a]Top row shows values for height/weight in feet and inches, and pounds. Bottom row shows values for height/weight in centimeters and kilograms.

Adapted from NCHS growth tables, National Center for Health Statistics (1976, U.S. Department of Health, Education, and Welfare, Rockville, MD).

and joints will be stronger and better able to handle demanding training. In contrast, Bill's body size may indicate that he is physically ready to handle a more challenging training program. As you will see shortly, however, assessing an athlete's developmental status involves more than simply considering his height and weight.

It's important to understand that the young distance runner's potential for reaching the highest levels of competition depends a great deal on body size and build. To illustrate, table 1.2 presents height and weight values for a group of elite 16-year-old female runners who were studied by Burke and Brush in 1979. Compared with the large sample of female subjects presented in table 1.1a, the elite runners are at the 50th percentile for height (about average), but they are at only the 10th to 25th percentile for weight (well below average). These elite runners, whose average mile-run time was 5:10, also have considerably lower amounts of body fat than nonathletic 16-year-old girls.

It's a simple fact that the best distance runners usually have long legs, small bones, and low percent body fat. No amount of coaching knowledge and skill can influence bone size, height, or leg length. For the most part, these factors are genetically determined. And, as we will discuss in both this and the next chapters, young runners who take drastic measures to reduce body fat risk their health. Coaches and parents can help young runners avoid negative health outcomes by adopting this philosophy: Through hard work and dedication, every runner can gain the satisfaction of personal achievement and self-improvement regardless of physique.

Table 1.2	Height and Weight for a Group of Elite Young Runners		
Subjects		**Height**	**Weight**
• 13 female runners		5'4" (162.2 cm)	107 lbs. (48.6 kg)
• Average age = 16.2 years			
• Average mile run time = 5:10			

Data from a study by Burke and Brush (1979).

MATURATIONAL AND BIOLOGICAL AGE CONSIDERATIONS

Maturation refers to changes in the body which lead to adult physical features, including breast development in females and the appearance of facial hair in males. The release of hormones during puberty triggers these sex-characteristic changes. Like growth, maturation favorably influences endurance performance in many young runners, particularly in boys. For example, during puberty, elevated testosterone levels result in muscular development and improved strength. Male hormones also stimulate the production of more hemoglobin, the oxygen-carrying compound in the blood.

Most girls don't improve their endurance capacity as much as boys as a result of pubertal changes, although they may benefit from slight increases in muscle mass and strength. Indeed, at puberty, girls experience other hormone-triggered changes that can impair running performance in some, but certainly not all, girls. These changes include increases in fatty tissue, widening of the pelvic bones, and slight declines in hemoglobin concentration. Negative health outcomes can result if girls take drastic measures to override natural biological changes such as increased body fat. For example, girls who increase their training and reduce calorie intake to lose fat can suffer from symptoms of overtraining and malnutrition. They become highly susceptible to injuries and illness.

Another set of health considerations for maturing girls who overtrain and reduce calories to lose body fat is delayed menarche (onset of menstruation) and amenorrhea (cessation of the menstrual cycle). Research shows that girls who train vigorously tend to have later average ages at menarche compared with the population of normally active girls. It's important to note, however, that researchers have not yet determined whether a definite cause-effect relationship between training and later maturation exists. It's likely that both genetic factors (e.g., family history) and diet contribute to delayed menarche in runners. Currently, researchers think that diet—specifically, an insufficient caloric intake—is a main factor contributing to amenorrhea in athletic girls and especially in distance runners. If runners don't replace the energy used in training, their bodies conserve energy by ceasing menstruation.

Should parents and coaches be concerned about negative health outcomes in girls who have late menarche and amenorrhea? Probably not. Very little scientific evidence shows any adverse long-term effects. In fact, some researchers think that women who experienced late menarche have a lower risk of developing breast cancer because their bodies have been exposed to relatively low levels of estrogen, a hormone that promotes cancer growth. Paradoxically, however, the female body also requires estrogen to maintain bone density. Thus, in conditions of delayed menarche and amenorrhea—both of which are associated with low estrogen levels, young female runners may be at risk for stress fractures in their legs and feet, if they continue to train hard without proper nutrition over many years into adulthood. As we'll discuss in detail in chapter 2, the keys to proper nutrition for maturing runners, both girls and boys, are to replenish the calories used in training and to eat a well-balanced diet that meets standard requirements for vitamins and minerals.

Coaches and parents must be sensitive to maturational changes, adjust training accordingly, and provide emotional support for maturing girls. Consider the case of Alice. Just after her 12th birthday, Alice experienced menarche and gained weight because of bone growth and increased body fat. As racing times slowed, she became disappointed, frustrated, and even considered quitting. The coach recognized that Alice was experiencing physical changes that were a natural, healthy part of development. While Alice might never become a world-class runner, she could still improve considerably and continue to enjoy running on the team. The coach gave Alice information about a healthy, low-fat diet and added some extra strength training to emphasize muscle development. In a short time, Alice regained her motivation and fitness, and her times began to improve again.

Only a physician can make a complete assessment of physical maturity, or *biological age*. One of the procedures involves taking x-rays to determine skeletal age, or the degree to which the bones have ossified. But before developing a training program for a runner, the coach must have at least a rough idea of his level of maturity. To help in this task, table 1.3 shows some of the distinguishing features, or "hallmarks," of maturation in boys and girls. The table also shows the average ages at which these pubertal events occur. As you read over the table, keep in mind that individuals mature at very different rates. For example, two individuals who are the same chronological age can be separated by four or five years in the age at which they begin puberty! For example, an early-maturing individual might reach puberty at age 11, while a late-maturing teammate might not reach puberty until age 16.

Table 1.3 Hallmarks of Pubertal Changes

Hallmark	Characteristics	Average age (years)	
		Girls	Boys
Beginning of pubertal growth spurt	Accelerated skeletal growth	10.5	12.5
Peak height velocity	Sharp increase in the rate of height gain per year	11.5-12.0	13.5-14.0
Growth spurt of the cardiorespiratory system	Accelerated growth of heart and lungs	11.5-12.0	13.5-14.0
Beginning of development of secondary sex characteristics	Changes in reproductive organs, breast development in females; lowering of voice in males	10.5-12.5	11.5-13.5
Menarche	Onset of menstruation	12.5-13.0	

Coaches must be aware of individual differences in maturation and adjust training and competitive experiences accordingly. For example, given advantages in size, muscle development, and certain physiological characteristics, early-maturers (both boys are girls) are usually able to handle more training than late-maturers. But late-maturers should not despair. Research shows that once they reach puberty, they often catch up to early-maturers in height and surpass them in endurance capacity. We'll have more to say about the importance of accounting for maturation level in chapter 9.

PHYSICAL AND PSYCHOLOGICAL FITNESS PROFILES

Many sport scientists agree that youths are naturally gifted with physical fitness for endurance activity. In laboratory tests, untrained youths have very high levels of *maximal oxygen consumption* or $\dot{V}O_2max$, a measure of the body's aerobic, or oxygen-utilizing, capacity (see chapter 3). Pound for pound, an untrained 12-year-old is able to utilize more oxygen than most 20-year-olds who exercise regularly! These high levels of $\dot{V}O_2max$ in youths are probably a product of age and high levels of everyday activity in games and sports.

While youths have a naturally high aerobic capacity, they are less fit to exercise under anaerobic conditions, or when oxygen is in short supply in the muscles—as in an all-out 400-meter sprint. Anaerobic fitness is related to the individual's maturational status. In fact, the ability to perform muscular work without oxygen improves dramatically following puberty. Thus, prepubertal youths respond well to aerobic, or moderate-intensity, running, but they are limited when doing anaerobic, or high-intensity, running.

Poor running economy, or efficiency, also limits the young athlete's physiological fitness. Young runners tend to waste energy as a result of flaws in technique. Another limitation is their inability to handle climatic extremes. Compared to adults, youths have higher surface-area to body-weight ratios and so are less able to warm their bodies in very cold weather and cool their bodies in hot, humid weather. Training and racing in hot conditions can be particularly dangerous for young runners if they do not drink enough water.

Despite their natural aerobic fitness for endurance sport, young runners lack the psychological fitness to train and race very long distances. Most beginners in distance running are not motivated to push themselves for long periods of time without resting—a fortunate limitation, actually, because it helps young runners avoid injury and psychological burnout. Youths must develop the motivation to endure physical stress progressively over time, following guidelines that we present later in this chapter. Young runners who are pressured to push themselves too hard are at high risk for getting hurt and losing interest in running. Of course, some beginners are very motivated to cover long distances in training and may even prefer the longer races, such as 10Ks. We feel that coaches and parents should strongly encourage these runners to start with relatively short distances and to take on the longer distances only as they develop.

EXPERIENCE IN TRAINING AND COMPETITION

In addition to considering biological age, coaches must consider young runners' *training age*, which refers to young athletes' experience in training and competition. Training ages are simply the number of months or years that runners have been training on a regular basis. Regardless of their biological ages, if runners are young in terms of training age, coaches should scale their programs appropriately. For example, mature 16-year-olds who have been training for only six months should not necessarily be expected to handle the same training load as mature 14-year-olds who have been training for two years.

Experience teaches coaches and runners to use the training methods and racing strategies that work best for them. For example, Coach Ed wanted to make sure that Perry, an elite 14-year-old, was able to use many different racing tactics for the 1,600-meter run. At the beginning of the track season she worked on even pacing. Perry learned to run splits of 82 seconds per lap for a time of 5:28. Even though Perry had run 5:16 the previous

Suzy Hamilton

Eugene, OR

Personal Bests:

800 meters	1:58.74
1,000 meters	2:33.93*
1,500 meters	4:04.53

*American record

©1995 Tim De Frisco

When she was 12 years old, Suzy Hamilton traveled with her coach and teammates from her home in Stevens Point, WI, to Philadelphia, PA, to compete in a national track-and-field meet for her age group. "I remember being so scared and nervous before the race started," she says. "But after the race I was happy because I had run my fastest time."

In her first national competition that day, Suzy ran 2:14 for 800 meters and placed third. Since then she has progressively lowered her 800-meter PR. In 1995, at age 27, she clocked 1:58.74, which was the 10th fastest time in the world. In her best event—the 1,500 meters—Suzy has won numerous NCAA and United States Track and Field (USTAF) titles. She made the U.S. Olympic team in 1992 in the 1,500 meters, racing with the world's best in Barcelona.

In talking about her steady improvement over the last 15 years (and her prospects for a bright future), Suzy emphasizes her love of running. "I'd always heard about 'burnout' in young runners who overtrained at an early age," she says. "But I never thought that I would burn out because I loved running so much. I looked forward to training every day and saw running as a way to learn about the world through traveling, to have fun with my friends, and to make new friends."

Suzy attributes her current success as a world-class runner to the same attitudes that made her a top young runner. She remembers learning at a young age that it's important to believe in yourself and not worry about what competitors do and think. "Going into a race, I say to myself, 'All I can do is my best.' And if I do my best, I'm satisfied." Suzy also cites the importance of support from family and coaches: "I feel lucky because all my coaches have been superb people. They never overtrained me, and they always stressed enjoyment. And my parents were my best supports. They never pressured me to run."

Although her workouts are much more demanding now than they were 15 years ago, Suzy's methods and focus in training are essentially the same. She has used weight training and technique drills since she was a teenager, and she emphasizes fast running rather than a lot of long, slow distance. Throughout her career, Suzy's coaches have made training fun by using games in workouts to develop skill and motivation. Suzy says that because her training experiences have been so enjoyable, she no longer worries or is afraid about competing.

"Don't be scared," she tells young runners. "Look at every race as a new experience and a chance to challenge yourself."

year, Coach Ed wanted her to hold back in early-season races and gain the experience of pacing and positioning in a crowded field of competitors.

During the middle part of the season, Coach Ed asked Perry to run very fast (73-second) laps at the start of the race, even if it meant slowing down over the last 800 meters. She learned that the front-running strategy was effective in "putting the hurt" on her competitors—not to mention herself! Coach Ed and Perry agreed that front running would be too risky in the championship meets at the end of the season. So they used a few late-season races to practice running at an even pace of about 77 to 79 seconds for the first three laps, and then accelerating over the last 400 meters.

They tried another strategy in which Coach Ed purposefully withheld splits from Perry. He knew that in big meets at the end of the season crowd noise and the commotion of running in a pack might make it hard for Perry to hear her splits. Coach Ed didn't want Perry to rely on the split times like a crutch. This strategy forced Perry to use her sense of effort and race strategy to adjust her pace and challenge her competitors. If the pace felt easy at 800 meters, Perry planned to make her move at that point by gradually accelerating and trying to break up the field over the next lap. If the pace felt fast, Perry planned to stay with her competitors until 300 meters remained before starting her kick.

For the state championships, Coach Ed and Perry decided to go with the strategy that made Perry feel most comfortable and effective. They thought that she could run fastest and place highest with a "pace-and-kick" strategy in which she would shoot for 77- to 78-second 400-meter laps over the first 1,200 meters and then accelerate over the last lap. With this strategy, Perry would shoot for a sub-5:10, a time that she and Coach Ed thought would win the race based on their analysis of the level of competition. To hit 77 seconds and 78 seconds for the first few laps, Perry had to let the pack go. But, even though she was 40 meters behind the leader, she felt confident in her plan; she knew that she would catch up, and the pace felt so easy. By 1,000 meters, Perry was right on pace, and she caught the struggling leaders

and gathered for her kick. She was feeling so good that she decided to accelerate with 500 meters to go. Perry set a personal record (PR) of 5:06 to win the race. It's certain that her experience with a number of strategies will help Perry succeed in the different competitive situations she faces in future years.

Beginners who have dreams of competing at Olympic levels must realize that it takes distance runners many years of training and competition to peak. In fact, most Olympic champions in the middle- and long-distance races are in their middle to late 20s and have been training for at least 10 years. Recently, many champions have been in their 30s. Consider that Carlos Lopes, the great Portuguese runner, won the 1984 Olympic marathon at age 37! The following year he broke the world record, running 2:07:51. You may be surprised to know that physiologically, Lopes was past his peak. In fact, research shows that physiological fitness for distance running, based on measures of maximal oxygen consumption, is optimal at age 25. How did Carlos Lopes continue to improve in his late 30s? What Lopes lost in physical ability he more than compensated for in experience. Encourage young runners who are motivated to take on the world to patiently work hard to achieve their short-term goals, while dreaming about the future.

© Ken Lee

DEVELOPMENTAL GUIDELINES FOR TRAINING AND RACING

Coaches help young runners develop by providing training *sessions for fitness* and *lessons for experience*. And as coaches work with individual runners over time, they get a sense of how far each athlete can go. Some may lack the ability and desire to continue competing beyond high school. Others may have what it takes to compete in college and at international levels many years down the road. Yet, regardless of the young runner's destination, the same basic principles should apply to development through training. Here are key developmental guidelines, based on the physical and psychological capacities of children and adolescents. As you read, keep in mind that a developmental approach means *gradual* progression toward the athlete's ultimate potential, with improvement from season to season and year to year.

> ▶ **Youngsters should wait until they have passed through many of the changes occurring with puberty to start training for distance running on a *regular* basis.**

No scientific evidence exists to support the belief that runners have to start training at a very young age to reach their ultimate potential as adults. In fact, many world-class runners did not begin training until they were in their mid- to late-teens. Considering the physical changes that occur during puberty, we recommend that youths wait until they are at least 12 to 14 years old before training on a regular basis. We define regular training as running three to seven days a week for several months at a time. By 12 to 14 years, most girls and boys will have experienced key pubertal changes that will make them better able to handle the repetitive musculoskeletal stress of distance running. But remember, because of differences in maturation rate among individuals, chronological age is not always the best indicator of readiness. Here are three of the most important indicators to look for in judging whether an individual is ready to start training regularly:

- Completion of the pubertal growth spurt
- Eagerness and self-motivation to train and compete

- Good general health as certified by a physician

> ▶ **Encourage prepubescent children who like to run to participate in organized age-group track and field.**

When we say that youths should not train regularly until ages 12 to 14, we certainly don't mean that they should completely avoid participating in track and cross-country until that age. Prepubescent children between 8 and 11 years old will benefit from an occasional run of one to three miles in physical education class or in special youth cross-country and road racing events. Adults should encourage those who express a keen interest in competitive running to participate in organized age-group track and field programs for a few months each year. In addition to competing in 800- to 1,500/1,600-meter races, the future distance runner will benefit from and enjoy the jumping, sprinting, and throwing events. We think that it's important for children to get involved in track and field at an early age, at about 8 years old or so. It's fun to be on a track team with friends and to try the different events, and the experience should promote positive feelings and motivation to join the team in following years. But the 8- to 11-year-old should not be on a daily training program designed specifically for the distance events. Remember, prepubescents are naturally fit for endurance activities. So, they can run an occasional one- or two-mile race without having to train and without risk of overexertion.

> ▶ **Early training experiences should promote *general* fitness and athletic skills.**

In addition to participating in track and cross-country, beginning runners should play a variety of sports throughout the year. As we'll discuss later in the book, coaches can even include sports such as soccer and basketball in the early-season training program. These activities develop *general* physical abilities and skills at a young age. By general, we mean abilities, such as endurance, speed, and strength, that are required for success in many different sports.

Several reasons exist for emphasizing general athletic skills at a young age. First, success in track and cross-country requires more than just cardiovascular endurance, which is gained through continuous running. Runners need upper body strength to absorb the impact forces generated by the leg muscles, especially during sprinting at the end of races and uphill running. They also need good flexibility and technique for optimal performance and injury prevention. Another reason for involving young runners in other sports at early ages is that the variety of activities will help prevent psychological burnout.

▶ Avoid early specialization in training.

The flip side of the developmental guideline just discussed is to avoid specialized training at early ages. Specialization means high-intensity work that stresses the energy systems that are used in competition. Thus, coaches should not assign many high-speed anaerobic workouts to beginners. While beginning runners should occasionally run fast in training, they should not run so fast and far as to cause excessive accumulation of lactic acid. Lactic acid is a chemical by-product of anaerobic energy production that causes fatigue during high-intensity running (see chapter 4).

Runners need a base of general fitness before undertaking training to develop specialized and anaerobic endurance (see figure 1.1). For beginners, training should focus on developing a solid base of endurance, speed, technique, flexibility, and strength. As runners gain fitness, experience, and maturity, a coach can safely add more specialized training methods (see part II).

▶ Increase training loads progressively.

We wish we could give you definite answers to questions such as "How far and fast should youths run in training?" and "How much should training loads be increased from season to season?" As long as individual differences in development exist, however, so will different answers for each athlete. We recommend that coaches increase amounts of training gradually based on detailed records of an athlete's training over the course of a single season, and from season to season.

In designing training programs, successful coaches decide on an appropriate load of work for each athlete based on his maturation level, training age, fitness, and previous training experience. Training loads are generally defined in terms of volume, intensity, and frequency. Volume means the total distance the athlete runs. Intensity refers to the effort and speed of the run. Frequency is how often the athlete trains.

Training Load =
Volume + Intensity + Frequency

Over time, training load must increase to account for athletic development. That is, as runners get older, fitter, and more experienced, they will be able to run farther, faster, and more often.

Consider Marsha, a 15-year-old runner who averages 20 miles a week in four days of training. To improve over time, Marsha should not do the same amount of training when she is 16. But

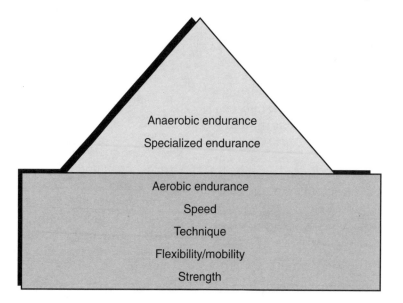

Figure 1.1 General and specialized elements of fitness for distance running.

neither should she jump up to 40 or 50 miles a week in the course of a year! A more appropriate progression in weekly mileage might be 26 at age 16, 32 at age 17, and 42 at age 18. As the total volume for a year's training increases, so should the intensity and frequency. At age 15, Marsha might be doing one fast interval session a week to prepare for track racing. By age 17 or 18, she may do two or three interval sessions a week. Marsha's overall frequency of training may increase from four to six days a week between ages 15 and 18.

An important key to ensuring sound development is to have a long-range focus. When planning training loads for the present, coaches should also think about how much training the athlete will be able to handle over the course of his running career. If, for example, a 12-year-old is allowed to run 50 or more miles per week, consider how much training he will need to continue improving at age 16 or 18. Over 100 miles? This athlete may stop improving because it may be impossible to increase training to such a high volume without injury.

> ▶ **Increase racing distances progressively.**

Up to this point, we have presented developmental guidelines for training only. Another key to ensuring proper development in racing is to increase the distances at which young runners race gradually from year to year. On the track, for example, beginners should start out focusing on short races such as 800 meters. With training and experience, runners can move up in distance if they show promise at longer races such as 3,000 to 5,000 meters. Why start out with short races? It is important for young runners to learn that successful racing means running as fast as they can for a given distance without slowing down and losing form. It's difficult for beginners to accomplish this objective in a long race such as 5,000 meters because most simply lack the concentration and pacing skills to maintain a fast pace for that long.

Table 1.4 provides guidelines for progression in track racing distances with chronological and training age. These guidelines are flexible. That is, 12-year-olds who have just begun competing don't always have to run 800 meters, the shortest distance. They will benefit from participating in other races, such as 400 and 1,500 meters, on occasion. In cross-country, 12-year-olds might

Table 1.4   Recommended Racing Distances by Chronological and Training Age

Chronological age	Training age	Racing distance
12 to 14	0 to 2	800 to 1,500/1,600 m
14 to 16	2 to 4	800 to 3,000/3,200 m
16 to 18	4 to 6	800 to 5,000 m

race distances longer than 1,500/1,600 meters. Nevertheless, a key focus in competition should be on covering the whole distance at the fastest pace possible, that is, at a pace that is neither too easy nor too hard to maintain without slowing. By starting out with shorter races, beginners will learn this lesson more quickly than if they try to master the longer events.

MAXIMUM DISTANCES

In the United States, no formal restrictions for the distances that youths can race exist. The British Athletic Federation, however, does not allow age-group runners to exceed these distances:

Distance (in meters)

Age	Track	Cross-Country
11-14	3,000 (boys) 1,500 (girls)	5,000 (boys) 3,500 (girls)
15-16	5,000 (boys and girls)	6,500 (boys) 4,000 (girls)
17-18	10,000 (boys and girls)	8,000 (boys) 5,000 (girls)

Data from Tulloh (1995).

> ▶ **Let elite adult distance runners serve as developmental role models.**

One of the best sources of inspiration and motivation for young runners is the world-class adult runner, who can serve as a developmental role model. Coaches and parents should expose young runners to the world of international-level track and cross-country. For example, coaches can bring running books and magazines to practice and tell their athletes about upcoming track meets and marathons on TV. Parents can take their young runners out to watch, or run in, local road races that feature elite adults. Beginners will be inspired by the strategies, technique, and accomplishments of top endurance athletes. Most importantly, young runners will learn that getting to the top means many years of smart, hard work. Now that's a great lesson for life as well as for running!

SUMMARY

The key to cultivating a developmental approach to training is to keep each element of development in mind when you are planning training and racing experiences. What are these elements?

- *Growth*. How does the runner compare to others his age in terms of height and weight? Has the runner experienced a recent growth spurt? Remember, training during growth spurts may increase the risk of injury.

- *Maturation*. Has the runner gone through puberty? Chronological age may not be a good indicator of maturation because individuals' maturation rates vary greatly.

- *Fitness*. Does the runner have the physiological and mental capacities necessary for long, intense training and competition? These capacities develop with maturation and training.

- *Experience*. Which training methods and racing strategies have proven to work best for the runner? The best approaches will emerge with experimentation and learning.

You'll be able to choose the right types and amounts of training with the background you've acquired on developmental factors. But our discussion of development does not end here. In the next few chapters on scientific foundations of distance running, we'll consider how developmental factors affect specific physiological, psychological, and biomechanical capacities. Then in part III, we'll use our developmental guidelines to provide more specific instructions in how to plan progressive training.

CHAPTER 2

Nutrition for Runners

The stress of distance running on the body is energy-draining. Runners need to consume certain types and amounts of foods to adequately restore the energy and nutrients depleted during training and competition. The knowledge you gain in this chapter will help you answer key questions about the optimal nutrition and diets for young runners:

- Should runners eat special foods?

- Is it important to load up on carbohydrates?

- How much fat and protein should runners eat?

- Are vitamin and mineral supplements necessary?

- What about the prerace meal?

- What fluids—water or sports drinks—should runners drink during training? And do they need to drink during races?

- Does an ideal body weight exist for runners? And how should runners go about gaining or losing weight safely?

In this chapter, we will answer these questions and many others about how nutrition affects endurance performance. You'll see that an understanding of the link between diet and performance is one key to designing effective training programs while ensuring optimal health.

NUTRITION FOR OPTIMAL PERFORMANCE AND HEALTH

Physiologically speaking, the name of the game in distance running is "energy." Energy is, in general terms, the capacity to do work. Or, for our specific interest in distance running, you might think of energy as the capacity to produce repeated, forceful muscle contractions for long periods of time. Successful endurance performance depends on whether the muscles can sustain a high level of "contractile force" over a long distance for an extended time. Fatigue, or the inability to maintain muscular force, is the opposite of energy. So, where does the energy to train, race, and defy fatigue come from? That's the story that we'll be telling you in this chapter and the following one. The story begins with nutrition. Fuel for the muscles comes from metabolic processes in the body that break down nutrients in food. In-

deed, because food makes energy for running, optimal performance for distance runners begins with good nutrition.

In contrast, poor nutrition can negatively affect performance, development, and health in young runners. During puberty, the need for nutrients to support growth and maturational changes is enormous. Add to these normal demands the energy spent in training for distance running and you can see that nutrition must be a major focus for coaches, parents, sports medicine professionals and young runners themselves.

Unfortunately, adolescents are at fairly high risk for poor nutrition because of the pressures of hectic lifestyles, commercial advertising to eat unhealthy foods, and society's focus on an ideal body image that is impossible for most people to attain. In addition, some young runners feel pressure to restrict nutrition because they've been told that their performance will suffer if they gain weight. More than anything, young athletes need guidance from adults to help them steer clear of negative pressures and to promote good attitudes and behaviors concerning nutrition. Coaches and parents can start by being good nutritional role models. This means eating healthy foods, encouraging young athletes to follow suit, and adopting the philosophy that any nutritional practice that compromises health should be avoided. For coaches, parents, and young runners, good attitudes and practices about nutrition begin with understanding the connection between diet and endurance performance.

FUEL FOR PERFORMANCE: CARBOHYDRATES, FATS, AND PROTEINS

The energy for physical work comes from the breakdown of the chemical building blocks of food—carbohydrates, fats, and proteins. These three energy sources are found in various kinds of foods and play distinct roles in supplying fuel for the exercising muscles. The proportions of carbohydrate, fat, and protein in the diet affect the runner's ability to work the muscles and to avoid fatigue. This is because the muscles selectively burn the three different fuels, depending on the intensity (speed) and duration (distance) of running. So optimal racing performance and quick recovery from demanding training sessions both depend on replacing the right energy sources in the right amounts.

Carbohydrates

Carbohydrates are the primary fuel source for high-intensity exercise. This energy source is abundant in starchy foods such as potatoes and in grain products such as breads, cereal, and pasta. They're also found in sweet-tasting foods such as fruits, syrup, and candy. As running speed increases, the amount of carbohydrates used by the muscles increases, while the contribution of the other major energy source, fat, becomes smaller (see figure 2.1).

In competitive events of up to 5,000 meters, most of the athlete's energy comes from *glycogen*, a storage form of carbohydrate found in muscle tissue and the liver. To be used in fueling muscle activity, glycogen must be broken down to a simpler form of carbohydrate, called *glucose*. Also known as "blood sugar," glucose circulates in the bloodstream and is the only fuel source that can be used by nerve cells in the brain and spinal cord.

The body contains limited amounts of carbohydrates. In an adolescent, stored glycogen and glucose can provide enough calories, or units of energy, to fuel about 10 to 12 miles of running at a moderate pace. It's important to understand that several days of hard training can deplete the body's stored carbohydrates if they are not restocked through the runner's diet. What happens when a runner's muscles are depleted of glycogen? The effect is like a car running out of gas. You can put the pedal to the floor, but you're not going to go anywhere! Glycogen depletion is a major cause of fatigue in distance running. Low glucose levels can also hurt performance. This is because nerve cells that signal the muscles to contract cannot work properly without energy from glucose.

Because carbohydrates are the primary energy source for events between 800 and 5,000 meters, and because they can easily be depleted during intense work, they should make up a large part of the runner's diet. Accordingly, sport nutritionists typically recommend that the endurance athlete eat a diet in which about 55 to 70 percent of the total calories come from carbohydrates. To give you an idea of how many calories make up these percentages, table 2.1 lists estimated calorie requirements for 12- to 18-year-old runners. The column for carbohydrates shows that the calorie intake required to meet these guidelines ranges from 1,485 to 1,925 (for a diet that is 55 percent

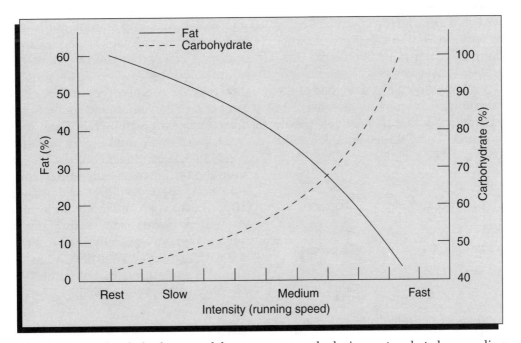

Figure 2.1 Contribution of carbohydrates and fat to energy needs during rest and at slow, medium, and fast running speeds.
Adapted, by permission, from Brooks, Fahey, and White, 1995, *Exercise Physiology: Human Bioenergetics and Its Applications* (Mountain View, CA: Mayfield Publishing Company), 117.

	Estimated daily requirements (in calories)			
Age/Sex	Total (100%)	Carbohydrates (55-70%)	Fat (15-25%)	Protein (10-20%)
12 to 14/Girls	2,700	1,485-1,890	405-675	270-540
12 to 14/Boys	3,000	1,650-2,100	450-750	300-600
15 to 18/Girls	2,700	1,485-1,890	405-675	270-540
15 to 18/Boys	3,500	1,925-2,450	525-875	350-700

Table 2.1 Estimated Daily Calorie Requirements for Runners: Carbohydrate, Fat, and Protein

Note: The total calorie requirements for young runners were obtained by adding 500 calories to the basic daily needs of normally active adolescents. (Basic daily needs from *The Swimmer's Diet: Eating for Peak Performance*, published by the Gatorade Sports Science Institute, Chicago, IL.) The 500 calories roughly estimate the energy expended during a 5-mile run at 7- to 8-minute-mile pace.

carbohydrates) and 1,890 to 2,450 (for a diet that is 70 percent carbohydrates) depending on the runner's age and sex. These values are based on adding the calories expended in running five miles (about eight kilometers) a day to the daily calorie requirements for normally active youths. We must emphasize that these are estimates, and that a runner who does more or less training will require fewer or greater calories, respectively.

One gram of carbohydrate contains about four calories. So, looking at table 2.1, you can see that a 15- to 18-year-old girl who runs five miles a day will require between 371 and 473 grams of carbohydrate a day (1,485 calories ÷ 4 calories per gram = 371.25 grams; 1,890 calories ÷ 4 calories per gram = 472.5 grams). To give you an idea of the carbohydrate content of various foods, tables 2.2a and 2.2b list some foods that are relatively rich in this energy source. Using these tables, let's add up the carbohydrates in a high-energy breakfast:

- 3 pancakes =   30 grams
- 1/8 cup of pancake syrup =   30 grams
- 1 banana =   27 grams
- 1 cup of orange juice =   26 grams
- 1 cup of low-fat milk =   12 grams
                                                        125 grams

The 125 grams of carbohydrate will supply roughly one-third of the required intake for the 15- to 18-year old girl runner. She can make up the rest of her daily carbohydrate needs at lunch, dinner, and with snacks between meals.

A great way to find out if you're in the right range for your daily intake of carbohydrates (and other nutrients) is to use nutrition information labels on food packages, which give you the number of grams per serving. And shortly, we'll provide more detailed guidelines and a sample menu for getting the required amounts of carbohydrates and other energy sources.

Tables 2.2a and 2.2b list carbohydrate content in its two forms: complex and simple. Complex carbohydrates—named for their long chains of molecules, make up starchy foods, grain products, and most vegetables. Simple carbohydrates make up sugary foods and fruits. Both forms can ultimately provide glucose for muscle activity; however, the complex type and fruits are healthiest because they are found in foods that contain fiber, vitamins, and minerals. These nutrients can be stripped away from highly processed sugary foods such as candy and donuts. Does this mean you should avoid sweets altogether? No, but nutrition experts recommend that no more than 10 percent of a person's total calorie intake should come from sweets made with highly processed sugar. This is an especially good rule to follow for preventing cavities. We'll have more to say about complex and simple carbohydrates later when we discuss the prerace meal.

Fats

Fats in the diet are broken down into *free fatty acids* to provide the muscles with energy. The

Table 2.2a   High-Carbohydrate Foods: Complex Carbohydrates

Food group	Serving size	Grams of carbohydrate[a]
Bread, cereal, pasta, and rice		
Whole wheat sandwich bread	2 slices	24
Bagel	1 (3 1/2" diameter)	36
Flour tortilla	1 (8" diameter)	20
Pancakes	3 (4" diameter)	30
Waffles	2 (3.5" × 5.5")	17
Boxed cereal (ready to eat)	1 cup	15-70
Oatmeal, cooked	3/4 cup	18
Spaghetti/macaroni, cooked	1 cup	40
Brown rice, cooked	3/4 cup	31
Vegetables		
Broccoli, cooked	1/2 cup	4
Carrot, raw	1 (medium)	8
Corn, cooked from frozen	1/2 cup	20
Peas, cooked from frozen	1/2 cup	11
Potato, baked	1 (medium)	51
Beans and nuts[b]		
Black beans, cooked	1/2 cup	20
Canned beans (white/navy), with sweet sauce	1/2 cup	27
Almonds, dry roasted	1/2 cup	16
Peanuts, dry roasted	1/2 cup	15
Sunflower seeds	1/2 cup	14

[a]To figure out the number of calories from carbohydrates in each of these foods, multiply grams × 4.
[b]Many nuts are high in carbohydrates but also high in fat and sodium.

contribution of fat to total energy needs during running increases as the pace gets slower (see figure 2.1). Thus, this nutrient plays a major role in fueling low- to moderate-intensity training runs as well as long races such as the marathon. Fat provides only a small part of the energy needed for events between 800 and 5,000 meters. Nevertheless, many advantages of burning as much fat as possible in these middle- and long-distance races exist. For example, fat is a highly concentrated source of energy. A gram of fat contains about nine calories, far exceeding both the energy in a gram of carbohydrate (four calories) and the energy in a gram of protein (also four calories). In addition, when the muscles burn fat, the body's limited stores of carbohydrate are spared. Carbohydrate sparing is important in

distance running because it delays the fatigue caused by glycogen depletion.

If fat is such a good energy source for running, why doesn't the body use it instead of carbohydrates at fast paces? The answer is that oxygen must be present in muscle cells for fat to be burned. When the runner's pace is fast, as in an all-out 800-meter race, the body cannot meet the oxygen demands of the muscles and uses only limited amounts of fat for energy. So carbohydrates become the dominant energy source because the body can burn them without oxygen. In chapter 3, we'll continue to examine how running speed and duration affect the body's ability to use fat and carbohydrates for energy. And we'll talk about how training improves the body's ability to use fat by increasing the rate of oxygen-rich blood flow to the muscles.

Table 2.2b   High-Carbohydrate Foods: Simple Carbohydrates

Food types	Serving size	Grams of carbohydrate[a]
Fruits		
Apple	1 (medium)	21
Banana	1 (medium)	27
Cherries	10	11
Grapes	1 cup	28
Orange	1 (medium)	16
Pear	1 (medium)	25
Raisins	1/3 cup	40
Fruit juices (apple, orange, grape, etc.)	1 cup	25-30
Dairy products		
Low-fat (2%) milk	1 cup	12
Fruit yogurt	1 cup	42
Sport drinks (e.g., Gatorade)	12 ounces	16
Soft drinks (e.g., colas, root beer)	12 ounces	36
Breakfast sweets		
Honey	1 tablespoon	17
Syrup	1/8 cup	30
Jams and jellies	1 tablespoon	14
Table sugar	1 tablespoon	13
Sweet snacks/pastries		
Chocolate candy	1 bar (1 ounce)	16
Chocolate chip cookies	4 (2 1/4" diameter)	28
Donut, glazed	1 (3 1/4" diameter)	27

[a]To figure out the number of calories from carbohydrates in each of these foods, multiply grams × 4.

Unlike its capacity to store carbohydrates, the body stores fat in abundant amounts. In healthy nonathletic teenagers, fat makes up about 12 to 15 percent of body weight in boys and 21 to 25 percent in girls. Studies have shown that, on average, teenage distance runners have body fat values of 8 to 12 percent for boys and 12 to 16 percent for girls (Butts 1982; Cunningham 1990; Sundberg and Elovainio 1982). How much energy can these stores supply? A runner who weighs 130 pounds and whose body is only 12 percent fat has enough energy to fuel approximately 650 miles of slow running without restocking fat stores!

Fat plays a major role in energy production and numerous other physiological functions. For distance runners, however, an excess amount of body fat wastes energy because its "dead weight" makes the muscles work harder to transport the body. So most sport nutrition experts recommend a diet in which only 15 to 25 percent of the total number of calories come from fat (but see the sidebar on page 21 for another view on fat intake).

THE HIGH-CARBOHYDRATE VERSUS HIGH-FAT DIET DEBATE

There's an interesting controversy brewing in the area of sport nutrition. Recently, some studies have challenged the conventional notion that distance runners should eat a high-carbohydrate diet. These studies support the new claim that a high-fat diet—composed of up to 40% fat—is optimal! This view, which is supported by some makers of high-energy "food bars," holds that because fat contains so much energy and its use spares glycogen depletion, runners should eat more of it. By eating more fat, runners will therefore train their bodies to burn it as a preferred fuel. Some studies do support this argument; however, the studies are not applicable to young runners. Subjects in these studies were highly trained adult runners who performed tests at relatively low speeds for long durations. The results suggest that eating a high-fat diet for a few weeks might improve performance for *highly trained adult marathon runners*. But young runners do not have the physiological capacities of elite marathoners. Because young runners compete at shorter distances and at relatively higher intensities compared to marathoners, they don't burn as much fat. Thus, *a high-fat diet won't improve the performance of young runners*. More importantly, a high-fat diet can lead to negative health outcomes because it is associated with heart disease.

Table 2.1 shows that the estimated number of calories from fat needed to meet these guidelines ranges from 405 to 525 (for a diet that is 15 percent fat) and 675 to 875 (for a diet that is 25 percent fat), depending on the runner's age and sex. Remember, one gram of fat yields nine calories. Thus, based on the values in table 2.1, a 12- to 14-year-old boy who runs five miles a day would need to eat about 50 to 83 grams of fat daily (450 calories ÷ 9 calories per gram = 50 grams; 750 calories ÷ 9 calories per gram = 83.33 grams). Most teenagers have little problem meeting the requirements for fat intake. In fact, it's easy to eat too much fat if you enjoy fast foods such as hot dogs, cheeseburgers, french fries, and pizza. To help you account for your fat intake, table 2.3 lists the fat content of some common foods.

As table 2.3 shows, dairy products—especially cheese and ice cream—have a high fat content. Runners whose diets tend to include more than the recommended 25 percent of dietary fat will benefit from switching to nonfat or low-fat dairy products. Note that even lean beef and pork contain a lot of fat. Low-fat alternatives are chicken and fish. But if these foods are cooked with butter or oils, their fat content skyrockets. For example, the fried fish sandwich that you can get at a fast food restaurant has around 20 grams of fat. The fish itself may have only one or two grams of fat, but the oil in which it's fried contains about 15 grams of fat per tablespoon. Another source of hidden fat is granola. Notice that the fat content in cereals ranges from 1 to 20 grams! Many granola cereals are at the high end of this range. To make sure that you're not getting unwanted hidden fats, read the nutrition labels on cereal boxes carefully. Finally, many snack foods such as potato chips and cookies are high in fat. If you enjoy these foods, you don't have to eliminate them from your diet altogether, but you should eat them sparingly so that you don't exceed your upper limits of fat intake.

Like carbohydrates, fats come in several different forms, some of which are healthier than others. Saturated fats and cholesterol are found primarily in animal products such as beef, bacon, and "nonskim" dairy products. These forms of fat contribute to the formation of fatty deposits on the inner linings of blood vessels in the heart. Over the years, the buildup of fatty deposits can clog these vessels and lead to heart disease. You may be surprised to know that this process begins during childhood! So nutritionists recommend that, beginning in childhood, the majority of our fat intake should come from *unsaturated* sources such as vegetable oils (e.g., canola, corn, safflower, and olive). Unsaturated fats pose less risk of heart disease.

Proteins

When carbohydrates and fats are in sufficient supply, the body uses very little protein for fueling the muscles during running. Only in cases of extreme glycogen depletion and starvation does protein metabolism occur to a large extent. Nevertheless, the runner must replace proteins on a daily basis because they undergo a process of continuous deformation or "turnover" in the

Table 2.3   Fat Content in Common Foods

Food group	Serving size	Grams of fat[a]
Bread, cereal, pasta, and rice		
Whole wheat sandwich bread	2 slices	1
Bagel	1 (3 1/2" diameter)	1
Boxed cereal (ready to eat)	1 cup	1-20
Oatmeal, cooked	3/4 cup	1
Spaghetti/macaroni, cooked	1 cup	1
Brown rice, cooked	3/4 cup	1
Dairy		
Milk, skim	1 cup	<1
Milk, 2% fat	1 cup	5
Milk, whole	1 cup	8
Yogurt (whole milk)	1 cup	7
Yogurt (nonfat milk)	1 cup	<1
Ice cream (16% fat)	1 cup	24
Cheese (cheddar, swiss)	1 ounce	10
Butter	1 tablespoon	11
Meat, poultry, fish, beans, nuts, and eggs		
Ground beef, broiled	4 ounces	20
Pork chop, broiled	3 ounces	19
Chicken breast, broiled (skinless)	4 ounces	5
Fish (tuna, shrimp)	4 ounces	1
Black beans, cooked	1/2 cup	<1
Canned beans (white/navy), with sweet sauce	1/2 cup	2
Almonds, dry roasted	1/2 cup	35
Peanuts, dry roasted	1/2 cup	36
Peanut butter	2 tablespoons	16
Sunflower seeds	1/2 cup	36
Eggs	1 large	5
Snacks		
Potato chips	1 ounce	10
Nacho chips	1 ounce	7
French fries (from fast food store)	1 large order	15
Cookies, chocolate chiip	4 (2 1/4" diameter)	10

[a]To figure out the number of calories from fat in each of these foods, multiply grams × 9.

runner's body. Protein is necessary for normal functions, including growth and repair of muscle tissue. In fact, muscle fibers are made primarily of protein, so the athlete needs this nutrient to rebuild and strengthen tissue torn down in training. Protein also makes up *hemoglobin* and *myoglobin*. These compounds are critical for high levels of endurance performance because they transport oxygen in the blood (hemoglobin) and muscle cells (myoglobin). Finally, specialized proteins called *enzymes* are needed to spark the breakdown of carbohydrates and fats during energy production.

Proteins are made up of compounds called *amino acids*. Twenty different amino acids are required to build the proteins that perform vital roles in the body. Although the body can synthesize 11 of these by itself, the athlete must include the remaining nine, called the essential amino acids, in the diet. The best protein sources are animal products such as lean meat, fish, poultry, eggs, and milk. Animal sources of protein are "complete" because they contain all of the essential amino acids. Many plant foods are good sources of protein; however, plant foods are "incomplete," or lacking in one or two essential amino acids. Are athletes on vegetarian diets at risk for insufficient protein intake? No, they can still get a complete supply of high-quality protein by eating a variety of plant foods daily, including beans, nuts, and whole grain products, such as corn, rice, wheat bread, and pasta.

For adolescent boys and girls, the Recommended Daily Allowance (RDA) for protein is .9 grams per kilogram (kg) of body weight. This means that an individual weighing 130 pounds, or 59 kg, would need about 53 grams of protein per day (59 kg × .9 grams per kg = 53.1 grams). The RDA is a liberal standard that an athlete can easily meet on a typical meat-eating diet. One four-ounce serving of beef, chicken, or fish contains about 30 grams of protein (see table 2.4). Add a serving of macaroni (7 grams) topped with one ounce of cheese (8 grams) along with a cup of skim milk (8 grams), and the total of 53 grams meets the RDA standard for adolescents in just one meal.

Young runners who are still growing and constantly breaking down muscle tissue in training need slightly greater amounts of protein than nonathletic youths. In fact, daily recommendations range between 1.2 to 2 grams per kg of body weight. Athletes usually meet their higher protein needs simply because they eat great amounts of food to replace the energy drained by training. So runners don't need to worry about supplementing the diet with protein pills or powders—as long as they eat a well-balanced diet with a sufficient number of total calories. As we have illustrated, it's easy to eat around 50 grams of protein in a single meal, particularly if it contains meat. As another general guideline for protein intake, about 10 to 20 percent of the young runner's calories should come from this energy source (see table 2.1).

PUTTING IT ALL TOGETHER: A DIET FOR OPTIMAL PERFORMANCE AND HEALTH

So far, we've covered the basics of how the energy sources are linked to running performance and how much they should contribute to the runner's diet. Now let's put it all together by constructing a diet for optimal performance and health. To do this, we'll rely on the most widely accepted and recommended standard for proper nutrition, the Daily Food Guide Pyramid (see figure 2.2). The Food Pyramid outlines the number of servings of different food groups for a healthy diet. At the base of the pyramid are complex carbohydrates such as breads, cereals, and pasta. Nutrition experts recommend eating six to 11 servings of these foods a day. At the second level from the bottom are vegetables (three to five servings) and fruits (two to four servings). The third level features dairy products such as milk, yogurt, and cheese (two to three servings) along with sources rich in protein such as meat, eggs, beans, and nuts (two to three servings). At the top of the pyramid are food groups that we should eat sparingly. These include fats, oils, and sweets.

Adolescents who eat a variety of foods from the first three levels of the Food Pyramid will meet their basic nutritional demands for optimal health. Runners, however, may need to *increase* the recommended number of food servings to replace

Table 2.4 Protein Content in Common Foods

Food group	Serving size	Grams of protein[a]
Bread, cereal, pasta, and rice		
Whole wheat sandwich bread	2 slices	4
Bagel	1 (3 1/2" diameter)	7
Boxed cereal (ready to eat)	1 cup	1-10
Oatmeal, cooked	3/4 cup	4
Spaghetti/macaroni, cooked	1 cup	7
Brown rice, cooked	3/4 cup	4
Dairy		
Milk, 2% fat	1 cup	8
Yogurt, low-fat	1 cup	12
Cheese (cheddar, swiss)	1 ounce	8
Meat, poultry, fish, beans, nuts, and eggs		
Ground beef, broiled	4 ounces	32
Chicken breast, broiled	4 ounces	32
Fish (cod, grouper, salmon), baked	4 ounces	28-32
Black beans, cooked	1/2 cup	8
Canned beans (white/navy), with sweet sauce	1/2 cup	6
Almonds, dry roasted	1/2 cup	12
Sunflower seeds	1/2 cup	16
Peanuts, dry roasted	1/2 cup	18
Peanut butter	2 tablespoons	8
Egg	1 large	7

[a]To figure out the number of calories from protein in each of these foods, multiply grams × 4.

the extra energy they use in training. The high end of the ranges for servings of each food group—11 for complex carbohydrates, 5 for vegetables, 4 for fruits, and so forth—will supply about 2,800 calories a day. Looking back at table 2.1 on page 18, you can see that this number of calories would be more than sufficient for 12- to 18-year-old girls who run five miles a day. But for girls whose training is more extensive and for 12- to 18-year-old boys, the highest number of recommended servings won't meet energy needs. How can you boost calorie intake? Start at the bottom of the Food Pyramid and add one or two servings of complex carbohydrates, fruits, and vegetables. But stay away from foods from the highest level of the pyramid because they're full of "empty" nonnutritious calories.

We've designed a sample menu on page 26 to meet the energy and nutrition requirements for a 15- to 18-year-old boy who runs five miles a day or who does other forms of training that demand as much energy. Here's how the diet shapes up in terms of number of servings from each food group:

- Breads, cereals, pasta, and rice = 14 servings
- Vegetables = 6 servings
- Fruits = 5 servings
- Dairy = 3 1/2 servings
- Meats, beans, eggs, and nuts = 3 servings

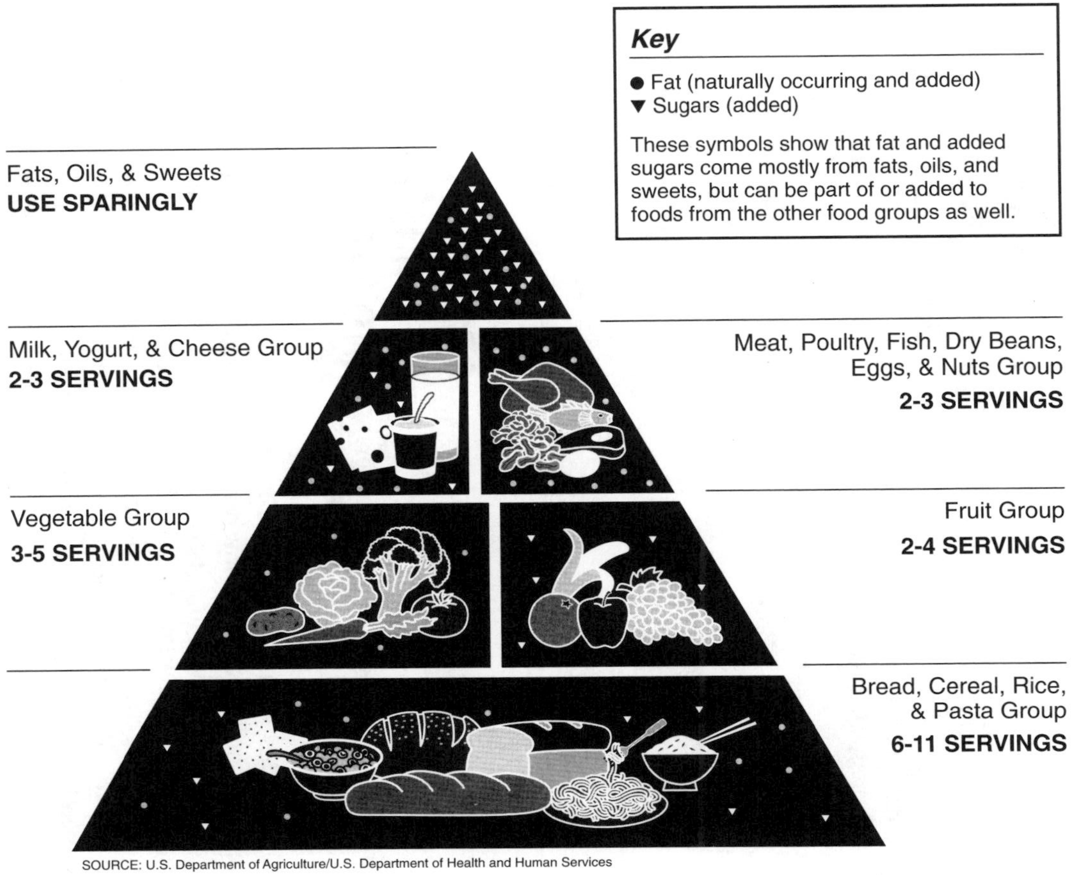

What Counts as One Serving?

The amount of food that counts as 1 serving is listed below. If you eat a larger portion, count it as more than 1 serving. For example, a dinner portion of spaghetti would count as 2 or 3 servings of pasta.

Be sure to eat at least the lowest number of servings from the five major food groups listed below. You need them for the vitamins, minerals, carbohydrates, and protein they provide. Just try to pick the lowest fat choices from the food groups. No specific serving size is given for the fats, oils, and sweets group because the message is USE SPARINGLY.

Food Groups

Milk, Yogurt, Cheese

1 cup of milk or yogurt   1 1/2 ounces of natural cheese   2 ounces of process cheese

Meat, Poultry, Fish, Dry Beans, Eggs, and Nuts

2-3 ounces of cooked lean meat, poultry, or fish   1/2 cup of cooked dry beans, 1 egg, or 2 tablespoons of peanut butter count as 1 ounce of lean meat

Vegetable

1 cup of raw leafy vegetables   1/2 cup of other vegetables, cooked or chopped raw   3/4 cup of vegetable juice

Fruit

1 medium apple, banana, orange   1/2 cup of chopped, cooked, or canned fruit   3/4 cup of fruit juice

Bread, Cereal, Rice, and Pasta

1 slice of bread   1 ounce of ready-to-eat cereal   1/2 cup of cooked cereal, rice, or pasta

---

Key

● Fat (naturally occurring and added)
▼ Sugars (added)

These symbols show that fat and added sugars come mostly from fats, oils, and sweets, but can be part of or added to foods from the other food groups as well.

Meat, Poultry, Fish, Dry Beans, Eggs, & Nuts Group
2-3 SERVINGS

Fruit Group
2-4 SERVINGS

Bread, Cereal, Rice, & Pasta Group
6-11 SERVINGS

Fats, Oils, & Sweets
USE SPARINGLY

Milk, Yogurt, & Cheese Group
2-3 SERVINGS

Vegetable Group
3-5 SERVINGS

SOURCE: U.S. Department of Agriculture/U.S. Department of Health and Human Services

Figure 2.2 The Food Pyramid: A guide for optimal daily nutrition.

SAMPLE MENU FOR A 15- TO 18-YEAR-OLD MALE RUNNER

Total calories: 3,500
% Carbohydrate: 65
% Fat: 15
% Protein: 20

Breakfast (typically eaten at home)
    1 1/2 - 2 cups Cheerios
        (ready-to-eat cereal)
    2 slices whole grain toast with:
        2 teaspoons margarine
        2 teaspoons jam
    1 banana
    12 oz orange juice
    1 cup skim milk

Morning snack (take to school in backpack)
    1 bagel
    1 apple (or other fruit)
    Water

Lunch (cold lunch at school)
    Chicken sandwich
        3 ounces baked chicken breast (skinless)
        2 slices whole grain bread
        Lettuce
        Mustard
    1/2 cup pasta salad with low-fat salad
    dressing
    1 slice of cantaloupe (or other fruit)
    1 carrot
    1 cup skim milk

Afternoon snack (take to school in backpack)
    1/2 cup canned fruit or 1/4 cup dried fruit
    6 graham crackers (3" square)
    Water

Dinner (eaten at restaurant or at home)
Cheeseburger
    3 ounces lean ground beef or turkey
    Whole wheat bun
    Tomato and lettuce slices
    1 slice cheese
    Ketchup and mustard
1/2 cup baked beans
Large salad
    2 cups lettuce/mixed greens
    1 cup mixed vegetables (tomatoes,
    cucumbers, carrots, peppers,
    mushrooms, etc.)
    2 tablespoons low-fat salad dressing
Iced tea (decaffeinated)

After-dinner snack or dessert
    1/2 cup low-fat frozen yogurt
    6 vanilla wafers

Note. If breakfast and dinner meals are too much food for one sitting, you can substitute a sandwich, fruit, or vegetable for a snack.

[a]Fresh spinach would be great for greens in salads.

The total number of calories in the sample menu is 3,500 (65 percent carbohydrate, 20 percent protein, and 15 percent fat). This may seem like too much food, and it might be too much for younger runners who train less than five miles a day or its energy equivalent. But it's also possible that the sample menu provides *too little* energy for runners whose training is more extensive. How do you know if you're getting the right amount of energy and nutrients? If you're maintaining a healthy body weight and good general health, you can be assured that you're eating right. Shortly, we'll discuss body weight and general health further.

OTHER KEY NUTRIENTS: VITAMINS, MINERALS, AND WATER

In addition to the energy sources described above, food contains other important nutrients, namely, vitamins, minerals, and water. None of these can be used directly for muscle fuel. Instead, they serve a number of different physiological functions in the body, including energy production and delivery, growth, healing, and protection against disease. In this section, we will examine these nutrients and their contribution to distance running performance. We will also answer key questions about whether runners need special supplements of these nutrients.

Getting Your Vitamins and Minerals

Vitamins are organic compounds found in many different kinds of meats, fruits, vegetables, and dairy products. A sufficient amount of these nutrients is essential for distance runners because they play a major role in *metabolism*, the conversion of food into energy. For example, several of the B-complex vitamins and niacin act like enzymes to speed up the metabolism of carbohydrates and fats. Vitamins play many other roles in maintaining high levels of performance and health. Vitamin C, found in fruits and vegetables, strengthens bones and connective tissue. This vitamin also protects the body against infections and common colds by boosting the immune system, the body's defense against disease. Vitamin B_1 (thiamine), found in meats, grains, and nuts, is involved in forming hemoglobin, the substance that carries oxygen in the blood to the muscles. Other vitamins are essential for young runners because they contribute to normal growth. As you may be aware, vitamin D, found in dairy foods and eggs, promotes bone growth.

Minerals are inorganic elements found in water, vegetables, and animal products such as dairy and meat. Among their major roles, minerals help to build bones, form enzymes, transmit neural signals, and produce muscle contractions. For runners, one of the most important minerals is calcium, which strengthens the bones and helps them grow. Calcium is also required to stimulate muscle contraction, so without it, the muscles can't produce force. Good sources of calcium include dairy foods, such as milk, yogurt, and cheese, vegetables, and whole grain foods, such as whole wheat bread.

Another important mineral for runners is iron because it plays a key role in forming hemoglobin. Iron is found in red meats, green vegetables, eggs, nuts, and whole grains. Endurance athletes can easily have low iron and hemoglobin levels. One way iron can be depleted is through sweating. Hemoglobin can be lost from red blood cells that are damaged simply as a result of the repetitive stress of footstrike during the running stride. Adolescent girls lose iron through menstruation as well. In fact, young female runners are at particularly high risk for iron deficiency. Several researchers have reported that more than 50 percent of female runners studied had insufficient iron levels. Extreme iron deficiency can result in *anemia*, a condition in which red blood cells and hemoglobin are decreased to dangerously low levels. Anemia severely reduces the oxygen-carrying capacity of blood cells, limiting the runner's endurance capacity. This condition can lead to serious health consequences if the runner does not boost iron intake.

Should Runners Take Vitamin and Mineral Supplements?

Since vitamins and minerals are so critical to good health and athletic performance many people think they should take supplements of these nutrients beyond their normal diets. At present, however, most nutrition experts agree that vitamin and mineral "pills" are not needed for young athletes if they eat a balanced diet. This means eating the required number of food servings from the Food Pyramid to meet energy needs. But, if you're at all concerned that you're not getting the necessary amounts of these nutrients, we recommend that you buy a generic brand of a multiple vitamin and mineral supplement that does not exceed 100 percent of the RDAs (the information labels on these products will tell you what percentage of the RDA they offer).

No strong scientific evidence exists to prove that runners can improve endurance performance by taking extra doses of vitamins and minerals. In fact, the body will simply excrete excessive amounts of most vitamins and minerals. For example, vitamin C and the B-complex vitamins are transported in water in the body. These and other water-soluble vitamins are eliminated in the urine when their daily intake exceeds the body's requirements. In contrast, the fat-soluble vitamins—A, D, E, and K—are stored in body fat. Harmful, and even toxic, effects can result when you take in excessive amounts (several hundred percent of the RDA) of these vitamins.

Major nutritional concerns for young runners are that their diets may consist of too much unhealthy junk food and that they may not be getting adequate amounts of vitamins and minerals. Like many adolescents, they may prefer sweets and high-fat fast foods to fruits and vegetables. Rather than relying on costly supplements, parents and coaches should strive to educate their young runners about nutrition, encouraging them to eat nutritious foods. It's no easy task, but it's worth the effort to ensure a lifetime of good health. Be aware, however, that sometimes runners may need vitamin or mineral supplements. For example, by eliminating red meat from the diet, vegetarians may not be getting enough iron. For such special cases, we recommend that parents seek guidance from their family physician, who may refer you to a nutritional specialist.

The Runner's Drink of Choice: Water

About 60 percent of body weight is made up of water, and this nutrient is a vital part of every cell, tissue, and organ in the body. Maintaining normal fluid levels is one of the most important nutritional concerns for runners because water is involved in many energy-making processes. When the body loses water, or dehydrates, the blood thickens and its flow through the vessels slows down, limiting oxygen and nutrient delivery to the working muscles. When dehydrated, the body places undue stress on the heart to pump more blood faster. Fatigue occurs rapidly in this condition, which can be life threatening.

Water in the blood is also required for cooling the body. The heat that accumulates in the muscles during running is released to the atmosphere through evaporation of sweat from the skin. Without sufficient water for cooling purposes, the body's core temperature can rise to levels that impair performance because the heat breaks down enzymes that help to make energy. In hot, humid weather, this situation can lead to heat injuries, such as heat exhaustion and heat stroke, which are very dangerous and demand medical attention. Young runners are particularly susceptible to heat injuries because of their large surface area to body weight ratio and low sweat production. Fur-

thermore, evidence shows that if young athletes are not reminded to stop and take fluids, they may not voluntarily drink enough to rehydrate the body. Therefore, especially in hot and humid conditions, coaches should insist that athletes drink water before, during, and after training.

As long as they have taken sufficient fluids in the hours leading up to competition, young runners usually do not need to drink during a race. Unlike the marathon and other adult races, youth events up to 5,000 meters are too short to cause dehydration in moderate temperature conditions. Likewise, athletes do not need to use glucose- or glycogen-containing sport drinks if they are getting sufficient carbohydrates in their diets. But sport drinks may be useful for replacing energy following demanding training sessions and races that have caused stomach upset or a short-term lack of appetite for solid foods.

© Terry Wild Studio

ENERGY FOR COMPETITION: THE PRERACE MEAL

It's an unfortunate, but fairly common, occurrence for runners to suffer disappointing racing results because of what they have or have not eaten in the hours before competition. For example, if athletes skip a meal on race day, they may feel tired and drained of energy even before the gun goes off. Eating too soon before a race or eating the wrong kinds of foods can cause an upset stomach or diarrhea.

How can runners avoid these sorts of problems? Generally speaking, they should eat the prerace meal about two to four hours before competing, consuming high-energy foods that satisfy the appetite and digest easily. Even for morning cross-country races, it's best for runners to wake up early and have a light breakfast because glucose and liver glycogen reserves can be partially depleted overnight.

The prerace meal should consist mostly of foods rich in complex carbohydrates, such as those listed in table 2.2a. Breakfast foods such as cereal with milk, toast and jelly, and pancakes or waffles with syrup are fine for morning competitions. It's okay to include small amounts of foods with fat and protein, such as butter and bacon, for taste. For afternoon or evening races, some runners prefer a plate of pasta (easy on the spices!) as the standard fare because this food has such a high carbohydrate content and digests easily. Water is the best drink to wash down the prerace meal. Caffeinated beverages such as cola sodas and iced tea have a *diuretic* effect, promoting water loss because caffeine increases urine production.

Years ago, athletes were told to eat sugary foods such as candy or honey in the minutes before competition for an energy boost. We now know that this practice can actually drain energy. The body responds to a high intake of simple sugars by removing glucose from the blood and transporting it into the muscles. The temporary drop in blood glucose levels, a condition called *hypoglycemia*, causes feelings of fatigue because it robs the brain of its energy source. This condition is more severe in individuals who are not accustomed to eating very much sugar at one time. Thus, hypoglycemia is likely to occur in runners who don't normally eat sugar but load up on it shortly before a race, thinking that they'll get an energy boost.

Perhaps the best advice to the young runner concerning the prerace meal is to go with what works best for you. A good strategy for figuring out your optimal prerace meal is to take note of what you ate before your best performances. You may find a pattern where you ate the same foods prior to races in which you felt really good and ran your fastest times. Stick with those foods in the future!

OPTIMAL BODY WEIGHT AND COMPOSITION

Simply by looking at runners of different abilities you know that a slight, lean build is a characteristic of many elite performers. Certainly, some athletes would reach a higher competitive level if they had the "ideal" runner's body. But while it's possible to alter body weight and shape by changing dietary and training practices, we advise great caution in doing so. Coaches and parents should provide close supervision in overseeing athletes who are trying to make these changes. And in many cases, nutrition and sports medicine professionals should be consulted.

The ideal weight for optimal endurance performance and health varies widely across individuals depending on their height, bone structure, and body composition, or the percent of muscle and fat tissue. In some cases, you can see that a runner is too light or too heavy just by the way he looks. Unfortunately, the "eye-balling" technique for determining whether a runner would benefit from gaining or losing weight is not always effective. For example, some runners who look tiny and thin may actually have a fairly high percent body fat and relatively little muscle mass. For such individuals, a plan to gain weight by eating more high-calorie foods may actually hurt performance.

An accurate determination of optimal weight requires measurement of body fat composition. In normally active adolescents, that is, those who don't train for distance running, a healthy body fat composition ranges from 10 to 20 percent in boys and 15 to 25 percent in girls. As mentioned earlier, studies have shown that, on average, teenage distance runners have 8 to 12 percent (boys) and 12 to 16 percent (girls) body fat. Recommendations for the minimal percent body fat in adolescent runners are around 6 percent in boys and 12 percent in girls. Lower values pose dangerous risks to health because the body relies on fat stores for normal physiologic functions.

For counseling runners who are trying to lose weight, sport nutrition experts consider the percent body fat at which the individual is starting out and then use health and performance guidelines such as the ones just discussed to set goals and suggest dietary changes. For example, let's say that Jackie, a 15-year-old who is five feet, four inches tall (1.63 meters) and weighs 120 pounds (54.5 kg), has 22 percent body fat. Jackie's body weight is therefore made up of about 26.4 pounds of fat (120 pounds × .22 = 26.4 pounds). It's important to stress that Jackie doesn't need to lose weight because her body fat is in the healthy range for adolescent girls of 15 to 25 percent. But she tells her coach and parents that she really wants to lose weight to improve her performance. Through the family physician, they contact a sport nutrition expert who plans a nutritious diet that will help Jackie lose 2 percent body fat over a period of two to four months. To go from 22 percent to 20 percent body fat Jackie would have to lose about three pounds of fat.[1]

It would be extremely dangerous for Jackie to attempt to lose enough fat to reach the minimal levels. In fact, she'd have to lose almost 15 pounds of fat to get to the 12 percent lower limit. To lose that much weight in a few months, Jackie would have to drastically cut her calorie and nutrition intake. You have to restrict calories considerably to lose even one pound of fat. This effort to perform better would backfire in a big way. Jackie would be denying her body the energy and nutrients it needs for fueling the muscles in training and for promoting regeneration and elevation to higher fitness levels. Furthermore, because of the nutrient restriction that would result from such drastic dieting, she would be at

risk for bone fractures, anemia, menstrual irregularities, and other disorders that can result from poor nutrition.

Having discussed the importance of body composition when considering optimal body weight for runners, we must emphasize that it's not so easy to obtain an accurate measure of the percent body fat in an individual. The measurement techniques, such as underwater weighing and the skinfold calipers method, require training and special instruments. If coaches are not trained and experienced in these techniques, they might ask a qualified athletic trainer or a local fitness specialist to take the measurements of their athletes.[2] We recommend that coaches consult specialists who know how to take and interpret body fat measurements because the techniques for assessment typically have large error ranges of 3 to 5 percent. It would be unfortunate if athletes altered their diets based on faulty measurements of body fat.

STRATEGIES FOR GAINING AND LOSING WEIGHT

Gaining and losing weight involve tilting the body's "energy balance." When your body is in energy balance, you eat about the same number of calories that you expend in resting metabolism and during training. To gain weight through changes in diet, you must eat more calories than you burn. To lose weight, the reverse must occur. You can also change your body weight by altering activity levels. For example, to lose weight, you can exercise more, thereby burning more calories. As a competitive runner, however, altering your activity level for the purpose of gaining or losing weight might interfere with your training plan itself.

Runners should gear effort to gain or lose weight toward safely attaining the values that we've listed for body composition in average teenage distance runners and normal, healthy teenagers. The most important general guidelines for safe outcomes are to change the diet very gradually

1. Jackie started out with a total body weight of 120 pounds, of which 26.4 pounds (22 percent) were fat. If Jackie lost one pound of fat, her total body weight would be 119 pounds, and the weight of her body fat would be 25.4 pounds. Thus, her body fat percentage would be 21.3 percent (25.4 pounds ÷ 119 pounds = .213 or 21.3 percent). A reduction of three pounds of fat would then result in 20 percent body fat because her total and body fat weights would be 117 and 23.4 pounds, respectively (23.4 pounds ÷ 117 pounds = .20 or 20 percent).

2. Because body fat assessment requires training and extensive practice, instruction in the techniques goes beyond the scope of this book. To learn more about body fat assessment, you can refer to an excellent resource called the *Practical Body Composition Kit*, published by Human Kinetics (see page 185 for reference information). Certification courses in exercise testing and prescription offered by the American College of Sports Medicine also provide training in measuring body fat.

Carla Borovicka

Bend, OR

Personal Bests:

2,000-meter
  steeplechase   6:34.54*
3,000 meters   9:08.32
5,000 meters   15:48.12

*American record

Few athletes in any sport are as serious about a healthful diet as is Carla Borovicka. Proper nutrition has been a fundamental part of her daily training for over 10 years, and the 33-year-old cites her diet as a key to her success as a world-class runner. Carla has competed all over the world, in events ranging from 1,500 meters to the marathon. She has been a pioneer in women's distance running by racing the steeplechase, an event only men ran in until 1990. In 1991 she set an American record of 6:34.54 in the 2,000-meter steeplechase.

Commenting about her long-term commitment to nutrition, Carla says, "My training sessions draw an awful lot of energy and require that I pay special attention to what I eat. Good nutrition offers me an avenue to bolster my immune system to protect against illness and injury." Carla first focused on nutrition as a high-school sprinter and hurdler in Beaverton, OR, where she grew up. "I was introduced to healthy, whole foods, and I gained awareness of the poor nutritional quality and damaging effects of food additives and processed foods," she explains. "However, it wasn't until my sophomore year of college that I really began to

look at food as a tool to improve my athletic performance." At about the same time, Carla switched from sprinting and hurdling to distance running. This transition involved changing her training and diet.

By reading books and taking college courses on nutrition, Carla discovered that eating good food could improve her body composition, boost her mental energy level, and keep her from missing training due to illness and injury. Since college, Carla has experimented with her diet to get the best health results. She avoids highly processed foods that have been stripped of nutrients and contain preservatives. "I choose fresh vegetables that have been organically grown and meats that are free of antibiotics and steroids. I also stay away from saturated fats and excess salt and sugar." Her diet consists of a variety of whole grains, fresh fruits and vegetables, seeds and nuts, cultured yogurt, nonfat soy and rice milk, and a limited amount of fish, chicken, and beef.

Carla shares her knowledge of and experience in nutrition and training with the young runners she coaches at La Pine High School in Oregon. She stresses education about nutrition. "Coaches can teach their runners about nutrition by taking them to restaurants with healthy foods when the team is traveling away from home for a race," she says. "And coaches should talk about nutrition and how it helps performance. Parents, too, can set good examples by eating healthy foods themselves."

and to meet daily requirements for all of the nutrients that sustain good health. Remember, drastic changes pose great risks to performance and health. To lose one pound of fat, you need to burn an extra 3,500 calories. That's a lot of energy! To lose that pound in one week requires cutting calorie intake by 500 calories a day, which would mean cutting out almost a full meal. Runners simply cannot afford that severe a deficiency in energy intake.

For runners trying to lose weight, a more sensible approach that won't endanger health and

performance is to cut calories by 50 to 100 a day, extending this reduction over a few months. The best strategy is to gradually cut out foods at the top of the Food Pyramid, the sweets, fats, and oils. In order to meet nutritional needs for vitamins and minerals, it's critical for athletes to keep eating a wide variety of foods from the first three levels of the Food Pyramid.

For most runners trying to *gain* weight, the key is to increase muscle mass. Regardless of whether you eat extra carbohydrates, protein, or fat, excess calorie intake will turn into fat unless you continue to exercise. So for runners who want to gain weight, we recommend increasing daily calorie intake by a small amount (100 to 200 calories) while maintaining training levels. You might even add a little extra resistance exercise such as circuit and weight training (see chapter 7) to promote muscle development. The increase in calories should come from adding an extra serving or two of high-energy, nutritious foods. Remember that no more than 10 percent of total calorie intake should come from highly processed sugars.

DISORDERED EATING AND PRESSURE TO LOSE WEIGHT

It's important to realize that genetic factors make it impossible for some individuals to attain the elite runner's body. Therefore, under no circumstances should coaches or parents pressure athletes to meet unreasonable standards for body weight or expect them to make unhealthy changes in diet. Coaches must understand that an overemphasis on weight loss and practices such as team weigh-ins strongly contribute to a condition called *disordered eating*. This condition, which occurs at alarmingly high rates in distance runners, encompasses abnormal eating behaviors that range from inadvertently falling below caloric needs to voluntary starvation. Extreme cases of voluntary starvation occur as anorexia nervosa and bulimia, diseases which are life threatening.

A main contributing factor to these eating disorders in young runners is coaches and parents who overemphasize weight loss as a means to perform better. Coaches who make derogatory remarks about athletes' bodies are the worst culprits. Even well-intended comments like, "If you lost a few pounds, you'd probably run a lot faster," can have very serious negative consequences. Thus, the desire to lose weight should come from athletes themselves in positive ways. For parents and coaches, the best

strategy for preventing disordered eating in young runners involves learning about nutrition and cultivating the philosophy that health comes before performance and body image. We encourage parents, coaches, and young runners to keep reading about and studying the interaction between nutrition, endurance performance, and health. There's a lot more to learn (see our reference list on page 185 for some excellent resources).

SUMMARY

An understanding of the connection between nutrition and endurance performance is vital to success in developing young runners. Let's recap the key links in this relationship:

- Because carbohydrates are the primary source of energy for runners who compete in events between 800 and 5,000 meters, they should make up a large part (around 55 to 70 percent) of young runners' diets.
- As long as runners eat a variety of foods with a sufficient amount of calories from the Food Pyramid, they don't need to supplement their diets with vitamin and mineral pills.
- Coaches must encourage runners to drink water before, during, and after training sessions.
- The ideal prerace meal, which runners should eat about two to four hours before competition, is high in complex carbohydrates.
- To determine the optimal weight for a runner, a qualified fitness specialist or exercise physiologist should take measurements to determine body fat composition.
- Parents and coaches should closely supervise runners who want to lose weight. Ideally, the athlete should consult a physician or professional nutrition expert.
- Coaches and parents should never pressure runners to lose weight.

CHAPTER 3
Running Physiology

From our discussion about nutrition and energy, you know that a good diet is the foundation for successful distance running performance. But how do the energy sources in food actually fuel the muscles and make them contract? Why is it that, despite eating a good diet, runners fatigue when trying to sustain fast paces? If nutrition were the only key to successful running performance, then training would probably mean just sitting around and eating good food! But, as you know, effective training for runners depends on repeatedly stressing the body to develop its energy-making systems. As you'll learn in this chapter, these physiological systems convert the energy from food into a fuel, called ATP, that makes the muscles contract. You'll also learn how two specific energy-making systems, the *aerobic* and *anaerobic* systems, contribute to helping runners do their best in 800- to 5,000-meter races. We'll talk about aspects of aerobic and anaerobic fitness such as $\dot{V}O_2$max, running economy, and the lactate/ventilatory threshold. This background on the physiological factors that determine running performance and cause fatigue will lead to a discussion of how the body adapts physiologically to training. Finally, we'll provide some applications of running physiology that you can use in training on a day-to-day basis. As you read, keep in mind that our lesson in running physiology is ultimately intended to help you choose the right kinds and amounts of training to improve fitness and performance, both of which are strongly related to the body's capacity to supply and use energy.

THE ENERGY SOURCE: ATP

From our discussion in the last chapter you know that energy for muscle activity comes from nutrients in the diet. The muscles, however, do not directly use the energy released during the breakdown of carbohydrates, fats, and proteins. Instead, it is harnessed, or stored, in a chemical compound called *adenosine triphosphate*, or *ATP*, that is stored in almost all cells in the body. Exercise physiologists refer to ATP as the "energy currency" because it is the only means through which the energy in food can be exchanged for physical work. Our muscles depend on ATP for running.

ATP and Muscle Activity

Because ATP is the key to muscle activity, you can imagine its value in athletic performance. This commodity is especially precious for distance runners because the resting body stores only enough ATP to fuel maximal exercise for about five seconds. Imagine what would happen if runners had to rely on these limited stores of ATP for energy. Total exhaustion would set in after only a few strides, so the longest race in a track or cross-country meet would have to be about 30 to 40 meters!

How, then, do runners get the energy to endure long distances? The answer is that ATP can be continually reformed and restocked in muscle cells through the breakdown of food nutrients. To illustrate this process, figure 3.1 shows that one molecule of glucose is completely broken down, or *metabolized*, in the muscle cell to produce 36 units of ATP. Notice that in this example oxygen (O_2) is used in the process and carbon dioxide (CO_2), water (H_2O), and heat are formed as *metabolic by-products*. These by-products are eliminated from the body in the breath and sweat.

The ATP units formed in the breakdown of glucose, fat, and protein must be "split" to make muscles contract. ATP splits in a process that begins when neural impulses from the brain tell the muscle to contract. When ATP splits, the energy released allows muscle fibers to shorten and produce "contractile tension" that is transmitted to the muscle's tendon. In turn, the tendon pulls on the bone to which it is connected, moving the limb. It is important to understand that the production of muscular force, triggered by the splitting of ATP, is the physiological basis of running. The runner's speed or pace is related to how much power his muscles can generate. So the ability to keep up a fast pace depends on how rapidly the body

$$\text{Glucose} + O_2 \rightarrow 36 \text{ ATP} + H_2O + CO_2 + \text{Heat}$$

Figure 3.1 When 1 molecule of glucose is broken down in the muscle cell in the presence of oxygen (O_2), it produces water (H_2O), carbon dioxide (CO_2), heat, and 36 units of ATP.

can produce ATP. Training increases the rate and efficiency of ATP production through many mechanisms—more on this later.

ATP Production Via the Energy Pathways

Figure 3.1 shows a simplified picture of how the body uses energy from food to form ATP. In reality, a sequence of many complex biochemical reactions must take place in muscle cells to break down carbohydrates, fats, and proteins. These reactions are referred to as the energy pathways (see figure 3.2 for a brief summary of the breakdown of glucose, a carbohydrate). You don't need to know all the names of the compounds in the energy pathways—unless you are studying for a PhD in exercise biochemistry! But it's important for you to learn about some of the reactions and the enzymes that trigger them. This information will help you understand how energy metabolism is linked to running performance.

Let's first examine how glucose gets broken down in the energy pathways to form ATP. The steps begin with a process called *glycolysis* that breaks down glucose into a chemical compound called *pyruvic acid*. Muscle cells will use pyruvic acid to make more ATP if there is sufficient oxygen and enzyme activity in the muscle cells where these reactions take place. If oxygen and enzyme activity are lacking in the cells, a chemical compound called lactic acid will be formed. You may be aware that lactic acid is a major contributor to fatigue in racing distances between 400 and 5,000 meters. You may be surprised, however, to find out that lactic acid itself is not the true cause of fatigue. Instead, hydrogen ions that dissociate, or break away, from the lactic acid compound are responsible for slowing the runner's performance.

As shown in figure 3.2, if glycolysis ends with lactic acid a single molecule of glucose produces only two ATP units. But if pyruvic acid is formed, ATP can be made in two new pathways, called the Krebs cycle and electron transport. These pathways allow the glucose molecule to

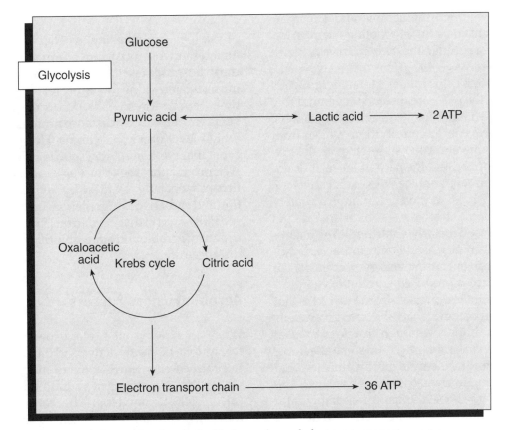

Figure 3.2 Breakdown of glucose in glycolysis, Krebs cycle, and electron transport.

be completely metabolized to produce 36 units of ATP. Keep in mind that greater amounts of ATP formed per unit of food nutrient translate directly into better endurance performance. So one goal of training for distance running is to help "steer" energy metabolism toward pyruvic acid (and the Krebs cycle and electron transport) and away from lactic acid. That's exactly what effective training can do.

Aerobic and Anaerobic Energy Contribution

From our discussion, you can see that oxygen plays a key role in determining how much ATP will be produced by the breakdown of food. Two terms with which you may be familiar, aerobic and anaerobic, are used to classify the energy pathways based on whether or not oxygen is involved in the reactions. In the aerobic pathway, oxygen is used to produce ATP from carbohydrates and fats. In the anaerobic pathway, oxygen is not required to produce ATP, and only carbohydrates can be used as fuel.

Both the intensity and duration of exercise determine how much the aerobic and anaerobic pathways will contribute to fueling the muscles. In distance running, the two pathways work together to provide ATP. How much each pathway contributes to the runner's total energy needs depends on the pace and distance covered. Table 3.1 shows estimated percentages of the aerobic and anaerobic energy contribution in races from 800 to 5,000 meters. You can see that as the distance gets longer, and the pace of the race slows, a runner uses more aerobic energy. At 5,000 meters, for example, most of the energy, approximately 93 percent, comes from the aerobic pathways. As racing distance drops, the contribution of anaerobic metabolism increases. For example, approximately 43 percent of the energy needed for an 800-meter race is produced without oxygen.

An important lesson taken from table 3.1 is that both the aerobic and anaerobic energy systems must be conditioned through training. Even in the longer events, runners rely on some anaerobic energy for midrace surges, sprint finishes, and uphill running in cross-country. As we will consider later in the book, the amount of aerobic and anaerobic training an athlete needs will depend both on level of development and event specialty.

Table 3.1 Estimated Contribution of Aerobic and Anaerobic Energy to Different Racing Distances

	Percent energy contribution	
Event	Aerobic	Anaerobic
100 meters	8	92
200 meters	14	86
400 meters	30	70
800 meters	57	43
1,500 meters	76	24
3,000 meters	88	12
5,000 meters	93	7

Data in second column are adapted from Péronnet and Thibault (1989, pp. 453-465) and Leger, Mercier, and Gauvin (1986, pp. 113-120) and were compiled by Martin and Coe (1991).

PHYSIOLOGICAL DETERMINANTS OF RUNNING PERFORMANCE

Physiologically speaking, what does it take to be a successful distance runner? You know that ATP must be produced at a high rate to keep the muscles contracting forcefully for long periods of time. Since more ATP is produced aerobically versus anaerobically, distance runners must have a high level of aerobic fitness. However, in the event that the anaerobic system is called upon for ATP production, they must also be anaerobically fit to prevent fatigue caused by lactic acid production and carbohydrate depletion. In the following sections, we will discuss various factors that contribute to aerobic and anaerobic fitness for young distance runners.

Aerobic Fitness Factors

When an athlete runs at slow speeds, relatively few muscle fibers are active and they do not have to produce very much force to move the body. Under these low-intensity conditions, the body can meet the demand for ATP aerobically. That is, the body can supply oxygen to the working muscles in sufficient amounts and at a fast enough rate to help make ATP. Oxygen transport involves the lungs, blood, and the cardiovascular system, which consists of the heart and blood vessels (see figure 3.3). As you know, we breathe oxygen from the atmosphere into the lungs through the mouth, trachea, and bronchi. In the lungs, the oxygen is transported into small, sac-like branches called *alveoli*. Through the alveoli run many small blood vessels, or *pulmonary capillaries*, that have thin walls. Oxygen diffuses through the thin-walled pulmonary capillaries into the bloodstream and attaches to hemoglobin.

Then this oxygen-enriched blood flows from the lungs to the left side of the heart. Next the heart pumps the blood through the aorta to the organs and tissues of the body. During running, the blood vessels channel up to 85 percent of the blood flow to the working muscles. Upon reaching the muscles, the oxygenated blood passes through capillaries to enter muscle cells. Aerobic metabolism takes place in a part of the cell called the *mitochondria*, also known as the cell's energy "powerhouse."

Under normal circumstances, breathing rate does not limit the capacity to transport oxygen. Our lungs normally work so well that we inhale a surplus of oxygen. Practically speaking, then, runners gain little by consciously changing their breathing patterns. The best advice is simply to let breathing occur naturally through the mouth or through both the mouth and the nose.

A Measure of Success: Maximal Aerobic Power or $\dot{V}O_2max$

An individual's potential for success in distance running is partly related to maximal aerobic power, or $\dot{V}O_2max$. $\dot{V}O_2max$ is the maximum amount of oxygen that can be used by the muscles in a given period of time. This measure is a product of the heart's pumping capacity and the muscles' ability to use oxygen to form ATP. $\dot{V}O_2max$ is assessed in laboratory tests in which

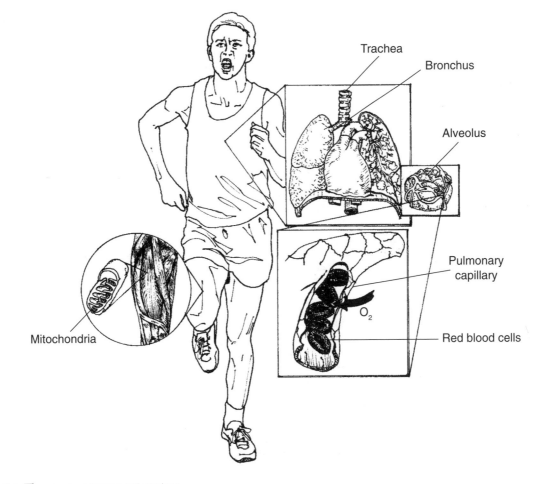

Figure 3.3 The oxygen transport system.

the athlete runs on a treadmill at increasing speeds. During the test, scientists measure the amount and concentration of oxygen that the athlete breathes in and out. As running speed increases, oxygen utilization by the muscles initially increases at a linear rate (see figure 3.4). Then, with further increases in speed, a point is reached at which oxygen utilization levels off: This is $\dot{V}O_2$max (point A in figure 3.4). The athlete, who is extremely fatigued at this point, can run a bit faster for a short while, but the energy to do so must come from the anaerobic pathways.

$\dot{V}O_2$max is measured in milliliters (ml) of oxygen used, expressed relative to the individual's kilograms (kg) of body weight, during one minute (min) of maximal exercise. A high $\dot{V}O_2$max is a good predictor of distance running ability. In fact, studies have shown that elite young runners have very high $\dot{V}O_2$max values of 60 to 70 ml $\cdot$ kg^{-1} $\cdot$ min^{-1}. In contrast, nonathletic youths have much lower values of about 35 to 45 ml $\cdot$ kg^{-1} $\cdot$ min^{-1}. Coaches don't necessarily need to have their athletes' $\dot{V}O_2$max measured to design effective training programs. But they should understand that training can improve maximal aerobic power. Endurance training increases $\dot{V}O_2$max by making the heart a more powerful pump and opening up blood vessels to deliver more oxygen to the working muscles.

Slow-Twitch Muscle Fibers for Endurance

An individual's aerobic power partly depends on the genetic makeup of the muscle fibers. Muscle tissue is composed of two distinct types of fibers, slow-twitch (ST) and fast-twitch (FT). ST, or Type I, muscle fibers are best suited for endurance activity and are therefore selectively "recruited" by the nervous system during low-intensity activity. ST fibers have a great capacity to contract for long periods of time without fatiguing. This is because they have high concentrations of mitochondria, aerobic enzymes, and myoglobin, which transports oxygen in muscle tissue.

It's important to understand that genetic factors determine the muscles' fiber type makeup. Thus, individuals who are born with a high percentage of ST fibers will have a natural advantage in endurance activities. In fact, studies have shown that many of the best adult runners in the marathon have over 80 percent ST fibers (Noakes 1991). Studies have not been conducted to determine the relationship between fiber type makeup and endurance performance in youths. This is because the "muscle biopsy" technique for determining fiber type composition is very painful and researchers are reluctant to perform it on children and adolescents.

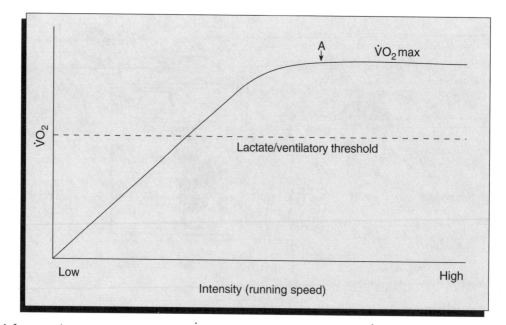

Figure 3.4 Increase in oxygen consumption ($\dot{V}O_2$) with faster running speeds. $\dot{V}O_2$max is shown at point A where oxygen consumption levels off. The broken line indicates the lactate/ventilatory threshold.

Although some controversy surrounds this issue, exercise physiologists believe that training cannot change fiber type. That is, you can't turn FT fibers into ST fibers by doing enough low-intensity running. All runners, however, regard-less of their fiber type composition, can improve their aerobic fitness through training. This is because endurance exercise can condition the ST fibers that are present in muscles, increasing their aerobic power.

Running Economy

As we mentioned in chapter 1, studies have shown that young athletes are notoriously inefficient runners. In other words, they have poor running economy. Exercise physiologists measure running economy as the amount, or "cost," of oxygen required to run at a given pace. Partly due to poor technique, young runners use excessive amounts of oxygen compared to adult runners. All other factors being equal, however, individuals with relatively good running economy can outperform inefficient counterparts. To illustrate, figure 3.5 shows values of oxygen consumption for two athletes (runners A and B) running at paces between 188 and 214 meters per minute, or approximately 8:30 to 7:30 per mile. Let's say that runners A and B have the same $\dot{V}O_2$max (60 ml · kg^{-1} · min^{-1}) as marked in the figure by the solid horizontal line.

Although these runners have the same $\dot{V}O_2$max, they differ in running economy. Note, for example, that at a pace of 201 meters per minute, or an 8:00-mile pace, runners A and B consume

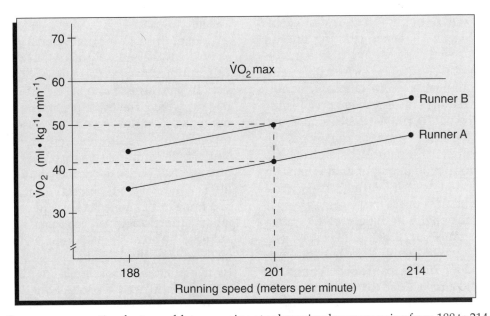

Figure 3.5 Oxygen consumption for two athletes running at submaximal paces ranging from 188 to 214 meters per minute, or about 7:30- to 8:30-mile pace. Runner A has superior running economy. (Adapted from Daniels 1985.)

42 and 50 milliliters of oxygen (per kg of body weight) per minute, respectively. We say that runner A has better running economy because he uses less oxygen than runner B to maintain the same pace. Because runner B is using more oxygen, he is closer to his $\dot{V}O_2$max than runner A. In fact, runner B is working at 83 percent of his maximal aerobic capacity ($50 \div 60 = .83$), while runner A is working at only 70 percent ($42 \div 60 = .70$). Poor running economy taxes the aerobic system and causes the athlete to rely more heavily on anaerobic energy, leading to fatigue. One cause of poor running economy is poor technique (see chapters 5 and 6).

Anaerobic Fitness Factors

With faster running speeds, more muscle fibers become active and their force output is greater. The increased muscle activity forces the respiratory and cardiovascular systems to supply more oxygen at a faster rate. For example, going from rest to high-intensity exercise, the young runner's breathing rate may increase by four times, from about 15 to 60 breaths a minute. High-intensity exercise may elevate the heart rate from about 70 to 210 beats per minute. During a maximum effort, the heart may pump about three to four times more blood per stroke compared to resting levels.

Despite the enormous increase in heart and lung output, the rate of oxygenated blood supply may fall short of the muscles' needs during intense running, like on the last lap of an 800-meter race. When oxygen supply and utilization can no longer increase with faster running speeds, $\dot{V}O_2$max is reached. As we have discussed, beyond this point ATP must be formed almost exclusively through anaerobic metabolism. Because fast running requires anaerobic energy, it is important for the young runner to be as anaerobically fit as possible. We stress the words "as possible" because of the natural limits on anaerobic energy production in prepubertal youths.

What determines an individual's capacity to perform anaerobic work? One of the major factors is enzyme activity in the glycolytic energy pathway. Enzymes are proteins that speed up ATP production. For example, the enzyme *phosphofructokinase*, or *PFK*, helps break down glucose to pyruvic acid and lactic acid during glycolysis. Levels of this enzyme increase markedly during puberty, partly explaining the improvement of anaerobic fitness with maturation.

Another factor that determines anaerobic work capacity is lactic acid. When lactic acid builds up to high levels, hydrogen ions, which dissociate from it, destroy enzymes in the energy pathways, weaken muscle contractions, and cause rather strong feelings of fatigue. This description of lactic acid may lead you to think of it as the "runner's nemesis." However, lactic acid actually plays a necessary role in energy production. When muscles work under anaerobic conditions, ATP simply cannot be formed, and therefore the muscles cannot contract, without converting glucose to lactic acid. It is a paradox of sorts, but runners need to produce lactic acid to sustain top speeds, even though its accumulation eventually leads to fatigue and slowing. As we'll consider shortly, training helps runners perform without having to produce so much lactic acid, and it helps reduce the negative effects of the lactic acid that does build up.

Lactate and Ventilatory Thresholds: The Onset of Fatigue

Even at relatively slow speeds, anaerobic metabolism actively supplies some of the runner's energy needs, producing lactic acid. But during easy running, the circulatory system easily removes the small amount of lactic acid formed in the muscle tissue. As the pace quickens, the body will reach a point at which lactic acid is produced faster than it can be eliminated from the muscles. Exercise physiologists refer to this point as the "lactate threshold."

The accumulation of lactic acid during high-intensity work is closely matched by a buildup of CO_2, another by-product of metabolism. CO_2 triggers an increase in ventilation, or breathing. The pace at which breathing becomes noticeably labored is called the "ventilatory threshold." This threshold occurs at about 60 to 70 percent of $\dot{V}O_2$max in untrained youths (see figure 3.4). In other words, the speed at the ventilatory threshold is about 60 to 70 percent of the speed corresponding to $\dot{V}O_2$max. Because the rapid accumulation of lactic acid is accompanied by a rapid increase in breathing, some exercise physiologists refer to these changes together using the term *lactate/ventilatory threshold*.

Why do you need to know about the lactate and ventilatory thresholds? A major objective of training is to increase the speed of running at which these thresholds occur. The goal is to be able to run at a faster pace without accumulating lactic acid and breathing very hard. You should design some training sessions for running at a pace that pushes these thresholds, raising them higher (see chapter 8). Later, we'll give you more detailed guidelines for how to determine this pace.

Fast-Twitch Muscle Fibers for Speed

During high-intensity work when movements demand great force, fast-twitch (FT), or Type II, muscle fibers are recruited into action. FT muscle fibers are large in diameter and can generate considerable tension rapidly. A naturally high percentage of FT fibers gives athletes an edge in sprinting and middle distances races such as 800 meters. This advantage is due to the high levels of anaerobic enzymes in FT fibers, which make them able to contract without oxygen. Given their anaerobic properties, however, such as inefficient glycogen use and lactic acid production, these fibers fatigue quickly. But like ST fibers, training can enhance the energy-making properties of FT fibers.

TRAINING SOLUTIONS TO THE "ENERGY PROBLEMS"

The following are the three major physiological elements that determine success in distance running:

- $\dot{V}O_2$max
- Lactate/ventilatory threshold
- Running economy

Young runners are far from their potential to perform at high levels because they have not yet developed these capacities. You might think of limiting factors like a low anaerobic threshold and poor running economy as "energy problems." It's important for you to understand how training solves the energy problems by improving physiological fitness and performance.

Adaptations to Aerobic Training

Table 3.2 summarizes some of the key physiological changes that occur following aerobic and anaerobic training in 12- to 18-year-olds. Studies have shown that $\dot{V}O_2$max can increase by 10 to 20

Table 3.2	Physiological Changes Occuring With Training in Youths
Type of training	Physiological changes
Aerobic	↑ $\dot{V}O_2$max ↑ Maximal cardiac output ↓ Resting and submaximal heart rate ↑ Size and number of mitochondria ↑ Aerobic enzymes ↑ Capacity to metabolize fat
Anaerobic[a]	↑ Anaerobic enzymes ↑ Maximal lactic acid production ↑ Capacity to buffer and remove lactic acid

[a]These changes are typically observed in postpubertal youths.

percent in youths who participate in a progressive program of moderate-intensity exercise for three to five days a week over a three-month period (Pate and Ward 1990). Aerobic training improves the heart's pumping capacity by increasing maximal cardiac output, or the greatest amount of oxygen-rich blood it can deliver to the muscles.

As a result of aerobic training, athletes experience a lowering of resting and low-intensity exercise heart rate, which also reflects better pumping efficiency, during rest and submaximal activity. Besides its cardiovascular benefits, aerobic training improves the ability of muscle fibers to extract and use oxygen to make ATP. These improvements are due partly to an increase in the number and size of mitochondria, the energy powerhouse in muscle cells. In addition, the concentration of aerobic enzymes increases in response to training, allowing the muscles to extract and use more oxygen. Because of this increased capacity to deliver and use oxygen, the trained runner's body can make greater use of fat as a fuel for muscle contraction. This is important because fat metabolism spares glycogen, delaying fatigue that can be caused by glycogen depletion.

Adaptations to Anaerobic Training

High-intensity training of postpubertal youths results in a greater capacity to perform anaerobic work. One of the most important changes is an increased amount of key anaerobic enzymes, like PFK. Another interesting training effect is an increase in the amount of lactic acid that can be produced during high-intensity work. Remember the paradox about lactic acid: It is necessary to sustain muscle activity, but it causes fatigue upon accumulation. While anaerobic training increases lactic acid production during top efforts, it also lessens the accumulation of lactic acid in muscles by producing chemical agents that buffer or reduce its harmful effects. High-intensity training also helps to remove the lactic acid from the active muscle fibers. The trained body can shuttle lactic acid from active to inactive muscle fibers and to organs, such as the liver and the heart, both of which use it for fuel.

Over time, high-intensity, anaerobic training can also produce some of the same changes that occur with aerobic training. For example, progressive increases in $\dot{V}O_2$max and cardiac output depend on increases in training intensity. These adaptations also help minimize the accumulation of lactic acid. Increases in $\dot{V}O_2$max result in a greater capacity to metabolize fat because greater amounts of oxygen are delivered to the mitochondria. This effect reduces the muscles' reliance on carbohydrates, sparing glycogen. Because the trained muscles use less glycogen, the fuel source for anaerobic metabolism, they produce less lactic acid.

APPLYING RUNNING PHYSIOLOGY TO TRAINING

Most of the information we have presented so far in this chapter comes from laboratory studies on the workings of chemicals, cells, energy pathways, and so forth. How can you use this information to plan and implement training? Later in the book we will present specific methods of training to develop the aerobic and anaerobic energy systems. For now, however, let's piece together our lesson in running physiology by examining some "real world" applications in day-to-day training.

Field Measurements of Physiological Responses

In the laboratory, exercise physiologists measure runners' responses to training. They use sophisticated and expensive equipment to assess $\dot{V}O_2$max, lactate threshold, running economy, and other physiological capacities. Most coaches do not have access to such equipment, but in most cases it doesn't really matter. In fact, coaches in the field can assess many of the same indicators of fitness and performance as exercise physiologists do in the laboratory.

For example, consider heart rates, which runners can use to gauge training intensity. It's much faster and more convenient for runners to count their heart rates during a workout than to hook them up to an expensive and cumbersome electrocardiogram machine. As another example, scientists use machines to analyze CO_2 concentration, determining the work level that corresponds to an individual's ventilatory threshold. A more practical field measure would simply be to note the pace at which breathing becomes noticeably labored.

Heart Rate

Heart rate is the best field measure of how a runner is responding physiologically during training. This is because heart rate increases in proportion to the need for oxygen in the muscles. So this measure provides a good clue of how hard the body is working and which energy pathways the muscles are using. Most importantly, coaches can use heart rate to gauge whether the athlete is running at the right level of intensity to meet training objectives for a given workout. Figure 3.6 shows the techniques for taking heart rate and pulse, which is like an echo of the heartbeat transmitted through the arteries. The pulse can be felt at the wrist (radial artery) and the neck (carotid artery). To take your pulse at the wrist, place your right hand in your left palm with the fingertips on your left thumb. Slowly slide the first two fingertips of your right hand along the edge of the thumb toward your wrist. Once your fingertips are off your hand and on your arm, feel for the pulse and count the number of beats for 15 seconds and multiply by four. To take your pulse at your neck, place your first two fingers of your left hand on your neck level with your Adam's apple. Slide your fingers back until they are in the groove between your Adam's apple and the large muscle running down the front of your neck. Press *gently* to feel your pulse (pressing too hard can cut off blood supply to your brain) and count the number of beats for 15 seconds and multiply by four. When you practice taking your pulse, you may find it easier to count the beats at one location compared to the other.

Another way to measure heart rate is to use a heart rate monitor that straps to the chest and digitally records the heart's output in beats per minute (bpm) on a wrist watch. Advancements in technology have made the heart rate monitor relatively inexpensive and easy to use. Heart rate monitors are especially useful during high-intensity workouts when it's difficult to count heartbeats because they're so rapid.

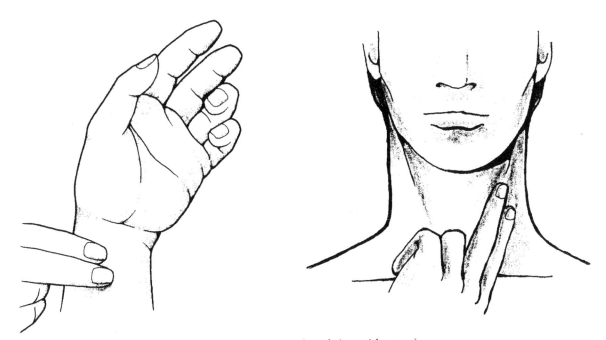

Figure 3.6 Taking the pulse at the wrist (radial artery) and neck (carotid artery).

Resting Heart Rate

You can measure your resting heart rate (RHR) by counting your pulse before getting out of bed in the morning. Remember, endurance training lowers RHR. Over time, it's possible for young runners' RHRs to decline from about 70 to 40 to 50 bpm. This adaptation reflects the greater pumping efficiency of the heart. RHR also gives an indication of how well athletes have recovered after the previous day's workout. If, on a given morning, RHR is more than five bpm greater than normal (and nightmares can be ruled out as the cause!) recovery may not be complete and they may need an easy day. Abnormally high resting rates also signal overtraining and impending illness. By having athletes record their daily RHRs, coaches will be able to make proper adjustments to training if necessary.

Maximal and Training Heart Rates

On average, maximal heart rate (MHR) for adolescents is 190 to 210 bpm. One way to estimate MHR is to use the equation MHR = 220 − age. An estimate for a 16-year-old is 204 bpm. Runners can more precisely determine MHR by counting the pulse immediately after completing a three-to five-minute run at an all-out effort. For this test, coaches should instruct their runners to set the fastest pace they can maintain for approximately one mile without slowing down at the end. The MHR from this test can then be used to prescribe the correct intensity for various types of training. This measure is called training heart rate (THR).

Scientists have discovered that THR is a good indicator of whether the runner's pace and effort are sufficient for developing aerobic and anaerobic fitness. Experts have established some general guidelines for youths' heart rates during training. As shown in table 3.3, to build aerobic fitness, THR should be about 65 to 75 percent of MHR. To raise the lactate and ventilatory thresholds, runners should train at heart rates that approximate 75 to 85 percent of MHR. Training at 85 to 100 percent of MHR builds anaerobic fitness. The last column in table 3.3 lists some calculations for target THRs for runners with MHRs of 204 bpm.

CALCULATING HEART RATE RANGES

To calculate heart rate ranges, multiply the individual's maximal heart rate times the lower and upper percentage values for a training response. Let's take the example of a runner whose maximal heart rate is 204 beats per minute (bpm). For developing aerobic fitness, the lower end of the range for this runner is about 133 bpm (204 × .65 = 132.6) and the higher end is about 153 bpm (204 × .75 = 153). On days when the training objective is to develop aerobic fitness, the runner should adjust pace so that heart rate stays within the range of 133 to 153 bpm.

SUMMARY

Congratulations, you made it through a pretty tough exercise physiology lesson! This background will help you apply the science of distance running to designing effective training sessions and programs. To illustrate this point, let's focus in on some highlights of the chapter:

- The aerobic energy system produces lots of ATP for a particular amount of food energy, so part of the training program should be geared toward developing this system.

Table 3.3 Recommended Heart Rate Ranges for Increasing Aerobic and Anaerobic Fitness

Training response	% of Maximal HR	Range for an individual with a max HR of 204
Increase aerobic endurance	65 to 75	133 to 153
Elevate lactate/ventilatory threshold	75 to 85	153 to 173
Increase anaerobic endurance	85 to 100	173 to 204

- Because some of the energy for races between 800 and 5,000 meters comes from anaerobic pathways, runners must also train for anaerobic fitness. The shorter the event, the greater the demand for anaerobic conditioning.

- Running economy is relatively poor in young athletes. Technique work is one way to improve running economy.

- Training to increase the lactate/ventilatory thresholds is essential because once these thresholds are reached, fatigue follows quickly.

- Physiological adaptations, including increases in $\dot{V}O_2$max and energy-producing enzymes, are the basis for improving performance.

- Coaches and runners can use measures of resting, maximal, and training heart rates to gauge how training affects the body.

CHAPTER 4

Running Psychology

© Ed Prytherch

We've all known runners who were in great physical shape, but raced poorly because they weren't mentally fit. In training sessions they showed the promise of new PRs—but on race day, with the pressure and challenges of competition, the promise was broken.

"I was in the best shape of my life," is the often-heard claim. "What could have gone wrong? How could I have run so slow and felt so bad after all those great workouts?"

We can easily explain disappointing performances by measuring indicators of physiological fitness such as $\dot{V}O_2$max and blood lactate levels. We can also design specific workouts to improve physiological capacities. But what if the runner's major limitations are psychological in nature? How can you measure motivation, confidence, or relaxation? Even more importantly, how can you design training to improve mental fitness?

In this chapter, we will focus on the key elements of mental fitness: perception (or thinking), concentration, relaxation, motivation, and racing tactics. Runners *can* improve their mental fitness through training. To help coaches plan such training, we'll present some techniques and strategies that can improve young runners' abilities to control effort and pace, to focus on appropriate strategic cues, to reduce nervousness, and to get "psyched up" to the right level.

WHY TRAIN FOR MENTAL FITNESS?

To appreciate the importance of mental fitness for distance running, you must understand that changes in mental state directly affect the body and vice versa. For example, when you are worried or afraid your heart and breathing rates increase, your muscles get tense, and your metabolism skyrockets. These so-called "fight-or-flight" responses, which occur when we think that a situation is threatening, are helpful for brief bursts of highly intense activity; however, they are counterproductive to good distance running. Endurance athletes perform best with a relaxed, focused, and unstressed state of mind. This mental state leads to an optimal physiological state characterized by relatively slow heart and breathing rates, efficient energy expenditure, and a powerful, yet relaxed, running stride.

Another example of how the mind affects the body involves your self-concept: A negative attitude about your abilities can cause poor technique. Runners who lack confidence tend to slouch their shoulders and focus their eyes on the ground directly in front of them. In contrast, runners who are confident in their abilities tend to have good posture and technique. They run "tall" with their shoulders squared and their eyes focused on the competition. So improved confidence can result in better running technique, which, in turn, improves efficiency and performance.

The flip side is that the body affects the mind. Consider the racer who starts out at a pace that she is not physiologically fit enough to handle. Early in the race, this runner will experience fatigue from lactic acid accumulation and muscle glycogen depletion. These sensations of physical fatigue open the door to negative thoughts, poor concentration, and loss of motivation. In contrast, a racer who is not overly fatigued physiologically will have the mental power to concentrate on positive thoughts and on the necessary strategies to accomplish goals.

THINKING ON THE RUN

Because of the interaction of body and mind, a strong connection exists between the way athletes think and how they perform. Let's look at how runners' thoughts about ability, pacing effort, and fatigue influence their performance. And let's consider some practical advice for helping runners think smarter.

Building Confidence

Confidence refers to thoughts about your ability to perform successfully. We all know about the importance of confidence in distance running. Without it, even the most physically fit runners won't reach their potential. But what makes runners confident? How can runners who lack confidence develop it? To answer these questions, let's consider three major factors that contribute to positive thoughts about ability. First, previous performance is a key. Athletes who were successful in their last race will likely be confident of running well next time. Second, training outcomes influence confidence. Runners who have accomplished their training objectives all week will bring little doubt to the starting line on race day. Third, perceptions of the coach, family, and friends affect confidence. Young athletes need plenty of positive reinforcement from "significant others."

Previous Performance

Because success in previous performance builds confidence, training and racing objectives should allow for improvement as the season progresses. With room for improvement, runners have the potential to experience repeated success. Certainly, with each new success, confidence will "snowball." To plan for improvement, coaches should design training so that runners experience their physiological peaks at the end of the competitive season when championship meets are held. (We'll discuss the details of peaking in part III of the book.)

One way to help ensure steady improvement and the confidence it instills is to set early-season performance goals that are relatively easy to achieve. Devote the first few competitions of each season to accomplishing technical and tactical objectives. As the season progresses, view each

© Terry Wild Studio

race as a "stepping stone" to reach the ultimate goal of a PR or a high finish in championship meets. Then, the confidence gained from running well at the end of the season will carry over to the next season of training and racing.

Success in Training

Perhaps the most important confidence-building factor is good training. There's nothing like a successful workout to boost the runner's self-concept and motivation. But how do you define a successful workout? Does it mean finishing ahead of all your teammates in an interval session? Do you have to set a new training PR for a five-mile course every time you run it? No, these should not be measures of success in training. Instead, successful training means running at the assigned pace and effort to accomplish training objectives for a particular day. It also means performing technique drills correctly, concentrating on the necessary cues to stay relaxed, and it even means eating the right postworkout meal.

To gain the confidence that comes from successful training, runners must know the objectives for each session and how to accomplish them. Coaches must clearly communicate the goals of training each day. Let's say Coach Catherine plans an easy three-mile run for Libby on Tuesday. The objective is to promote recovery from a hard interval session on the previous day. Coach Catherine must communicate to Libby that if she pushes herself and runs too fast on the recovery run, she has *not* been successful in accomplishing her training objectives. The confidence Libby might gain from running hard in the recovery session may be short-lived because, if she doesn't recover properly, she may not have the energy to successfully complete upcoming workouts in which the objective will be to push herself and run fast.

Coaches should provide plenty of feedback during and after workouts so that their runners can tell whether they have actually accomplished their training objectives. This feedback includes times run in interval sessions, videotapes of running technique, and charts that show progression in training over time.

Influence of Significant Others

Even when training and racing are going well, confidence can be shaken by negative criticism from coaches, parents, and friends. Young runners need to hear the words, "You can do it. I believe in you." When training sessions and races don't go so well, coaches and parents should repair the emotional wounds of disappointment with constructive, rather than negative, criticism. Especially after poor performances, runners can regain their lost confidence if the coach is there to tell them that a bad race is just a temporary setback. To restore confidence, coaches must help their athletes focus on successes in previous races and workouts.

Judging Pace and Effort

The best distance runners excel at judging their pace by sensing their effort and speed. They tend to pace themselves evenly from the start to the finish of races. Pacing skills are critical for two reasons. First, runners must be able to judge their paces in order to attain time goals, especially in track races. Second, uneven, erratic pacing can waste precious energy. Figure 4.1 illustrates the importance of good pacing skill. It shows the 400-meter split times for Ethiopian Haile Gebreselassie's 5,000-meter world record (set on August 16, 1995). Many track experts consider this performance to be the most impressive of the long-distance records. Notice the consistency of the splits and how they got faster as the race progressed. Gebreselassie's 1,000-meter splits were 2:34.04, 2:34.66, 2:34.22, 2:31.23, and 2:30.24! So the last half of the race was faster than the first

half, a pattern called "negative splits." Most record performances are characterized either by even pacing throughout the race or by negative-split pacing. These pacing strategies keep runners from wasting energy and fatiguing prematurely.

Especially in track racing, pacing skill involves making calculations and decisions about whether to maintain a given pace, slow down, or speed up. Smart runners quickly calculate their splits when cumulative running times are called during races. Let's say Taro is prepared to run 3,200 meters in 10:24, which is 78 seconds for each 400 meters. If Taro hears the timer call "2:36" at 800 meters and "3:57" at 1,200 meters, his thought process might be as follows: "That last lap was 81. I need to average 78s, so I should have been at 3:54 for 1,200. I'm three seconds off pace, but I'm feeling good. I'll try to drop the pace to 77 for a few laps to get back on target before I start my kick over the last 400."

Of course, in some racing situations, the runner will have to base decisions on adjusting the pace in order to stay in contact with competitors. Runners who completely ignore the competition and focus only on their split times can limit themselves. This is because competition can bring out hidden potential. So, especially when you're feeling good in the late stages of a race, it's a good idea to forget about split times and focus on competing. It's when runners get caught up in the competition that they achieve big performance breakthroughs. Most of the time, however, runners feel strongest in the late stages when they have paced themselves properly early on.

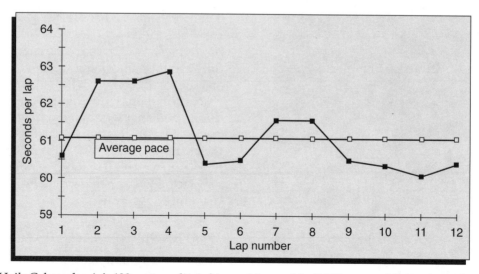

Figure 4.1 Haile Gebreselassie's 400-meter splits in his world record for 5,000 meters (12:44.39). Gebreselassie's last 200 meters, which is not shown on the figure, was 29.7 seconds.

Young runners won't learn pacing skills by themselves. Coaches must teach these skills and provide training to reinforce them. As a first step, runners should learn the split times required to attain their performance goals. To help, coaches can hand out pacing charts such as the one in table 4.1 and quiz athletes to make sure they have memorized their goal splits. Coaches should also design specific training sessions to help athletes better control their pace (see chapter 8).

Dealing With Fatigue and Pain

Earlier we said that running may be fatiguing, but that it should not be painful. Fatigue is a general sense of muscular weakness and lack of energy. When fatigued, runners know they can keep going. To avoid slowing down, they'll have to exert a lot more mental effort. In contrast to fatigue, pain is a danger signal from a specific part of the body—perhaps a sprained ankle, a pulled muscle, or a sharp aching in the shins. Runners should be trained to endure and push through fatigue, but not pain.

What kind of training is necessary to endure common sensations of fatigue in distance running? The traditional approach for coaches was to stress mental toughness by constantly pushing runners to their physical limits and degrading them with the criticism, "You're just not tough enough." However, research in sport psychology and the experiences of elite adult runners show us that the traditional approach doesn't work very well. The way to push through fatigue is not simply to think tough. Instead, runners must "think tough and smart."

Two keys to smart thinking help runners defy fatigue. The first is to eliminate fear and anxiety. When we are afraid or highly anxious our sense of fatigue is heightened. In contrast, when we have little or no fear, our sense of fatigue is greatly reduced. Soon we'll discuss ways to get rid of fear and anxiety. The second key to defying

Table 4.1	Pacing Chart							
				Meters				
200	400	800	1,000	1,500	1,600	3,000	3,200	5,000
:30	1:00	2:00	2:30	3:45	4:00	——	——	——
:32	1:04	2:08	2:40	4:00	4:16	8:00	8:32	——
:34	1:08	2:16	2:50	4:15	4:32	8:30	9:04	14:10
:36	1:12	2:24	3:00	4:30	4:48	9:00	9:36	15:00
:38	1:16	2:32	3:10	4:45	5:04	9:30	10:08	15:50
:40	1:20	2:40	3:20	5:00	5:20	10:00	10:40	16:40
:42	1:24	2:48	3:30	5:15	5:36	10:30	11:12	17:30
:44	1:28	2:56	3:40	5:30	5:52	11:00	11:44	18:20
:46	1:32	3:04	3:50	5:45	6:08	11:30	12:16	19:10
:48	1:36	3:12	4:00	6:00	6:24	12:00	12:48	20:00
:50	1:40	3:20	4:10	6:15	6:40	12:30	13:20	20:50
:52	1:44	3:28	4:20	6:30	6:56	13:00	13:52	21:40
:54	1:48	3:36	4:30	6:45	7:12	13:30	14:24	22:30
:56	1:52	3:44	4:40	7:00	7:28	14:00	14:56	23:20
:58	1:56	3:52	4:50	7:15	7:44	14:30	15:28	24:10
:60	2:00	4:00	5:00	7:30	8:00	15:00	16:00	25:00

Note: Rows show minutes and seconds for even-paced running across standard track distances.

fatigue is learning to control mental focus, or concentration.

ATTENTION AND CONCENTRATION

A major aim of mental training is to gain control over your thoughts by focusing attention, or concentrating. Coaches tell runners to concentrate all the time. But concentration is a very difficult skill in competitive running because so many cues compete for your attention. We can categorize these cues by whether they are outside (external cues) or inside (internal cues) the body (see table 4.2). Which cues should you concentrate on? If you focus on external cues—other competitors, upcoming hills and turns, instructions from the coach—you may not attend to what's going on internally. If you focus on internal cues—running form, thoughts about pacing and strategy, feelings of fatigue—you may lose sight of what's going on around you. The key to concentrating effectively is to focus on the right cues at the right moment as the race unfolds.

Focusing Attention

Sport psychologists often compare attention to a beam of light that can be varied in direction and width. An individual can vary the direction of attention by focusing on internal or external cues. The width of attention changes on a continuum of narrowly focusing on a small number of cues to broadly focusing on many cues. A runner with a "narrow internal" attention style might concentrate on his technique, excluding other internal and external cues. In contrast, a runner with a "broad external" attention style might open his focus to include other competitors, the coach's instructions, and the encouragement of spectators.

The best attention strategy for distance runners is to be flexible in the way they concentrate. Sometimes the focus of attention has to be internal and narrow. For example, when approaching a steep hill in a cross-country race, you should concentrate on good technique. Your attention might be directed internally to pushing forcefully off the ground with the driving leg. But after establishing good hill-running technique, you must shift your focus to external factors such as the competition. Consider what might happen if a competitor decides to break away by surging up the hill while you are concentrating only on technique?

The ability to quickly adjust the direction and width of the attention beam is critical to successful racing. By focusing on the right cues at the right moment runners are mentally "in the race." Such skill in concentrating actually reduces feelings of fatigue and keeps negative thoughts out of the mind. To help runners develop better concentration, table 4.3 presents some strategies that coaches can implement in training. The first strategy is to take regular inventory of body cues such as breathing rate, muscle tightness, and even the sound of footstrike. (Heavy, plodding footstrikes indicate that the runner's form is breaking down.) These internal cues tell you how hard you are working. And they help you adjust your effort to save energy and improve technique. For example, if you sense too much tension in your shoulders, you can consciously relax these muscles.

Table 4.2 Focusing Attention	
Internal cues	**External cues**
Technique	Other competitors
Feelings of fatigue and muscle tightness	Coach's instructions
Sense of pace and effort	Demands of the course (cross-country)
Thoughts about strategy	Spectators' cheers

Table 4.3 Training Strategies for Improving Concentration

- Take regular inventories of body cues: breathing rate, muscle tightness, sound of footstrike, technique.

- Practice calculating split times.

- Practice running in a crowd.

- Practice running alone.

- Know the cross-country course.

For the second strategy in table 4.3, practicing calculating split times, we suggest that after coaches call out cumulative running times in selected workouts, a runner can call back his split times. For example, let's say that the coach calls out "1:17" after the first 400 of a 1,600-meter repetition and "2:36" at the 800-meter mark. Immediately after hearing the 800 time, the runner would calculate the split and call out "1:19." Our guess is that as the runner's pace gets faster, his math gets worse!

The third and fourth strategies, practicing running in a crowd and running alone, help runners shift concentration from internal to external cues and vice versa. Practicing running in a pack challenges athletes to shift focus from their positioning (to avoid tripping and running too wide on curves) to cues that indicate how their competitors are doing. For example, by listening to the breathing rate of other runners in the pack, you can tell whether they're having trouble with the pace. Practicing running in a pack also helps runners relax and move along with the flow of their competitors without being distracted. As you may know from watching elite adult races, when the pace is fast and steady, running in a pack gives runners a tremendous advantage; the runners work together and pull each other along. It takes, however, considerable skill in focusing attention and maintaining relaxation to gain this advantage.

It's also important to practice running alone to prepare for races in which the pack gets away. In selected interval training sessions, coaches can stagger runners so that they start by themselves. These sessions will challenge runners to keep their focuses open, staying in mental contact with those who are ahead. Mental contact refers to the feeling that, even though your competitors are ahead, you have the energy, confidence, and focus to not let them get away.

Finally, a strategy for improving concentration in cross-country is to practice running on race courses. Knowing the course helps you anticipate shifts of attentional focus that you'll need to make as the race unfolds. There's nothing like an unexpected, steep 400-meter hill to break your concentration! When traveling to cross-country races, it's essential to preview the course on the day before the meet or during the warm-up. Visualizing or mentally rehearsing your performance on a particular course is a great way to be prepared for it—more on this shortly.

"Psyching Up" and Attention

All runners know that it's important to be "psyched up," or mentally energized, to do their best. But young runners may not yet understand the importance of fine-tuning their level of mental energy for optimal performance. Some runners don't get psyched up enough. On the other hand, many get too psyched up, becoming overly nervous. It's important to understand that your level of mental energy directly affects your ability to concentrate. Recalling our analogy of attention as a beam of light, when mental energy is low the attention beam widens and it becomes difficult to focus on important cues. Runners who aren't psyched up enough have trouble concentrating. In contrast, when mental energy is high, the attention beam narrows and can't easily change direction. In this state, runners may overlook important cues as the race unfolds. For young runners, being too psyched up is the most common problem in controlling mental energy.

It takes experience and training to learn to control mental energy. Through trial and error, runners will associate their best performances with an optimal level—one that is neither too low nor too high. Coaches can help in several ways. They can use motivational strategies for athletes who don't seem to get psyched up about competing, some of which we'll present shortly. Yet, coaches should protect runners from getting too psyched up before races. Unlike athletes in sports that require short bursts of energy, distance runners do not benefit from precompetition pep talks that unleash fiery emotions. Remember, those emotions will narrow the focus of the athlete's attention and trigger physiological responses that may burn precious energy.

Another key to optimizing mental energy is to have a familiar prerace routine that promotes concentration and relaxation. A routine warm-up, consisting of a certain duration of jogging, specific stretching exercises, strides, and so forth, helps runners control their emotions and focus on their preparations without worrying about the competition. During the warm-up, some runners tune their mental energy levels by listening to music. This strategy works well as long as the music doesn't overly energize the athlete. For some runners, warming up with teammates before the race helps to settle the mind. Others like to be alone as they prepare. Coaches should encourage runners to discover the psyching up strategies that work best for them and to use those strategies every time they race.

REDUCING ANXIETY AND FEAR

The suggestions for finding the right level of mental energy are also helpful for reducing anxiety and fear. Anxiety refers to the stressful feelings that come with being too psyched up. Fear is an emotion that is felt when one expects a negative outcome such as embarrassment, criticism, or physical discomfort. Keep in mind that these negative emotions trigger energy-wasting physiological responses, increase the perception of fatigue, limit concentration, and, ultimately, hurt performance.

Putting Failure and Success in Perspective

How can runners reduce anxiety and fear? First, failure has to be put in its proper perspective. When runners who lack mental fitness don't reach their competitive goals, they may feel anxious about upcoming races and may even fear another poor outcome. Mentally fit runners don't fear failure because they know that it is often the foundation for success. When you race poorly you're forced to think about the reasons why. Then, when you see your mistakes, you're able to correct them in future races. Failure can also be the source of powerful motivation to try harder next time. Above all, when runners don't fear failure, they are willing to take chances. By taking chances, runners make breakthroughs! So coaches and parents should always emphasize that it's okay to fail as long as you've tried your hardest, have learned from your mistakes, and are willing to take some chances in the future.

Besides putting failure in its proper perspective, young runners must learn what success means. As we have emphasized, success should be measured by self-improvement—not by winning. Runners who are taught this important lesson learn to focus on the processes required to improve and reach their goals: eating nutritious foods, training to enhance fitness, mastering technique and tactics. Focusing on process eliminates the anxiety and fear that

accompany the viewpoint that "winning is everything."

Eliminating Uncertainty Through Visualization

For many runners, uncertainty about performance outcomes is a source of fear and anxiety. Runners who are uncertain about their fitness and ability to achieve their goals are often overly anxious about competing. To eliminate this sort of anxiety, runners must be thoroughly prepared for the physical and mental demands of competition. As a part of an effective mental preparation, visualization is very useful for reducing uncertainty. In this technique, athletes mentally rehearse competition by using their imaginations.

In a quiet setting, you should close your eyes and see, hear, and feel yourself running, as if you were watching a movie. The movie will be much clearer if you are relaxed before visualizing! The idea is to visualize positive outcomes and the ways to achieve them. For example, to prepare for an upcoming race, you might use your imagination to "see" yourself running with good form, "hear" the split times you're shooting for, and "feel" the effortless movement. Or you can watch good, old movies, so to speak, by visualizing your best races in the past. By practicing visualization several days a week for as short as five minutes each time, you can replace uncertainty about performance with positive expectations.

Relaxation

The final key to getting rid of anxiety and fear is relaxation. Like concentration, relaxation is a critical skill for distance running, but one that is hard to master. Coaches tell their athletes to relax all the time, but it's hard to do because running involves tension. In fact, as we discussed in chapter 3, the key to successful performance, physiologically speaking, is generating forceful muscle contractions or tension. So how can runners relax when the objective is to create tension?

Before each training session and race, runners should cultivate a general relaxed state of body and mind. For almost all young runners, the best way to relax before training and racing is simply to do quiet activities that are enjoyable. Some of

Lynn Jennings

Newmarket, NH

Personal Bests:

3,000 meters	8:40.45*
5,000 meters	15:07.92
10,000 meters	31.19.89

*American indoor record

© 1993 Tim De Frisco

When Lynn Jennings started running in her first year of high school, it was simply something fun to do. "Initially, I just loved discovering my ability to run," she says. "I loved running on the country roads and being in control of my little body." Running with her springer spaniel over hilly terrain in her hometown of Harvard, MA, Lynn worked herself into good shape without giving much thought to serious training or competition.

By her senior year in high school, however, she was a national-class runner, racing the mile in 4:39 and dreaming about becoming one of the best distance runners in the world. That dream has come true for Lynn, who won the World Cross-Country Championships in 1990, 1991, and 1992. Among her many achievements in a running career that has spanned 22 years, Lynn won a bronze medal at the 1992 Olympic Games in Barcelona, and she has won the U. S. Cross-Country Championships eight times.

Speaking with passion, Lynn sees no secret to making dreams come true. "From an early age, my whole approach to running has focused on discipline, hard work, and progression." It's an approach that she learned from her high school coach, John Babington, who has worked with her since 1975. Together, they view training as a way for Lynn to develop the fitness and skills to make her a complete runner—one who can respond successfully to any competitive challenge.

Becoming a complete runner is a never-ending quest for Lynn. "I've always had a great kick, but I'm finding out that I can't rely solely on my kick when I'm running against the best athletes in the world," she says. "So, I'm learning how to make moves by changing paces in the middle of the race so that I can pull away and still have something left for a kick at the end."

Lynn learns these skills through very focused training sessions in which her goal, in her words, is to "develop a mind that masters the body and a body that is trained to do what the mind asks of it." For developing control over pacing, Lynn maintains a predetermined pace over a set number of laps during her track sessions. As an aid to her concentrating on the effort and pace, Lynn's coach blows a whistle to signal the correct pace for each 100 meters, which is marked by a cone placed on the track. Lynn's goal is to reach the cone as the whistle blasts. For developing the ability to surge, Lynn does 200-meter repetitions in which she accelerates at three points along the way.

Lynn thinks that young runners should focus on developing their skills to become more complete racers. But her main advice to young runners is to enjoy and take pride in their approach to distance running and becoming part of a rich tradition. She especially likes "the pure and simple things that make up the tradition of the sport—our ideals, beliefs, and how we conduct ourselves." Lynn recommends that young runners learn about this tradition by reading books and running magazines, also finding out how great runners approach the sport.

the best preperformance activities are reading, listening to relaxing music, talking with friends, and watching TV. Then, the goal during training and racing is to relax specific muscles that are not involved in the running movement itself. Athletes should focus attention on detecting and reducing tension in the shoulders, hands, and the facial muscles. Coaches can help by analyzing each runner's technique and expressions for tightness and strain. The coach's cues to relax should be specific to the body part that looks tight, such as "relax your shoulders" or "loosen your hands."

MOTIVATION

Consider a sleek, aerodynamic race car with a powerful and fine-tuned engine. While the car may be built for high speed, it won't go anywhere without a driver! Likewise, it doesn't matter how much physical ability a runner has if he is not driven or motivated to succeed. Motivation is a complex part of psychological fitness because it involves the athlete's reasons for training and racing. And when you ask 10 young runners to list the reasons why they run, you're likely to get 10 different sets of answers.

For coaches, a key to boosting motivation in runners is to make training and racing experiences consistent with each individual's reasons for participating. Consider runners who run mainly for fun and to be around friends. A sure way to discourage these athletes and decrease motivation is to always stress competitive success. In contrast, coaches should encourage runners who are mainly motivated to succeed in races to stay focused on their competitive goals. Effectively setting goals is another key to boosting motivation for all athletes. Goals help runners direct their mental and physical energy toward a purpose—whether it is to win the state championship or to break 6:30 in the mile. In chapter 9, we'll help you set motivating goals as a part of the process of designing training.

Indeed, the best sources of motivation are the feelings of satisfaction and accomplishment young runners will experience from improving and achieving their goals. These feelings develop intrinsic motivation, which sport psychologists emphasize as a key to mental fitness. Parents and coaches can help develop intrinsic motivation in young runners by regularly drawing their attention to the connection between hard work and the feelings that accompany self-improvement. Frequent praise helps: "You took five seconds off your PR! See how the hard training paid off?"

Sport psychologists tell us that extrinsic rewards, such as trophies, T-shirts, and other material prizes are less effective at increasing motivation than intrinsic rewards. Nevertheless, when they accompany intrinsic rewards, these prizes can be good motivators because they are material reminders of achievement. A T-shirt awarded for completing a summer training program or running a PR can be a source of great satisfaction and motivation to keep working hard.

RACING TACTICS

Too often young runners go to the starting line of races without a strategy to follow. Without well-tested and effective racing tactics, runners may not feel confident in their ability to achieve their goals. In addition, they may lack concentration because they are uncertain of the right strategic cues to focus on. Ultimately, without a plan, runners are likely to be short on motivation. After all, if you don't have a road map to your destination, you won't make much of an effort to get there!

Successful racing means using the best tactics for a given situation. And because no two races are ever the same (in terms of the competition, weather, course conditions, and the like), runners should train to master many different racing tactics including even pacing, front running, kicking, and surging. Consider the case of Marie, an elite runner whose only plan was to lead the pack from the start. Front running worked perfectly in small, local races where Marie was superior to her competitors. She would open up a large lead and hold on to win—even though she slowed in the final stages of the race. But in championship races against other runners of comparable ability and fitness, the strategy backfired. Marie couldn't break away from her competitors early. She would lose concentration because she was frustrated by the jostling in the pack. Furthermore, because she couldn't shake the other runners as the race progressed, Marie lost confidence and began to question her ability to win. When the other runners began sprinting to the finish line, Marie was left behind. She didn't have a finishing kick because she never practiced one.

Marie exemplifies many runners who are fit and talented enough to win or place high in races yet lack the tactical skill to reach their potential. Perhaps the best plan for Marie in championship races would be to run with the pack for at least half of the race. Then, at some predesignated point—say with 1,000 meters to go—she could use her front running ability to break up the field with a long, controlled kick to the finish. Next, we'll outline some different racing tactics to help you decide on the best plans for different competitive situations.

Racing for Time

In track racing, the best tactic for *most* young runners is "racing for time." This is because runners can best gauge their improvement by the stopwatch; self-improvement is the best motivating factor for developing athletes. Using this tactic, the coach and athlete decide on a goal time that is challenging yet achievable, considering the athlete's fitness, the point in the competitive season, and the weather. We have to stress the importance of considering the weather. Sometimes extreme conditions prevent even the fittest athletes from accomplishing their time goals. On such days—when it's too hot and humid, or too

cold and windy—tactical skill means making adjustments from an "ideal" plan.

On the track, the key to racing for time is even-paced running. Let's say Tonya's goal is to run under 5:05 for 1,500 meters, a time that requires an 81-second 400-meter pace. Tonya will have to concentrate on the effort needed to hit 81s and use split times to stay on pace when she starts to fatigue in the middle of the race. If other runners sprint the first 400 meters, she'll have to let them go. If Tonya's early pace is on target but faster than her competitors' pace, she'll have to run in front. Most importantly, she'll have to concentrate on running her own race while staying aware of what her competitors are doing.

Runners who maintain an even pace usually pass their competitors, rather than get passed, as the race unfolds. Passing boosts confidence. One way to capitalize on this confidence is to finish fast. When running for time, you should use the even-pacing strategy until a point in the race when you feel as if you can sustain a kick to the finish. All young distance runners should practice the strategy of running at an even rhythm, picking up the pace over the last stages of the race. It's the best way to run fast times. But keep in mind that the objective for this strategy is not to jog for most of the race and then unleash a mad sprint to the finish. From the start, your pace should feel fast and steady, and when you start your kick, you should feel tired but in control.

Racing for Place

While running for time is often a good strategy, sometimes the young runner should shoot for a certain finish place. Let's say Brad's goal is to place in the top 25 of a cross-country race. Cross-country racing requires a keen sense of effort and position in the field as the race unfolds. Brad has to know the demands of the course and have a plan for how much effort to put into running different segments of the race. During the race, he has to gauge his success by his position relative to his competitors. If Brad finds himself running with the lead pack, and the pace feels too fast, he will have to slow down. Or if Brad isn't even in the top 50 by the middle of the race, and he is feeling good, he'll have to pick up the pace. With feedback from the coach about his place as the race unfolds, Brad will be able to make the right adjustments so that he doesn't wind up at the finish line with too much or too little energy left.

It's much easier to run for place on the track because typically fewer runners compete at the same time than in cross-country races and it's easy to see and count your competitors. Still, we do not recommend settling into a particular place at the start and trying to hold it throughout. On the track, it's better to run for time early in the race, using even pacing, positioning yourself for place in the latter stages. Of course, runners should not limit themselves to a particular place if they can surpass it with a fast finish.

Racing for First Place: Front Running, Surging, and Kicking

If your goal is to finish in first place, you might use one of several strategies including front running, surging, and kicking. Front running is leading the pack from the early stages of a race. This tactic is like a double-edged sword. It can cut your competitors by breaking their spirit and shaking their confidence, but it can cut you if you wield it improperly. Front runners must be supremely fit and confident that they can cover the distance alone.

Front runners can also use a surging tactic, in which they speed up—or run in surges—over certain segments of the race in order to shake competitors and break their confidence. Plan surges to catch the competition off-guard and to make them think that you're in control of the race. To learn this strategy, young runners should watch the world-class Kenyan athletes, who have used surging tactics to dominate the endurance events in international competitions such as the Olympic Games.

Another strategy for winning races is kicking. Kickers feed off the energy and momentum of the other runners by tucking themselves in the pack in the early stages of the race. Then, they use their fitness and speed to sprint away from competitors over the final stages. Runners should practice starting their kicks from different distances. For example, runners who lack basic speed might experiment with a long, controlled sprint from 400 to 600 meters out. Runners with good speed might wait until the last 100 to 200 meters to start an explosive sprint.

Experimentation is the key to mastering racing strategies. Runners who can't adapt tactics to different competitive situations limit themselves to performing well only when the conditions suit them. In addition, the same plan race after race can get boring, limiting motivation. In contrast, runners who are skilled at many different racing strategies have potential for superior performances every time they toe the starting line. And it's fun to try different approaches on a regular basis.

TACTICAL TIPS

Here are some additional strategies to help runners at critical points in races:

• *Be prepared for a fast, safe start.* For runners who are in contention for winning a race or placing high, it's important to establish a good position early, especially in the middle-distance track races, such as the 800- and 1,500-meter runs. The keys are to start out at a fast, but controlled pace (not a mad sprint!), and to be aware of competitors who might jostle or trip you up. To avoid getting knocked around in a track race that does not have a staggered start, you might work your way to the outside edge of the pack, even if it means running a little wide on a turn. As soon as you establish your position, try to move closer to the inside lane and settle down to a more manageable pace. For the longer track races, such as the 3,000- and 5,000-meter runs, and for cross-country, it's not as critical to establish your position at the start. These races are long enough to give those who start out a little behind the pack plenty of time to catch up.

• *Avoid getting boxed.* Be aware of what competitors around you are doing, stay clear of trouble, and avoid struggling to get out of a box if you're in one. For example, let's say you're on the inside of the first lane behind two runners. You hear and see a pack of several runners moving up on your right side. To avoid getting boxed, you might pick up the pace and pass the runners in front of you, going ahead of the pack. Or, if you don't want to lead the race at that point, you could slow down and let the pack pass you. As soon as they are a few strides clear, you should move to the outside shoulder of the last runner in the pack. This is the best position to be in to avoid getting boxed. The only problem with running on the outside shoulder of the competitor in front of you is that you will have to run an extra distance on the curves. It's best to avoid running wide unless it causes you to be boxed in at a point when you want to strike and establish the lead (such as coming off the last curve before the finish). If, however, you are boxed in and hugging the inside lane at a point when you don't want to lead, be patient and move along with the pack until a position opens up for you to move to the outside.

• *Run the shortest distance.* In track racing when you're running in a group, the best position is just on the outside shoulder of the competitor in front of you. Ideally, you shouldn't be so far outside that you're in the second lane. This position helps you avoid both getting boxed and tangling up your legs with your competitor's legs. If you are running on your own, however, the best position is to hug the inside of the first lane, without stepping off the track, because it's the shortest distance. In cross-country and road racing, the key tactic is to run the tangents, or the lines that create the shortest distance between two points (while staying on the actual course, of course!).

• *Run through the finish line.* Always run as hard as you can through the finish. If you get accustomed to letting up in the last few strides before the line, you may find yourself getting nipped at the tape on a regular basis.

SUMMARY

Psychological foundations of distance running lie in two main themes:

• First, for runners to reach their potential they require a high level of mental fitness. They must have self-confidence, a flexible attention style, strong pacing and strategic skill, and optimal levels of mental energy and motivation.

• Second, training can improve mental fitness.

This improvement depends on carefully planned training and racing experiences that go beyond simply conditioning the body's physiological systems. When planning these experiences, coaches should always question how they will affect the runner's mind. Indeed, every training session should be geared toward developing mental as well as physical fitness. Developing key aspects of mental fitness such as confidence, concentration, and pacing control are essential components of a successful training program. When we discuss the details of designing training in parts II and III of the book, we'll integrate this background in running psychology. Before we get to talking specifically about training, however, we'll cover one last scientific foundation of running in the next chapter: biomechanics.

CHAPTER 5

Running Biomechanics

A major part of training in many youth sports is geared toward improving technique, or the proper form for carrying out movement skills. For example, right-handed golfers work on keeping a straight left arm during the swing. Basketball players spend hours perfecting the "follow-through" portion of the jump shot. In track and field, athletes in the technical events—jumps and throws—refine their form by performing special drills over and over again.

How important is technique in distance running? Are there features of the running movement that characterize optimal form? If so, what cues and advice should coaches offer runners to help them improve their skills? An understanding of the biomechanics of running helps to answer these questions. For example, a skillful stride can improve endurance performance as well as help prevent injuries. Throughout this chapter, we'll illustrate examples of common technical flaws and features of good form. We'll suggest ways to analyze running technique so coaches can help their athletes break bad habits and improve their form. Finally, we'll present 10 "tech tips" for optimal running biomechanics.

TECHNIQUE AND OPTIMAL PERFORMANCE

The most basic objective in distance running is to move the body at the fastest possible speed that does not cause marked fatigue and slowing. In other words, the secret is to run fast without running out of energy. Many endurance coaches are surprised to learn that this twofold objective requires considerable motor skill. It's easy to overlook the importance of technique because of the great physiological and psychological demands of running. Furthermore, many coaches perceive running as a simple or "natural" skill that doesn't need to be practiced. But just like a golf swing or basketball jump shot, an effective and efficient running stride requires plenty of practice to develop.

One reason that running requires skill is that the movement involves hundreds of muscles and most of the limbs and joints in the body. In the to-and-fro motion of the limbs, muscles have to "turn on," or contract, and "turn off," or relax, in the proper sequence and at the right instant in

time. Efficient running depends in part on precise timing among antagonistic muscle groups, which are located on opposite sides of the same limb and move the limb in opposite directions. For example, the hip flexors in the thigh and pelvic area and the hip extensors in the buttocks and hamstrings are antagonistic muscles (see figure 5.1). These muscle groups lift (hip flexors) and lower (hip extensors) the leg in the running stride.

Figure 5.1 shows that after pushing off the ground, the runner's leg moves forward due to contraction of the flexor muscles. During the forward-swinging action, the runner bends and lifts her knee in front of her body to prepare her foot for ground contact. For an unrestricted forward-swinging motion to occur, the runner must allow her hip extensor muscles to relax. If they begin to contract while she is still lifting her thigh in front of her body, the two muscle groups

Figure 5.1 Antagonistic muscle control: If the hip extensors contract while the hip flexors are still raising the thigh, counterproductive work results.

will be working against each other. In this example of counterproductive work, energy is wasted as poor technique forces the hip flexors to pull against the contracting extensors. At the same time, insufficient knee lift will reduce the runner's stride length and speed.

To appreciate the skill involved in running, you need only watch world-class adult runners performing. It is truly remarkable how they can run so fast and appear to be moving effortlessly. Streamlined technique is certainly fundamental to high levels of performance. Thus, developing the skill to run fast and efficiently should be a goal for all young runners.

Running Fast

Running speed is related to two key biomechanical factors—stride length and cadence. Stride length can be measured as the distance covered between the landing points of opposite feet. Cadence, or stride rate, refers to the number of strides taken in a particular period of time. Runners may differ markedly in these two measures due to individual variations in height, leg length, flexibility, and strength. No optimal standards exist. Nonetheless, any increase in stride length or cadence results in faster running speed. One of the goals of technique training is to improve speed by lengthening the stride if it's too short and picking up the cadence if it's too low.

It takes plenty of skill and strength to run fast and optimize the striding pattern simultaneously. For example, it's difficult to pick up the pace by increasing cadence without suffering a reduction in stride length at the same time. When an unskilled runner attempts to increase stride length, overstriding often results, wasting energy. The developing runner will get faster naturally with growth and maturation. But without specific technique training, youths can waste valuable energy when running at fast speeds.

Running Efficiently

Some of the key physiological responses to training result in saving energy. For example, with training, the runner will be able to use more fat to fuel muscle activity, sparing energy in the form of glycogen. The energy that is conserved through training allows the athlete to run faster and farther without fatiguing. What does all this revisited physiology have to do with biomechanics? Simply put, poor technique wastes energy, limiting performance.

The young runner's inefficient, uneconomical stride can be partly explained by unnecessary and counterproductive movements. Figure 5.2 illustrates overstriding, a common energy-wasting flaw in running technique. It occurs when the foot strikes the ground in a position far in front of the center of gravity, the most concentrated point through which gravity acts to pull the body down to the ground. During running, the center of gravity is located just above the center of the pelvis. As the figure shows, in overstriding, the front leg strikes the ground in a "propping" or "braking" position. This action greatly reduces the runner's forward momentum and costs the muscles extra energy to reaccelerate the body to push off the ground. Later in the chapter we'll illustrate some other flaws in technique that waste energy, hurting running performance.

Figure 5.2 Overstriding: an energy-wasting technical flaw.

TECHNIQUE AND INJURY PREVENTION

Besides improving running economy and performance, good technique is essential for injury prevention. Every footstrike challenges the muscles of the lower body to absorb large impact forces and generate their own propulsive forces. Given the repetitive nature of the running stride, a flawed pattern of movement can load affected muscles, bones, tendons, and ligaments with undue stress. When overstriding, for example, runners subject their quadriceps and knee joints to extreme jarring. In contrast, a smooth and powerful stride prevents overloading any one muscle group or joint structure.

Many common running injuries are caused by a combination of structural abnormalities and poor technique.[1] Misalignment of the foot, shin, thigh, and pelvis characterize most structural problems. When the leg is not vertically aligned, its joints will bear a greater amount of stress on one side compared to the other. Elite runners usually have straight legs. Not surprisingly, they tend to have fewer injuries than runners of lesser ability.

An uneven loading of force, caused by structural and biomechanical problems, can twist and strain joints of the lower leg upon footstrike

---

1. Faulty training methods and improper footwear are other major causes of injuries.

(see figure 5.3). In a normal landing the foot hits the ground and pronates, or rolls inward at the ankle joint (see figure 5.3a). A slight amount of pronation is beneficial because it lowers the whole foot to the ground and helps to cushion the shock of impact. Excessive pronation, however, pulls the foot out of alignment with the lower leg (see figure 5.3b). This places great stress on the arches, Achilles tendon, and connective tissue supporting the ankle and knee joints. Runners with flat feet or low arches, knock-knees, and weak ankles tend to overpronate. These runners also tend to suffer injuries such as stress fractures of the foot and shin, plantar fascitis (arch pain), Achilles tendinitis, and runner's knee.

Another biomechanical problem that can occur during footstrike is excessive supination, or outward rolling of the foot. Supination, which follows pronation in a normal landing, puts the foot into position for a forceful pushing-off action. On landing, some runners supinate without allowing the foot to pronate and absorb impact forces (see figure 5.3c). This causes undue stress on the lateral side (outside) of the ankles, knees, and hip joints. Runners who supinate excessively typically suffer injuries such as iliotibial band syndrome (lateral knee and hip pain), Achilles tendinitis, and calf muscle strains. Coaches should refer young runners who have excessive pronation or supination to a physician who specializes in

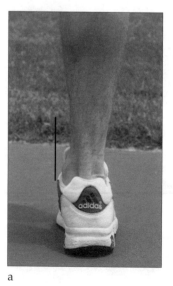
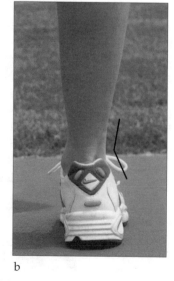
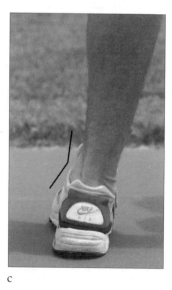

a   b   c

Figure 5.3 Footstrike positions: normal (a), excessive pronation (b), and excessive supination (c).

sport-related injuries of the lower extremities. The doctor may prescribe a common solution to biomechanical problems that originate at the feet—orthotics. These are shoe inserts that are made out of shock-absorbing materials and are sculpted to guide the foot through its most efficient and least stressful movement pattern.

In many cases, orthotics are not necessary to prevent injuries caused by structural and biomechanical flaws. Instead, the solution may be a good, supportive pair of running shoes that are specially designed to correct problems such as excessive pronation and supination. Many sports medicine specialists know about the best running shoes, and they can refer you to local running stores where knowledgeable salespersons can help with proper selection and fitting.

Because genetic factors play a major role in determining an individual's bone and joint structure, runners with structural abnormalities must work to optimize their form and to prevent injuries by training properly. Besides working on technique, all runners should regularly perform exercises to make the joints stronger and more stable. A good warm-up routine with proper stretching exercises is also critical to injury prevention. We'll discuss these components of training further in the following chapter.

ANALYZING RUNNING TECHNIQUE

Technique work should be included as a regular part of the young runner's program. Technique sessions allow the athlete to work on correcting technical flaws and making improvements on features of good form. During these sessions, the coach must be able to detect biomechanical problems and cue the athlete to make appropriate changes.

To effectively analyze technique, focus on the key actions that make up the stride. This is a real challenge because running involves so many rapidly moving body parts. At fast paces, for example, the foot is in contact with ground less than one-half of a second. Critical flaws such as overstriding are easy to overlook because the action happens so quickly. You may have already

guessed that the solution to this problem is the video camera. Coaches can film their athletes and then view the tape in slow motion, freezing the action with the VCR pause button. Given its accessibility, video has become a common aid for coaches in all sports.

Phases of the Stride Cycle

When analyzing a runner's technique, it's helpful to break the striding action down into distinct segments or phases. The stride can be divided into two major phases—support and nonsupport, and several smaller subphases. The support phase is made up of the actions that occur while the foot is in contact with the ground. In the nonsupport, or recovery, phase, both feet are off the ground and the body is in flight. Shortly, we'll describe how the limbs move during a stride cycle, which is made up of the movements occurring between two successive landings of the same foot. To help you identify important biomechanical features and to detect flaws in form, figure 5.4 illustrates the subphases of the runner's stride cycle beginning and ending with right footstrike.

a   b   c   d

Figure 5.4 The phases of a stride cycle.

Support Phase

The support phase begins when the foot contacts the ground and ends with the pushing-off action that propels the body into flight. Figure 5.4a shows the landing subphase of the support phase for the right leg. Notice that the runner's right ankle, knee, and hip joints are bent or flexed. This action cushions the impact of landing and stretches the muscles of the calf, quadriceps, and buttock. Like pulling on a rubber band, the stretching builds up "elastic energy" in these muscles and their tendons. The energy can be "returned" for a powerful shortening contraction in the pushing-off segment of the stride.

An instant after landing, the hips pass over the foot and the driving subphase of support begins. The body is propelled forward and upward as the drive leg pushes against the ground, exerting force in a backward and downward direction (see figure 5.4b). Note that the ankle, knee, and hip joints straighten or extend in this subphase. To increase stride length and speed, the runner would have to produce a more forceful driving action and greater extension of the leg joints. As we'll discuss in later chapters, a runner can develop a more powerful driving action with weight training and hill running.

Nonsupport, or Recovery, Phase

After pushing off the ground, the runner's body is in the nonsupport, or recovery, phase. The extended drive leg moves from its takeoff position to prepare for another landing in a sequence of three subphases: follow-through, forward-swing and foot-descent. Figure 5.4c illustrates the follow-through action of the right leg after it pushes off the ground with the foot trailing the body. After follow-through, the direction of leg movement is reversed as the thigh swings forward and the knee is raised in front of the body (see figure 5.4d). Finally, in the foot-descent subphase, the thigh is accelerated downward, lowering the foot to the ground for the next support phase.

Arm Action

The runner's arm movements are coordinated with the legs to balance the body and counteract rotational forces. Figure 5.5 illustrates the importance of good arm action. As the runner's left knee is lifted in front of the body, the hips naturally rotate in a clockwise (left to right) direction. To offset the turning action of the hips caused by lifting the left knee, the right arm simultaneously moves forward, stabilizing the torso. Balance is maintained as the runner's right arm moves in "synch" with the left leg and vice versa.

To minimize unnecessary motion of the upper body, the arms must swing naturally from the shoulders in a fairly straight direction, forward and backward. Throughout the arm-swinging cycle the runner should hold the elbows at about a 90 degree angle, keeping them close to the body. The hands should be relaxed, moving in front of the body but not crossing over its vertical mid

Figure 5.5 Upper body and arm action.

line. As the running speed increases, the runner needs to use a more forceful, extensive, and rapid swinging action to coordinate arm movement with the longer strides and faster turnover of the legs. Effective uphill running also demands vigorous arm action.

TECHNIQUE TIPS

Marked differences in size, strength, flexibility, coordination, and bone-joint structure characterize young runners. Thus, it's inappropriate to try to change one runner's technique to match another's exactly. In fact, because of individual differences, no single "ideal" distance running form exists. Nonetheless, runners should work to acquire a number of sound biomechanical features, correcting common flaws to enhance performance and reduce the risk of injury. This section presents 10 important "tech tips" to help coaches instruct their athletes to make changes in form, if they are necessary. In the next chapter, we'll show you some specific exercises and drills for developing good technique.

TECH TIP #1:

▶ Relax muscles that are not active in the running movement.

Just as baseball coaches tell players to "keep your eye on the ball," distance running coaches are known for cuing runners to "relax." It's critical to eliminate tension in the muscles that do not contribute to the running movement because their activity can result in counterproductive work. When coaches cue runners to relax, they should be specific to the part of the body that looks tense. They might say "Loosen your shoulders," or "Relax your hands." Besides telling runners to relax, it's important to encourage them to stay on pace. Tired runners can easily mistake the word "relax," for "slow down." They may loosen muscles all over the body, including those that generate propelling force. If runners relax too much, they will shorten their stride lengths and slow down.

TECH TIP #2:

▶ Keep the body in an almost upright position, squaring the shoulders and holding the head level.

As shown in figure 5.4, the runner's upper body should be almost vertical with only a slight forward lean. By squaring the shoulders, the arms can swing freely to counteract hip rotation. The head should be level without turning or bobbing, and the eyes should be focused 20 to 30 meters in front. To reinforce good posture, coaches should remind the athletes to run "tall." They can also cue the runners to imagine that they are being pulled upward by a rope attached to the very top of the head.

TECH TIP #3:

▶ Drive the arms and legs in a backward and forward direction along a fairly straight line.

Any excessive side-to-side movement of the arms and upper body will cause a turning or weaving motion that wastes energy. As mentioned earlier, the hands may pass in front of the chest but should not cross over an imaginary vertical line that divides the body into right and left halves. Likewise, the inner sides of the feet should not cross over the midline.

Upon striking the ground and during push-off, the foot should be pointed straight ahead rather than turned inward or outward. Note, however, that runners who "toe-in" or "toe-out" due to a structural misalignment may have difficulty positioning their feet straight. Trying to change the pattern of foot placement in these athletes may cause a painful twisting of the ankle and knee joints. Keep in mind that in any situation where changes in technique cause joint pain, it's best to let the runner use the style that feels most comfortable.

TECH TIP #4:

▶ Let runners select their natural stride length and cadence.

With training and experience most runners naturally choose stride lengths and cadences that optimize performance. Unless runners are obviously overstriding or taking short choppy steps, they don't need to alter their strides at a steady pace. For many runners, the best technique for speeding up is to consciously increase stride length by generating greater propulsive force in the driving subphase. This can be accomplished through training that enhances strength and flexibility.

TECH TIP #5:

▶ Minimize downward sinking or upward bouncing motions.

One of the most common technique flaws for young runners is a large lowering and lifting of the center of gravity with every stride. Biomechanics experts call this excessive vertical oscillation. Runners who lack leg strength and neuromuscular skill display an extreme sinking or lowering of the hips immediately upon footstrike. The ankles, knees, and hip joints bend too much because the support leg cannot withstand the force of impact. Correct this problem with strength training, technique drills, and a conscious effort to produce a fast and forceful driving action. To help athletes focus on a powerful takeoff, the coach should try cuing them to imagine being on a hot track: They'll need fast feet to avoid getting burned.

While some runners sink, others bounce like a pogo stick. This action occurs during the driving subphase when runners exert too much vertical force against the ground. Bouncy runners will benefit from technique drills that promote pushing force in a more backward than downward direction.

TECH TIP #6:

▶ When running at fast speeds, the runner should land and push off on the middle to the front of the foot.

An effective stride begins with foot positioning upon landing. The best technique is to strike first on the outer edge of the ball of the foot. The whole foot is then naturally lowered to the ground for an instant, allowing for slight pronation and shock absorption. Finally, the driving action occurs when the runner raises the heel and pushes off from the front of the foot.

The best runners tend to be midfoot and forefoot strikers. That's why you often hear coaches cuing their athletes to "get up on your toes." Heel strikers spend too long on the ground, losing forward momentum by rolling into position for push-off. It's important to note, however, that an optimal landing requires great strength in the lower extremities. The arch, ankle joint, and Achilles tendon must be able to withstand considerable force. Thus, heel strikers who want to convert to midfoot or forefoot strikers will have to improve their strength and flexibility first.

Some runners, particularly those with flat feet, will have great difficulty landing on the front part of the foot. Again, because of the risk of injuries, never force runners to alter technique if the change causes pain.

TECH TIP #7:

▶ The foot should strike the ground close to the hips with an active landing.

In an effort to increase their stride length, some runners make the mistake of swinging the lower leg forward in a kicking action just prior to landing. You can detect this flaw because the foot appears to be reaching out to the ground. The result of this action is overstriding, which we defined as foot placement well in front of the center of gravity. For a smooth and efficient style, the foot should land only slightly in front of the hips, as shown in figure 5.4a (page 66).

Overstriding is linked to another technical flaw: forward movement of the foot at the instant it strikes the ground. From elementary laws of physics, we know that for every action there is an equal and opposite reaction. So if the foot is moving forward upon landing, the ground returns force in a backward direction, slowing the runner down. This flaw is called a passive landing. In contrast, if the foot is already moving backward as it lands, the ground reaction force will help to propel the body forward. This technique is called an active landing (see figure 5.6). A runner can develop the active landing skill through drills and the conscious effort to bring the foot toward the body as it is lowered to the ground.

TECH TIP #8:

▶ **For a powerful stride, the driving action should come from good extension of all the leg joints.**

You can imagine how little propulsive power would be generated if runners used only one joint—the ankle, for instance, in the driving phase of the stride. An effective stride requires extension, or straightening, of each of the three major leg joints—ankle, knee, and hip. You can tell if runners are achieving good ankle extension by whether their toes point downward as their feet leave the ground. For good knee and hip extension during fast running, you should be able to draw a straight diagonal line from the ankle joint to the hip joint on a side view of a runner. At relatively slow speeds, however, runners do not need to completely straighten their leg joints.

TECH TIP #9:

▶ **A high knee-lifting action helps to increase stride length and running speed.**

In the recovery phase of the stride, knee flexion raises the foot off the ground and hip flexion brings the knee up in front of the body (see Figures 5.4c and 5.4d on page 66). Especially during fast running, a high knee-lifting action is critical because it brings the foot into proper position for the next landing and driving subphases. Runners who have poor knee-lift drop the foot to the ground too quickly after takeoff. This shortens stride length by limiting the amount of time over which force can be produced by the opposite driving leg. One of the drills we'll present in chapter 6 can help increase knee lift.

Figure 5.6 An active landing occurs when the foot is moving backward as it hits the ground.

TECH TIP #10:

Good uphill and downhill running require alterations of the technique used on flat surfaces.

On tough cross-country courses, hill running technique can greatly affect performance. Going uphill, runners should try to maintain their rhythm and pace without straining. The key technical adjustment for uphill running is to lean slightly forward and forcefully extend the drive leg as it pushes off the ground. Coaches should cue their runners to focus on straightening the driving leg during push-off. Arm action should also be more vigorous going uphill. Finally, the eyes should focus 20 to 30 meters ahead. When runners' eyes turn to the ground, it's a sure sign that the hill has defeated them, instead of the other way around.

Downhill sections on cross-country courses allow runners to relax and maintain pace with little effort. For good downhill form, runners should lean backward slightly and allow their strides to increase in length. To avoid injury caused by jarring, the action should be controlled, rather than reckless. Good downhill runners have the strength and technique to use the hill to pick up speed and pass competitors.

SUMMARY

Proper technique improves distance running performance and prevents injuries. While no single, optimal form for distance running exists, our "tech tips" can help young runners race faster and stay healthier. For coaches, the keys to helping runners improve their technique are detecting flaws in runners' strides and prescribing technique training to correct them. Watch for these key flaws:

- Overstriding—the foot lands well ahead of the hips

- Passive landing—the foot is moving forward as it hits the ground

- Excessive vertical oscillation—the hips sink deeply upon footstrike

- Counterproductive upper body action—the shoulders turn excessively and the hands cross the body's midline

Remember, never force a change in technique if it causes discomfort or pain!

In part II of the book, which is just around the corner, we'll introduce specific training methods for improving running technique. Then, in part III, we'll show you how to implement these methods in the young runner's weekly training program.

PART II

ESSENTIAL TRAINING METHODS

Training for distance running is a journey. Through training, athletes get from where they are now to where they want to be in the future. Just as cars, planes, and trains take us from one geographical location to another, training methods are the vehicles that allow runners to travel from their current level of performance to their goals, or final destinations. Because distance running performance depends on many physiological, psychological, and technical abilities, coaches must include a number of different methods in the training program to ensure a successful journey.

Here in part II, we'll introduce and describe the most effective training methods for developing runners. In chapter 6, we'll present general principles and terminology of training and cover four fundamental methods: flexibility, mobility, technique, and recovery. In chapter 7, we'll discuss two more fundamental methods that build the runner's training base: strength endurance and aerobic endurance. Finally, in chapter 8, we'll present advanced training methods, including specialized interval running, to add to the fitness base to prepare the runner for the specific demands of competition.

Part II will introduce you to the key vehicles for the training journey of successful runners. The specific road maps for success in reaching each destination will follow in part III.

CHAPTER 6

Training Fundamentals

Let's talk training! First, we'll introduce the most important rules, or principles, that explain and predict how training adaptations occur. Then, we'll present terms that will help you understand our discussion of training throughout the rest of the book. Finally, we'll describe fundamental training methods for developing four basic elements of fitness for distance running:

- Flexibility
- Mobility
- Technique
- Recovery

We call these methods "fundamental" because they promote the basic fitness required to undertake aerobic endurance and strength endurance training (see chapter 7) as well as advanced training (see chapter 8).

The fundamental methods don't necessarily simulate the exact movements and physiological and psychological demands of cross-country and track racing. Neither do these methods require the high-intensity effort that racing demands. Instead, the fundamental methods lay down a base, or foundation, of fitness for more advanced training that *does* simulate racing. The stronger the runner's base, the greater potential she will have to develop specialized, or race-specific, fitness using advanced methods. A strong base also lessens the risk of injuries that can occur during high-intensity training.

Because the fundamental methods are used to prepare runners for more specialized training, they are emphasized in the early phases of preparation for competition. Then, as the competitive season draws near, the contribution of the advanced methods gradually increases. We'll discuss the details of how much fundamental and advanced training runners should do while in different stages later in the book.

PRINCIPLES OF TRAINING

The responses to specific types of training can vary considerably from athlete to athlete. For example, one youth may develop muscle mass after weight training while another may not. Generally speaking, however, the effects of training are highly predictable if coaches use training

methods properly. The two youths who performed weight training, for example, will both gain strength if they lift optimal loads over a sufficient period of time with the right amount of recovery in between training sessions. We can predict the results of certain types of training because coaches and scientists have observed and recorded these outcomes over many years. This study of training adaptations has led to the development of a number of laws, or principles, of training. These principles are useful in helping coaches implement training methods for optimal results.

> **▶ Principle of Individual Differences:**
> **Each athlete will respond to a particular type of training in a unique way.**

Differences in age, maturational status, body size, and genetically determined physiological capacities make each young runner distinct in terms of how he will adapt to training. So it doesn't make sense to adopt a training program merely because it produced good results for another runner. The principle of individual differences means that each athlete has distinct training needs. Coaches must design training in a way that allows each youth to capitalize on his individual strengths, while developing fitness in his weak areas. For example, a runner who has poor form will need extra technique work. A runner who lacks a base of endurance will need to emphasize aerobic training. For coaches, the key to selecting training methods that meet individual needs is assessing each athlete's developmental status and current fitness levels (see chapter 9).

> **▶ Principle of Specificity:**
> **A particular method of training will develop some physiological and performance capacities but not others.**

For example, weight training results in increased strength in the specific muscles that perform the work. Lifting weights, however, won't have much of an effect on aerobic endurance. This element of fitness is developed with moderate-intensity training, such as long-distance running, that stresses the heart and circulatory systems over prolonged periods. According to the principle of specificity, however, such training doesn't improve muscle strength, particularly in the upper body.

One important implication of this principle is that fast running should be included in young runners' programs so that they can run fast in races. It takes a proper amount of high-intensity, anaerobic training to condition the fast-twitch muscle fibers that will be recruited in fast-paced racing and sprint finishes (see chapter 8). Of course, coaches must also consider individual differences when assigning high-intensity training. Keep in mind that beginners and physically immature individuals may be at risk for injury when the anaerobic workload is too high.

> **Principle of Overload-Regeneration:**

For runners to elevate their levels of fitness, training overload must be followed by adequate rest and regeneration of their bodies.

Overload means that the training "dose" has to be potent enough to stress the body to its "threshold for improvement." To develop aerobic fitness, for example, the athlete must run far enough and fast enough to trigger adaptations of the heart, blood vessels, and aerobic enzymes. If the training dose is below the threshold for improvement, the level of fitness will not increase.

Figure 6.1 illustrates how fitness improves by the principle of overload-regeneration across cycles of training and recovery. The flat line of segment A_1 to B_1 reflects the athlete's level of fitness *before* a training session. The overload segment (B_1 to C_1) shows that training actually lowers fitness by depleting energy and causing fatigue. In fact, if training continues without recovery, symptoms of overtraining—poor performance, injury, illness, and psychological burnout—can result because the body lacks the energy to withstand the physical stress. Without adequate recovery following demanding training sessions, a runner may end up in the "overtraining zone" (segment C_1 to D_1). However, with recovery (segment C_1 to E_1) and replacement of nutrients, the athlete can avoid overtraining and restore energy to normal levels (segment E_1 to F_1). Note that with regeneration the athlete's fitness does not simply level off at point F_1, the initial level of fitness. Instead the fitness level continues to increase from F_1 to A_2, the new starting point. This increase in fitness beyond initial levels is called "super regeneration," or "super compensation." Over time, with new cycles of overload (segment B_2 to C_2), recovery (segment C_2 to D_2), and regeneration (segment D_2 to A_3), training elevates fitness to higher and higher levels.

In practice, the overload-regeneration principle means that a "hard" training day in which the workout demands considerable effort and energy should be followed by an "easy," or recovery, training day. Or the coach can vary the pattern, depending on each individual's level of fitness and training objectives. For example,

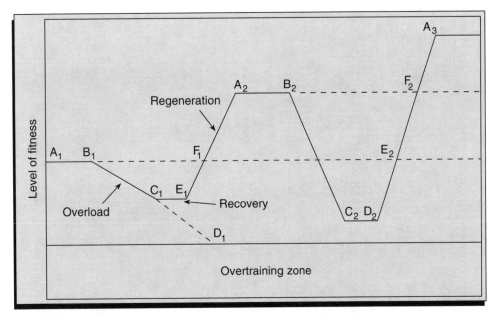

Figure 6.1 Overload-regeneration pattern.

consider the case of a highly fit runner who is preparing for a track meet in which she will race on consecutive days (e.g., a trial on Friday and the final on Saturday). At some point in training, this athlete might do two hard days in a row, followed by one or two easy days.

> **Principle of Progression:**
> In order for the runner's fitness and performance to improve, training loads must be increased gradually over time.

As you know, sharp increases in training can result in injury, illness, and burnout. If the training load remains at the same level over time, however, the runner's fitness and performance will stagnate. No concrete rules exist to guide how much training should be increased from season to season and year to year. Yet, by keeping in mind the athlete's developmental level and abilities, coaches can make good decisions on how to progressively increase training. Of course, we'll help by providing examples of progression as we talk more about training in the remainder of the book.

> **Principle of Reversibility:**
> "Detraining" occurs when a runner stops training to allow an injury to heal or takes a planned off-season break.

In other words, the effects of training are gradually lost. It's difficult to say exactly how much and how quickly fitness will be lost since the decline depends on the initial fitness level and the length of the layoff. However, when training is stopped completely for more than two or three weeks—especially after an injury—runners should not try to pick up where they left off. Instead, their training should resume slowly, beginning with fundamental methods.

TRAINING TERMINOLOGY

In our discussion of training methods in this and the next two chapters, we'll present sample sessions to illustrate the basics of how these methods are applied. In doing so, we'll use specific terms to describe the training dose, which refers to the amount and difficulty of training in a given session. To ensure clear communication when sharing ideas and details about training young runners, it's critical to have common, accepted definitions for the elements of training. Therefore, we'll introduce terms that best describe components of the training dose and are currently accepted among coaches, training theorists, and exercise scientists.

• *Duration*, or *volume*, refers to the length of a whole training session or a part of it. Duration can be measured by time (e.g., seconds, minutes, and hours) or by distance (e.g., miles or kilometers). For example, the total duration of a continuous aerobic endurance run might be 35 minutes or five miles (about eight kilometers). Duration might also refer to the length of one run or "repetition" in an interval training session.

• *Intervals* simply refer to a type of training that is broken up into a number of repetitions separated by recovery periods. We use the term interval to describe the recovery period itself.

• *Frequency* refers to the number of times a repetition is performed in a training session. The frequency of repetitions must be noted when planning circuit training, weight training, and interval running sessions (see chapters 7 and 8). For example, an athlete might do four repetitions of a 600-meter run, a session that is written as 4 × 600 meters.

• *Intensity* refers to how much effort is required to complete a repetition or a whole training session. When we describe training methods involving running, we will define intensity by "pace" or "percentage of maximal heart rate." So, the sample session might be further developed as 4 × 600 meters @ 2:00 (the "@" sign can be read either as "at" or "in"). When we describe strength endurance training methods (circuit and weight training), we'll define intensity by the "load lifted." Athletes can increase their intensity of training by extending more effort or by decreasing the recovery interval between repetitions during interval workouts.

• *Recovery* refers to the activity performed and the duration in between repetitions during interval training. We can add a recovery interval to complete our sample session: 4 × 600 meters @ 2:00 w/ a 2:00 jog recovery. In this session, the athlete would jog for two minutes after each 600-meter repetition.

METHODS FOR DEVELOPING FLEXIBILITY AND MOBILITY

Because of the nature of running movements themselves, perhaps the most fundamental elements of fitness are flexibility and mobility.

Flexibility is the ability to move the limbs through an extensive range of motion. Mobility is the ability to make coordinated, goal-directed movements in various planes (e.g., forward, sideways, diagonally). Because running does not demand the flexibility of gymnastics or ballet and because the limbs move mostly in one plane, many coaches and runners pay little attention to developing flexibility and mobility. It is a mistake, however, to overlook these fundamental elements in training.

Stretching: The Key to Flexibility

Movement through a full range of motion occurs when the muscles and connective tissue can stretch to their fullest natural extent. Thus, the training method for improving flexibility is stretching. It's very important for distance runners to stretch in order to prepare their muscles for activity and to avoid injury. Many injuries occur because the running stride can be fairly limited in range of motion. For example, when covering long distances at relatively slow speeds, runners don't lift their knees very high so their hamstrings don't stretch very much. Repetitive movement through such limited ranges of motion can lead to tightness that can result in muscle strains and tears when runners extend their stride for faster running in workouts and races. Runners who stretch regularly lower their risk of injuries by increasing their ranges of motion. These runners also benefit from stronger muscles because stretching increases force production.

Pages 78 through 82 illustrate a routine of 13 flexibility exercises that stretch key muscles for distance running. The first six figures are called "dynamic" stretching exercises because they involve continuous movement of the limbs through wide ranges of motion. The last seven exercises are called "static" stretching exercises because you hold the stretching position without movement. Before using these exercises, take careful note of the following general guidelines for stretching:

• **Always warm up the muscles by jogging before stretching:** 10 to 15 minutes of easy jogging will increase circulation to the muscles and prepare them for stretching. To help warm up the muscles before stretching on cool days, jog in warm clothes that cover the legs.

• **Use the same stretching routine for both training and racing**: A familiar stretching routine will help make you comfortable and relaxed during the prerace warm-up when competitive anxiety can distract your attention and make it difficult to concentrate on proper preparation. Because stretching should be relaxing, spend 10 to 15 minutes stretching, never rushing the routine.

• **Stretch before and after training:** It's important to stretch *after* training and racing—not simply before. Stretching after training is especially critical when the workout involves relatively long, slow running. It loosens tight muscles for the following day's workout.

• **Perform dynamic stretching** before static stretching: The order in which you perform stretching exercises is critical. Stretch large muscle groups at major joints, such as the hips, before smaller muscle groups, such as the calves. We recommend performing the 13 exercises in the order that they appear. The first six are dynamic stretching exercises that loosen up the joints and prepare the muscles for static stretching. The movements in dynamic stretching should be slow and gentle, rather than fast and "ballistic." Do 10 to 15 repetitions of each dynamic exercise. When performing static stretching, hold the position steady for about 20 to 30 seconds without making rocking or bouncing movements. Stretching should never be so vigorous that it causes quivering or pain in the muscles.

Perhaps you've heard of another type of stretching, called *proprioceptive neuromuscular facilitation,* or *PNF* (not illustrated in the figures). In PNF, a partner stretches a muscle by pushing or rotating a limb at the joint until the stretch is near maximum. Then, the athlete being stretched produces a forceful muscle contraction while the partner keeps the limb in the same position. This technique allows the muscle to stretch to a greater extent than in standard stretching exercises. While some athletic trainers assert that PNF is an essential form of stretching, it is not widely used by distance runners. The severe stretch combined with the vigorous resistive contraction can be very uncomfortable. Moreover, if athletes perform this type of stretching incorrectly, the greater degree of force that PNF generates can result in muscle injuries. We recommend that coaches and runners consult their school or club's athletic trainer for advice and guidance in using PNF stretching.

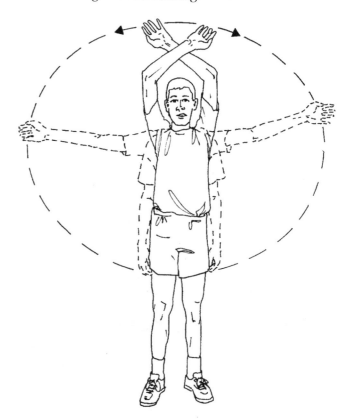

Arm Reach and Swing

Extend the arms above the head and then down to the sides in a wide, sweeping action.

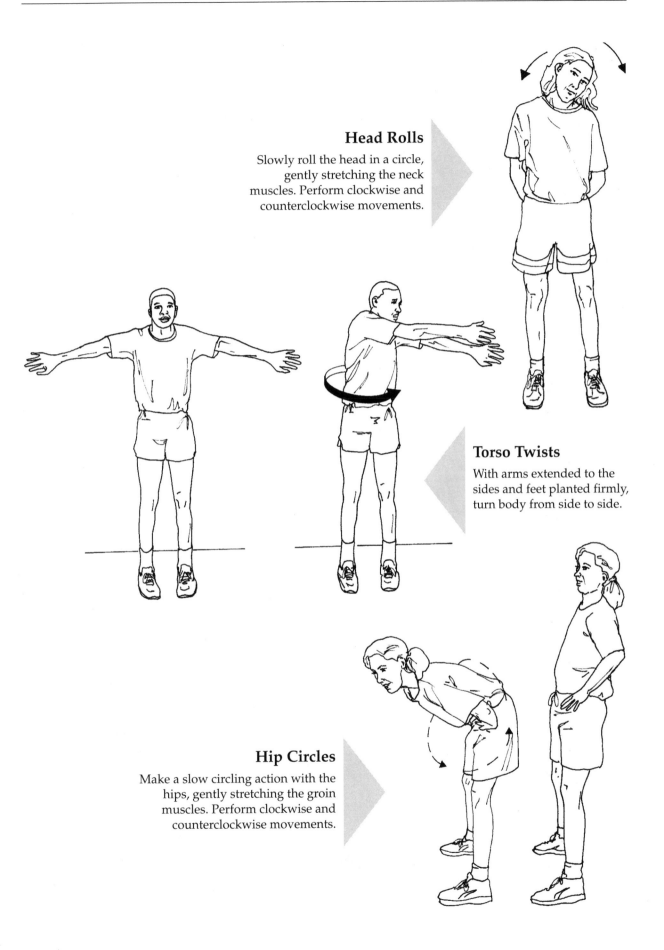

Head Rolls

Slowly roll the head in a circle, gently stretching the neck muscles. Perform clockwise and counterclockwise movements.

Torso Twists

With arms extended to the sides and feet planted firmly, turn body from side to side.

Hip Circles

Make a slow circling action with the hips, gently stretching the groin muscles. Perform clockwise and counterclockwise movements.

Leg Swing

With the left foot firmly planted and the left leg straight, swing the right leg in a kicking action. Keep the right leg as straight as possible. Hold on to a support (e.g., fence, tree) to maintain balance. After repetitions for the right leg, repeat the swinging action with the left leg.

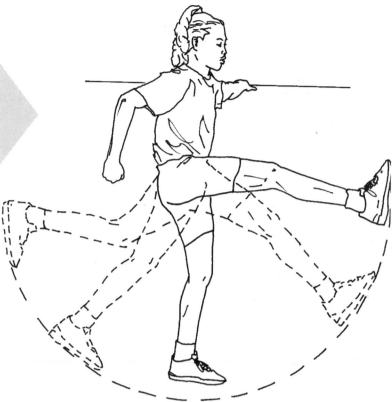

Ankle Swing

Starting with the right foot pointed downward, make a slow circling motion with the foot, gently stretching the ankle. Repeat with the left foot.

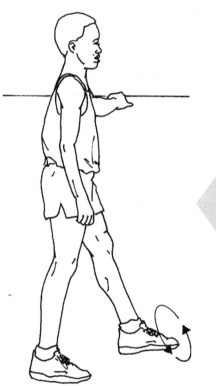

Hurdle Stretch

In the hurdle position with the left leg forward, lean forward gently to stretch the right quadricep and left hamstring.

Hip and Butt Stretch

After performing the hurdle stretch for the right quadricep and left hamstring, lie on back and cross the right knee over the body's midline. Reverse the hurdle position to perform the hurdle stretch for the left quadricep and right hamstring. Then perform the hip and butt stretch for the left side.

Groin Stretch

Sit with the soles of the feet together and press downward on the inside of the thighs.

Hamstring Stretch

Reach forward, keeping the legs straight. Don't strain to reach the toes.

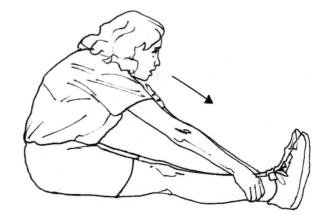

Lower Back and Spine Stretch

Pull the knees toward the chest and shoulders while elevating the hips off the floor.

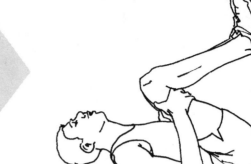

Quad Stretch

Holding on to a support (e.g., fence, tree) with the left hand, pull backward on the top of the right ankle. The right knee should be pointed downward. Repeat with the left leg.

Calf and Achilles Tendon Stretch

Against a supporting surface such as a fence or wall, plant the left foot firmly behind the right foot and bend at the left ankle by pushing downward with the shin. Repeat on the other side.

Increasing Mobility to Reduce Injuries

Although the running action occurs mostly in the *sagittal*, or straight-forward plane, it is important for runners to have good mobility in other planes of movement. The main reasons for training to improve mobility are to strengthen muscles and connective tissue that surround the joints and to prevent injuries. Runners who lack mobility are at risk for ankle and knee sprains when training and racing on uneven surfaces. Poor mobility can also lead to injury when the primary muscles used for running become fatigued, activating weak, untrained supplemental muscle groups. Mobility training is a way to condition these supplemental muscles.

HOW TO PLAY ULTIMATE FRISBEE

Ultimate Frisbee, or "ultimate" for short, is a noncontact game played on grass by two teams. In official games, the teams each have seven players. For purposes of training and fun, you don't need to have seven players on a side—simply pick sides among the runners on your team. For the offense, the object of the game is to score goals by throwing a Frisbee to teammates and advancing it across the opposing team's goal line, like in American football and rugby. You can only advance the Frisbee by passing because the player who catches it is not allowed to take any steps. But the game has plenty of running and action because players are trying to get free from defenders to catch the Frisbee. The defense tries to intercept the Frisbee by covering offensive players who are trying to get open for a pass. If the defense intercepts the Frisbee, they become the offense and try to score. The Frisbee also changes direction if an offensive player drops it, or if it hits the ground on an incomplete pass.

An official field is 70 by 40 yards (64 by 36.5 meters), but you can adjust the field according to the number of players and to your training objectives. A longer and wider field will challenge runners to cover more distance and build speed endurance through long sprints. Shorter and narrower fields are good for quick bursts and rapid changes in direction.

To prevent injuries, coaches should stress that ultimate is a noncontact game!

Many formal drills for developing mobility exist, but the best method for young runners is playing games, such as basketball, soccer, flag football, and "keep-away." Games are best because they involve running and jumping movements in different planes—not to mention they're fun! One of our favorite mobility games is "ultimate Frisbee," which is a mixture of rugby and American football (without the tackling!). A 15-minute session of ultimate Frisbee once or twice a week during early phases of preparation is a great way to improve mobility while beginning to develop a base of speed and endurance.

DEVELOPING TECHNIQUE: DRILLS AND STRIDES

Technique training should be a regular part of a young runner's program because good technique is essential for both optimal performance and injury prevention. One method for improving running form involves "technique drills" that isolate key parts of the running stride such as knee lift and ankle extension during the drive phase. Figure 6.2, a through d, illustrates and explains four key technique drills, specifically intended for the distance runner. The objective of performing these drills is to develop the neuromuscular pathways that underlie efficient movement patterns for running.

Runners should always precede technique sessions with a complete warm-up that includes both jogging and stretching. If a coach plans more than one type of training on a particular day, such as technique drills and a weight workout, athletes should do the technique drills at the beginning of the session when they are fresh and rested. Coaches should carefully supervise runners during technique drills, providing detailed instructions and feedback. Too often, young athletes perform technique drills incorrectly and actually reinforce inefficient movement patterns in their running stride.

The sample sessions on page 85 show workouts involving the four technique drills that are illustrated in figure 6.2. For these sample sessions and those that follow in the next two chapters, we define developmental levels for young runners in terms of chronological and training age as follows:

Figure 6.2a High knees. Performing rapid, short strides, produce the running motion with an exaggerated knee-lifting action and forceful pushing-off during the drive phase. Most of the movement is up and down, so don't move forward very quickly. The upper body should be vertical, and the arms should pump vigorously. Beginners who are learning this drill should perform a "marching" high knee action. With practice and skill acquisition they can then perform the running motion.

Figure 6.2b Skipping. Just as a child would skip, land on the heel and roll off the ball of the foot. The knees should be fairly straight but not rigid. The objectives are to roll quickly from the heel to the forefoot and to push off the ground forcefully by rotating at the ankle and driving the foot downward.

Figure 6.2c Butt kicks. Produce the running motion with an exaggerated follow-through action in which the heel lightly touches the buttocks. The action occurs by bending the knee, which should not be lifted as in a normal stride.

Figure 6.2d Fast feet. The objective is to take the smallest, yet fastest, steps possible while coordinating the arms with the legs. The drill is performed on the toes; the heels should never touch the ground.

	Chronological Age	Training Age
• Beginner	12 to 14 years	0 to 2 years
• Intermediate	14 to 16 years	2 to 4 years
• Advanced	16 to 18 years	4 to 6 years

The sample sessions in this part of the book present *general* guidelines for training during the early phases of the "preparation period," or the first few weeks of a season. While these sessions illustrate developmental progression over the years, they don't provide guidelines for progression within a single season from the preparation period to the competition period or to the racing season. We'll briefly address such within-season progression for each method in this part of the book. Then, in part III, we'll present more detailed guidelines on how to organize training in specific phases of the preparation and competition periods.

Following the principle of progression, it's important to gradually increase the amount of tech-

A REMINDER: ADAPT TO THE INDIVIDUAL

We think the sample sessions presented in this and the next two chapters are appropriate for most runners at their respective developmental levels. Remember, however, that these sessions are only general guidelines and are not meant to be "written in stone." It's likely that some youths will find the sessions too easy, while some will find them too difficult. Therefore, coaches should adapt the doses of these workouts to meet the specific abilities, needs, and training responses of individual athletes.

nique training over time. As shown in the sample sessions below, the distance covered in the drills should increase from year to year. In our example, the total volume for advanced runners (570 meters) exceeds the total volume for beginners (270 meters) by slightly over 100 percent. Coaches should have runners progressively increase the

SAMPLE SESSION: TECHNIQUE DRILLS

Duration: 10 to 100 meters
Frequency: 3 to 6 repetitions per drill
Intensity: Fast, but controlled
Recovery: Walk or jog back to starting position

Sample Sessions for the Preparation Period

Drill	Beginner CA[a] = 12-14 TA[b] = 0-2	Intermediate CA = 14-16 TA = 2-4	Advanced CA = 16-18 TA = 4-6
High knees	3 × 20 meters	3 × 30 meters	3 × 40 meters
Skipping	3 × 40 meters	3 × 60 meters	3 × 80 meters
Butt kicks	3 × 20 meters	3 × 30 meters	3 × 40 meters
Fast feet	3 × 10 meters	3 × 20 meters	3 × 30 meters

[a]CA = chronological age in years.

[b]TA = training age in years.

High knees drill develops the hip flexor and extensor muscles for powerful hill running and sprint finishes. The powerful arm action develops upper body technique

Skipping drill develops the muscles and connective tissue in the feet, ankles, and calves. Strength and endurance in these areas are necessary for an active landing and a forceful pushing-off action in the drive phase.

Butt kicks drill develops the hamstrings that can be weakened—compared to the quadriceps—during long, continuous running. The hamstrings come into play during short, fast running—such as in 800-meter races—and sprint finishes.

Fast feet drill develops the muscles and connective tissue of the feet and trains the nervous system to issue rapid and forceful commands to arms and legs.

Steve Holman

Arlington, VA

Personal Bests:

800 meters	1:44.98
1,500 meters	3:32.01
Mile	3:50.76
3,000 meters	7:46.27

© 1995 Tim De Frisco

Like many adult elite runners, Steve Holman started training and racing because he enjoyed running in elementary school and because he was good at it. "I always excelled at running in gym class and in what we called the 'track-o-rama' day in school," he says. "But I never trained on a daily basis until I was 14."

Since then, Steve has taken a progressive approach to training. Good high school and college coaching and smart training account for Steve's rise to the highest levels of international competition. In 1995, when he was 25, Steve ran 3:50 for the mile and was the fourth-ranked 1,500-meter runner in the world. Having started running relatively late and having used progressive methods of training, Steve feels he's just now beginning to peak.

Steve stresses fundamental training methods, like technique work and strength training, for young runners. "I did a lot of dips, sit-ups, pull-ups, and push-ups as a young runner," he says. "I'd encourage young athletes to get into the habit of doing different types of training, not only to avoid injury but also to add variety and break the monotony of just running every day."

Steve believes in a high-intensity training program, with a little bit of fast running on a regular basis. However, he cautions against doing high-intensity training without first developing a base of fitness. In addition, Steve tells young runners to make sure they get enough recovery time between demanding training sessions. "With high-intensity training, recovery is especially important. To get the most from workouts, you need to be pretty well-rested. So take it easy on your recovery days," he advises.

Steve trains carefully to improve his pacing and strategy, and he urges young runners to do the same. "I would advise paying attention to how you train because chances are that's how you race. An athlete who runs the first few repetitions in an interval session fast and then fades, I'll bet, does the same thing in races. Everyone has strengths and weaknesses in practice, so it's the coach's and runner's job to devise a race plan that will exploit the athlete's strengths."

A strong proponent of fundamental training methods, Steve also thinks the key to getting the most from fundamental training is to have fun. "Perhaps the most important training advice for young runners," he says, "is to have fun."

amount of technique work during a single training season. We have designed the technique sessions for the early phases of preparation. As the preparation period progresses, you can increase the volume by adding distance to individual repetitions and by adding more repetitions. Keep in mind that progression must be individualized. Athletes who demonstrate good technique and ease in handling the load should increase their training volume. Others who are having difficulty with the drills may need to keep their load constant until their technique improves.

Another method of technique training involves sessions in which the athlete runs repeated "strides" over short distances (100 to 150 meters) at race pace and faster. Technique strides can reveal and correct flaws in the pattern of movement. During these sessions, the coach looks for problems in the runner's form, gives instructions for correcting the problems, and provides feedback after each stride. As we suggested in chapter 5, it would be ideal to provide immediate feedback on the strides using video. This type of technique work must be highly individualized because each runner will have unique flaws in form.

To show you how technique strides can be used in individualized training, let's consider the case of a runner who overstrides, has a passive landing, and brings his arms across the front of his body, causing rotation of the torso. A sample session for this athlete might involve 15 repetitions of a 150-meter stride with complete recovery between repetitions. To work on correcting each flaw, the session can be divided as follows:

- 5 × 150 meters at 1,500-meter race pace, with a focus on correcting the overstriding problem by planting the foot closer to the body;

- 5 × 150 meters at 800-meter race pace, with a focus on performing an active landing; and

- 5 × 150 meters at a controlled sprint, with a focus on driving the arms in a straight line without crossing over the body's midline.

As with drills, athletes should do technique strides when they are rested. Fatigue limits the ability to perform, and thereby, learn, optimal motor patterns. Coaches, however, should pay special attention to runners' techniques during training sessions that are designed to cause fatigue, especially anaerobic sessions (see chapter 8). After all, the objective of technique training is to apply it to racing situations when fatigue occurs. To keep runners focused on form during high-intensity training sessions and races, coaches should use the types of verbal cues we recommended in presenting the "tech tips" in chapter 5.

RECOVERY METHODS BETWEEN TRAINING SESSIONS

It may seem odd to include recovery as a method of training; however, it makes good sense when you consider that running fitness is actually developed during the time *between* training sessions. As you know from our discussion of the principle of overload-regeneration, fitness doesn't come from training alone; it comes from the proper combination of training and recovery. During the recovery period between workouts, the body replaces the energy spent and repairs muscle tissue that was broken down. In addition, recovery refreshes the athlete's psychological outlook and motivation.

Regeneration occurs naturally with proper nutrition and adequate rest, including a good night's sleep. Runners can, however, accelerate regeneration by using specific recovery methods, including light exercise, massage, and ice and heat treatments. Recovery sessions on days following intense training actually make regeneration occur faster than a complete break from training. Twenty to 30 minutes of easy exercise (e.g., jogging, cycling, or swimming) along with stretching increases the rate of oxygen- and nutrient-enriched blood flow, restoring energy to tired muscles. This type of training session should not drain energy; it is simply meant to accelerate regeneration from the previous day's training. So athletes can run, cycle, or swim as slowly as they please!

Other methods that speed recovery include massage, cold treatment, and heat treatment. Athletes can massage their own tired and sore muscles, or the school or club athletic trainer can administer the massage. Massage decreases tightness and accelerates blood flow through the muscles, effectively "washing away" damaged cells and metabolic by-products. The application of cold or heat also speeds recovery by increasing the rate of blood flow to damaged muscle tissue. Generally speaking, use cold applications (e.g., ice packs, ice whirlpool) immediately following training, especially when muscles and joints are sore or injured. In most cases, apply heat prior to a training session to warm the muscles and prepare them for activity. Coaches should seek specific guidelines for applying cold and heat treatments from the school or club athletic trainer.

SUMMARY

You've covered a lot of ground learning about the principles, terminology, and fundamental methods of training in this chapter. Let's review the key points:

- Why is it important to understand the principles of training? By knowing principles like specificity and overload-regeneration, you'll feel confident both in choosing the right methods to develop specific elements of fitness and in planning recovery periods so that runners can restore energy and increase their fitness after demanding workouts.

- What are the key components that make up the training dose?

- Volume (or duration)—the amount of time or distance of training.
- Intensity—the speed and effort of training.
- Frequency—how often repetitions are performed.

- What are the reasons for using the fundamental methods of training? By developing better flexibility, mobility, and technique, runners lay down a base of fitness that allows them to undertake more advanced, specialized training with a low risk of injury. By using recovery methods to restore energy following training, runners will gain the greatest benefit from both fundamental and advanced methods.

To continue our discussion of fundamental training, we introduce and describe two more methods for building the base—strength endurance and general aerobic endurance—in the next chapter.

CHAPTER 7

Building a Base: Strength and General Aerobic Endurance

The methods for developing fundamental abilities such as flexibility, mobility, and technique are essential to building a strong base of fitness. Recalling our analogy of training as a journey, however, these vehicles allow runners to cover only short distances toward their final destinations. In this chapter, we'll introduce methods for developing two elements of fitness, strength endurance and general aerobic endurance, that further build the training base and help runners cover much more ground.

Why do runners need to develop strength endurance? One key reason is to prevent lower extremity injuries that can result from the repetitive stress of footstrike. Consider that in one mile of running, each foot may strike the ground as many as 500 times. Under such repetitive pounding, injury can result if the muscles fatigue and cannot maintain the structural integrity of lower extremity joints. By conditioning the muscles to withstand repetitive stress, strength endurance training helps to prevent lower extremity injuries.

With a greater capacity to withstand impact stress, the runner will be able to endure greater volumes of training—an ability that is essential to developing general aerobic endurance, or conditioning of the cardiovascular system. A high level of cardiovascular fitness allows the muscles to work without having to rely heavily on anaerobic energy. Furthermore, because successful distance running performance depends so heavily upon bypassing the anaerobic system, general aerobic endurance training makes up a large part of the training program.

DEVELOPING STRENGTH ENDURANCE

Strength is the ability to exert maximum muscular force, such as bench-pressing a heavy barbell one time. Strength is related to the cross-sectional area and mass of the muscles. For athletes, the importance of strength and muscle mass depends on the demands of the sport. For example, offensive linemen in football need big muscles and their extraordinary strength to successfully block defensive opponents. In contrast, distance runners don't need much strength because they do not exert maximum force in the running stride. That's why runners don't need large, bulky

muscles to be successful. Runners need a combination of strength *and* endurance; that is, they need to produce moderately high levels of muscular force over long periods of time. This important component of fundamental fitness is called strength endurance.

Keep in mind that strength endurance training helps prevent injuries. Another key reason for developing strength endurance is to improve running technique. Poor technique often results from weak lower extremity muscles that fatigue easily. For example, poorly conditioned calf muscles can be the cause of flat-footed running and heel striking. Weakness in the hip flexors may limit the height of knee lift. Strength endurance exercises that isolate and strengthen weak leg muscles will improve the runner's technique.

Good technique also depends on upper body strength endurance. During the running stride, muscles in the arms, abdomen, and lower back repeatedly contract to absorb the shock of landing and counteract rotational and side-to-side movements. Runners can reduce these counterproductive movements, enhancing efficiency and therefore racing performance with strength endurance training.

Strength endurance training involves exercises that place greater loads on the muscles than they normally have to resist. Since the objective is to gain a combination of strength and endurance, the training dose is critical. Runners develop strength endurance with low-intensity, high-volume training. This means that you should perform exercises with relatively light resistive loads and a large number of repetitions. In fact, many of the best exercises for developing strength endurance, such as push-ups and abdominal curl-ups, involve lifting your body weight only. The combination of low resistance and high repetitions allows you to perform the exercise for a long duration to gain endurance in addition to strength. Note that this approach differs from the high resistance and low repetitions method used to develop maximum strength and gain muscle mass—training results that distance runners generally should not seek. We'll introduce two kinds of strength endurance methods for runners—circuit training and weight training.

But first—you may be familiar with another form of strength endurance training called *plyometrics*. This type of training involves vigorous jumping movements that place great loads on the muscles for brief periods. Because we think the method is of questionable value for young distance runners, we will not cover it in the book. Our main concern is that severe injuries can result unless plyometric drills are performed with nearly perfect technique.

Circuit Training: Building Strength Endurance Through Body-Weight Resistance

Circuit training consists of a routine of strength endurance exercises organized in a sequential pattern that, as the name implies, is called a circuit. You can arrange a series of stations mak-ing up the circuit on the infield of a track, in a gymnasium, or wherever space permits. The sample sessions below show circuit training work-outs for runners of different developmental lev-els during the preparation period. You can set up this circuit, consisting of nine body-weight resis-tance exercises placed at three stations, in a grassy field or park that has exercise bars for chinnies and dips (see pages 92 through 94). As you read the instructions, keep in mind that proper tech-nique is essential in circuit training because, ironi-cally, these exercises, although intended to pre-vent injuries, can actually cause them if they are performed incorrectly. Always precede circuit training sessions with a complete warm-up that includes jogging and flexibility exercises.

SAMPLE SESSION: CIRCUIT TRAINING

Duration: 10 to 45 minutes
Frequency: 10 to 30 repetitions per exercise
Intensity: Fast, but controlled; >70% HRmax
Recovery: 20 to 30 seconds between exercises

Sample Sessions for the Preparation Period

	Number of repetitions		
	Beginner CA[a] = 12-14 TA[b] = 0-2	Intermediate CA = 14-16 TA = 2-4	Advanced CA = 16-18 TA = 4-6
Station 1			
Push-ups	10-12	14-16	18-20
Curl-ups	18-20	22-24	26-28
Squats	18-20	22-24	26-28
400-meter run	1	1	1
Station 2			
Chinnies	10-12	12-14	14-16
Back extension	10-12	14-16	18-20
Heel raisers	18-20	22-24	26-28
400-meter run	1	1	1
Station 3			
Dips	10-12	12-14	14-16
Leg raisers	18-20	22-24	26-28
Step-ups	10-12	12-14	14-16
400-meter run	1	1	1

[a]CA = chronological age in years.
[b]TA = training age in years.

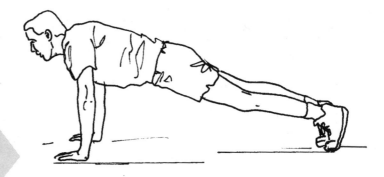

Push-Ups (Station 1)

With the back and legs straight, lower the body to the ground and then push up to starting position.

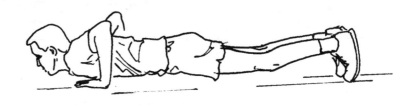

Curl-Ups (Station 1)

Lie on the ground with the arms at the sides and palms face down. The fingertips should just touch the close edge of a strip of cardboard or wood measuring 30 inches by 4 1/2 inches. Raise the body by curling the trunk until the fingertips have reached the far edge of the strip.

Squats (Station 1)

Standing upright with the feet flat on the ground shoulder-width apart, lower the body by bending at the hips, knees, and ankles. At the end of the lowering action, the thighs should be close to parallel to the ground. Keep the back and head as straight as possible. Return to starting position by straightening the hips, knees, and ankles.

Partner-Assisted Chinnies (Station 2)

With assistance from a partner, lift the body so that the chin rises over the top of the bar. Slowly lower the body back to the starting position. The partner should provide enough help so that at least 12 repetitions can be performed.

Back Extension (Station 2)

Lying face down with the hands behind the head, slowly raise the head and torso off the ground. Lower the body, returning to the starting position. If needed, a partner can hold the legs down.

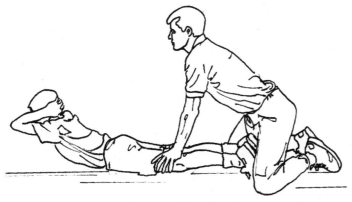

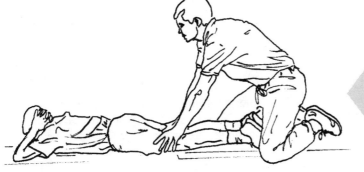

Heel Raisers (Station 2)

Starting with the heel flat on the ground and the balls of the feet placed on a two-by-four block of wood, raise the heels by extending at the ankles and pushing down with the toes. Lower the heels to return to the starting position. For balance, hold on to a fence, pole, or partner if necessary.

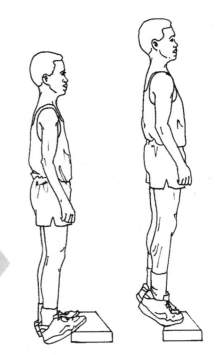

Partner-Assisted Dips (Station 3)

With assistance from a partner, lower the body by bending the arms at the elbows. Keep the back straight. At the end of the lowering action the upper arms should be parallel to the ground. Lift the body upward by straightening the elbows. The partner should provide enough help so that at least 12 repetitions can be performed.

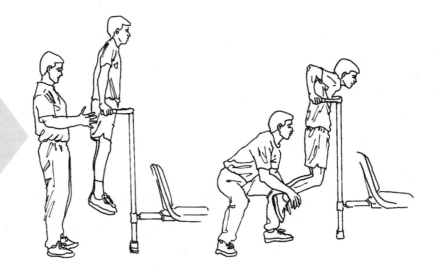

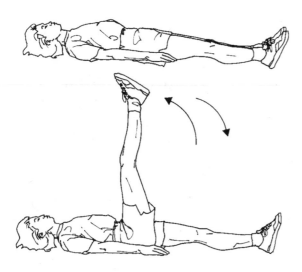

Leg Raisers (Station 3)

Lying flat on the back, lift the right leg by bending at the hip. The leg should be straight throughout the movement. Lower the leg to the ground in a controlled manner. After completing the repetitions for the right leg, switch sides.

Step-Ups (Station 3)

Begin with the right foot on a step or wooden box high enough so that the thigh is parallel (but not beyond parallel) to the ground. Keeping the back straight, step up onto the step or box, and then step down. The arms can be kept at the sides or, to help maintain balance, they can perform a pumping action as in the running stride. After all the assigned repetitions are completed with the right leg, switch sides.

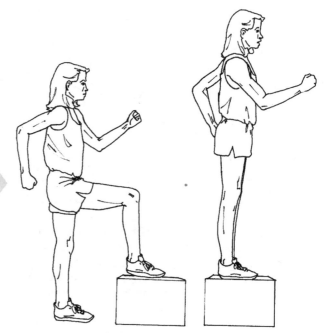

Types of Circuit Training Exercises

For the sample circuit training sessions, we've selected exercises that stress key muscle groups used in running. Each station includes an exercise for the arms, torso (abdomen and back), and legs. Note the rotating pattern in which the different parts of the body are stressed at each station: Exercises for the arms, torso, and legs are ordered sequentially, allowing time for recovery before working the same body part again at the next station. If you use the same muscle groups consecutively at a station, excessive localized fatigue can result. This fatigue can reduce the number of repetitions you can perform, limiting the desired endurance effect. Incidentally, to promote strength endurance, we have added a twist to the sample circuit—a 400-meter run after each station. We'll have more to say about this part of the session shortly.

Most young runners really enjoy circuit training because it adds variety to daily workouts, it's physically challenging, and it produces visible results, such as enhanced muscle tone and a more powerful stride. Even so, it's important to be creative and vary the exercises included in the circuit over time. For example, to develop the calves, you can replace heel raisers with rope jumping. Instead of doing push-ups for developing the chest and arm muscles, you might do medicine ball chest passes with a partner. For conditioning the abdominal muscles, you can change the type of curl-ups or sit-ups in the circuit. While the number of exercises in a circuit should be in the range of 8 to 12, the exercises themselves can vary greatly as long as they stress the muscle groups used in running.[1] Finally, the circuit might be more enjoyable if some of the exercises require teammates to pair off and help each other. The partner-assisted exercises illustrated on pages 93 and 94 are good examples.

Circuit Training Dose

Depending on the type of exercise and the athlete's developmental level, the number of repetitions will range between 10 and 30. You should perform repetitions at a fast, yet controlled, rate.

Going too fast can result in sloppy technique, increasing the risk of injury. In between exercises at each station, you should take 20 to 30 seconds for recovery. This short recovery period, during which you can walk, jog lightly, or stretch, will help develop the desired endurance effect by keeping the heart rate elevated. So will the 400-meter run at the end of each station! Perform this run at a fast, steady pace, but not as an all-out sprint. If you do the exercises properly, they will elevate your heart rate to at least 70 percent of maximum throughout the circuit.

One complete circuit of the exercises should take 12 to 15 minutes. At the start of a training season, you should perform only one circuit in a workout. Over time, and with improved fitness, you can repeat stations until you can perform two to three circuits. You can see that this type of training can be quite lengthy. For example, if you do three circuits, the session can take up to 45 minutes. When you consider the effects of circuit training on the cardiovascular system and on the muscles performing the resistance exercises, these workouts are very demanding. But they are extremely valuable in terms of building a fitness base.

Exercises that require moving your body weight generally offer sufficient resistance for developing strength endurance. However, well-conditioned intermediate or advanced young athletes (i.e., with a training age over two years) can increase the intensity, or load, by doing circuit exercises with weighted vests, medicine balls, dumbbells, sand bags, or any other object that will create an extra load on the muscles. The added resistance should be light enough to allow the athlete to perform at least 15 repetitions with good technique before fatiguing. If you cannot accomplish 15 repetitions without straining or losing form, you should lighten the load.

Progression of Circuit Training

As shown in the sample circuit training sessions on page 91, year-to-year progression involves increasing the number of repetitions of each exercise. Remember, you can also increase the training intensity over time by adding extra loads to the body. Across the preparation period of a single season, the key to progression is repeating stations, so that you perform up to three circuits as you gain strength endurance from week to week. For example, once you can perform one circuit

1. For alternative exercises, we refer you to *Strength Training for Young Athletes* by William Kraemer and Steven Fleck (Champaign, IL: Human Kinetics. 1993.). This book features illustrations and detailed instructions for performing numerous circuit and weight training exercises.

(stations 1, 2, and 3) without difficulty and muscle soreness, you can repeat a station (station 1, 2, 3, and 1) in the next circuit session. As the preparation period progresses, you may be able to handle up to three complete circuits.

Weight Training: The Next Step in Building Strength Endurance

As in circuit training, the objective of weight training for distance runners is to build strength endurance for improved performance and injury prevention. So most of the same principles and guidelines for circuit training apply to weight training. For example, the weight training dose should be low in intensity and high in repetitions. As usual, precede the workout with a complete warm-up, including flexibility exercises. Keep in mind that distance runners should not lift weights to increase muscle mass or develop maximum strength. Instead, the goal, as in circuit training, is to develop muscular strength *and* endurance.

Weight training can be used to supplement circuit training as the training season progresses and the athlete gains strength endurance. Some drawbacks, however, may limit the use of weight training. First, this method may not be appropriate for beginners and youths who have not reached physical maturity. Heavy loads pose a slight risk of injury to growing bones in prepubescent youths, especially if they perform the exercises with poor technique. Therefore, we recommend that beginners in their first year and physically immature athletes use circuit training exclusively. Once athletes become proficient with the technique involved in circuit training and are physically mature, they can begin weight training.

A second limitation is that weight training does not offer the convenience of circuit training. You may not have access to a gym with weight machines and free weights. Even if you do have access to such equipment, it is often not designed for youth. Weight machines are typically built for adults and free weights on long bars may be too cumbersome and difficult for youths to control. So if you don't have access to weights, or if the equipment is inappropriately sized, circuit training with added resistance (e.g., weight vests, medicine balls, dumbbells) will suffice as an excellent means of developing strength endurance. If, however, you do have access to weight training equipment that is appropriately sized, you should consider including weight training in your program. It's fun and challenging to lift weights. Certainly, young athletes enjoy the skill and benefits of this type of training.

So the type of weight work you do will depend on the available equipment. You may have access to weight machines, free weights, or both. If properly sized, machines offer the advantage of isolating specific muscle groups and minimizing the risk of injury. This is because the path over which the movement occurs is controlled by pulleys and other mechanical devices. In contrast, free weights require considerable balance and technique to isolate key muscles and stabilize the movement. Because the technical demands are much greater for free weights, experts recommend starting out on machines and progressing to free weights over time.

Types of Weight Training Exercises

The sample sessions on page 97 show weight training workouts for intermediate and advanced young runners during the preparation period of a season. The sessions involve nine exercises using both free weights and machines (see pages 98 through 100). As in circuit training, weight training should stress the muscle groups involved in the running movement (legs and arms) and those that stabilize the body (abdomen and lower back). The order of exercises should allow for recovery of a given muscle group before it is stressed again. Therefore, the sample sessions alternate exercises for the upper body, torso, and legs. Stress large muscles first in the training session, then small muscles.

Like circuit training, weight training can prevent injuries; however, injuries can occur during this type of training if coaches don't supervise the exercises closely, providing instruction and feedback on technique, ensuring that athletes perform them with the proper form. Several free weight exercises require spotters to help position the bar and to assist athletes if they experience difficulty lifting the weights. Ideally, the spotters should be adults. But youths who demonstrate knowledge and skill in spotting techniques can assist their teammates during training sessions.

One key to a successful weight training program is variety. You can add variety to workouts by periodically replacing the exercises used with others that stress the same muscle groups. (See

Strength Training for Young Athletes by Kraemer and Fleck for detailed information on spotting techniques and additional weight training exercises for distance runners.)

Dose for Weight Training Exercises

Keeping in mind our objective of developing strength and endurance at the same time, weight training sessions should be low in intensity and high in repetitions. A concept called *repetition maximum*, or RM, should guide coaches in determining the appropriate dose for each individual. As an example, the 12 RM dose is the amount of weight that an athlete can lift 12—but not 13—times, without excessive straining and loss of good form. To develop strength endurance, distance runners should perform 8 to 15 repetitions of each weight training exercise with one to two minutes recovery in between exercises. As shown in the sample sessions below, we recommend using a 10- to 15-RM load. For example, to determine how much weight to lift for a 12 RM, start with a very light load that can be lifted at least 20 times. Then, after resting for several minutes, increase the weight by approximately 10 to 15 percent and perform the repetitions until fatigue sets in. Repeat this process, with sufficient rest periods, until 12 repetitions is the maximum number that you can perform.

The lower end of the repetition range for the exercises allows athletes to refine their lifting technique without becoming too fatigued. For example, if you perform 10-12 repetitions of barbell squats with 15-RM loads, you will not have to strain during the last few lifts. Athletes should never do exercises such as squats that involve many different joints and require coordinating the whole body under conditions that

---

SAMPLE SESSION: WEIGHT TRAINING

Duration: 20 to 50 minutes
Frequency: 8 to 15 repetitions per exercise
Intensity: 10 to 15 repetition maximum
Recovery: 1 or 2 minutes between exercises

Sample Sessions for the Preparation Period

	Training dose	
	Intermediate CA[a] = 14-16 TA[b] = 2-4	Advanced CA = 16-18 TA = 4-6
Bench press	12-15 reps/15 RM[c]	10-12 reps/12 RM
Incline sit-ups with twist	12-15 reps	12-15 reps
Barbell squats	12-15 reps/15RM	10-12 reps/12 RM
Overhead press	10-12 reps/12RM	8-10 reps/10 RM
Good mornings	10-12 reps/12RM	8-10 reps/10 RM
Knee extensions	12-15 reps/15RM	10-12 reps/12 RM
Knee curls	10-12 reps/12RM	8-10 reps/10 RM
Dumbbell arm pumps	12-15 reps/15RM	10-12 reps/12 RM
Barbell heel raisers	12-15 reps/15RM	10-12 reps/12 RM

Note: No sample workout is given for beginners because we recommend that most youngsters whose training age is under 2 years use circuit training rather than weight training.

[a]CA = chronological age in years.

[b]TA = training age in years.

[c]RM = repetition maximum (see text for explanation).

Bench Press

Lying on a flat bench with the feet flat on the floor, grip the bar so the hands are about shoulder-width apart. Lower the bar to the upper chest in a controlled manner. Press the bar upward to the starting position. Do not raise the back or buttocks off the bench.

Incline Sit-Ups With a Twist

Lying on the back on an incline sit-up board, raise the body by curling the torso. Right before the end of the lifting movement, twist the torso by touching one elbow to the opposite knee. Lower the body slowly and repeat the lift, switching the twisting direction.

Barbell Squats

Stand with the bar resting on the spines of the shoulder blades and the hands and feet spaced slightly greater than shoulder-width apart. Keeping the back as upright as possible, lower the body by bending at the hips, knees, and ankles until the thighs are almost parallel to the floor. The lowering movement should be slow and controlled. Lift the body to the starting position by straightening the lower extremity joints. During the lifting movement keep the feet flat on the floor.

Behind-the-Neck Press

Beginning in the same position as in barbell squats, press the bar above the head until the arms are straight. Lower the bar slowly to the starting position. During the lowering and lifting movements, keep the feet flat on the floor.

Good Mornings

Beginning in the same position as in barbell squats, with the knees slightly bent, slowly bend forward at the waist until the torso is almost parallel with the floor. Slowly raise the body back to the starting position. During the lowering and lifting movements, keep the back straight.

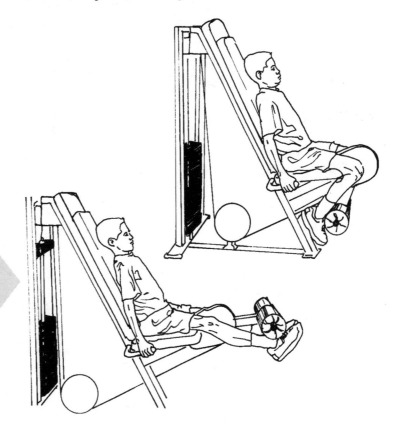

Knee Extension

Sitting with the knees over the edge of the machine seat, lift the weight by straightening the legs. Hold the position at the top for two seconds. Slowly lower the weight to the starting position. During the lifting and lowering movement, keep the back flat against the seat.

Knee Curls

Lie face down on the machine bench with the knees hanging slightly over the edge and the heels under the pads. Lift the weight by slowly pulling the heels to the buttocks. To lower the weight, straighten the legs in a controlled manner.

Dumbbell Arm Pumps

Standing with one foot propped up on a bench or chair for balance, pump the arms rapidly using the same motion as in the running stride.

Barbell Heel Raisers

Beginning in the same position as in barbell squats, with the feet pointed straight ahead, raise the heels by extending at the ankles and pushing down with the toes. Lower the heels to return to the starting position.

compromise good technique. When form breaks down, the risk of injury increases. Therefore, it's best to reduce the number of repetitions when you are still perfecting technique or if you experience excessive fatigue.

Progression of Weight Training

The year-to-year progression of weight training involves increasing the intensity, or the load lifted. You can accomplish this objective by reducing the RM load over time. For intermediate runners, 15-RM loads are appropriate because they are light enough to allow mastery of technique, yet heavy enough to increase strength endurance. The relatively light load also reduces stress on growing bones in those youths who may still be maturing. Advanced runners who are more physically mature and have learned the proper technique will benefit from relatively heavier weights such as 10- or 12-RM loads.

Within a season, runners should not begin weight training until they have done at least 8 to 10 circuit training sessions over a period of three to four weeks. Circuit training helps build a base of strength endurance to prepare athletes for more intense weight training. When first used in a training season, the weight session should include only one set, such as a circuit in circuit

training. As the training season progresses, athletes may perform two or three sets. In addition, the RM loads will have to increase periodically as athletes gain strength endurance. It is very important to keep detailed records of weight training workouts so that athletes can increase their RM loads systematically.

DEVELOPING GENERAL AEROBIC ENDURANCE

Endurance refers to the ability to sustain physical activity for a long time without fatiguing. In this section, we'll discuss general aerobic endurance, which is the ability to perform any type of exercise at low to moderate intensities for prolonged periods. In the next chapter, we'll distinguish between general aerobic endurance and specialized endurance, which refers specifically to running at high intensities that tax the aerobic and anaerobic systems.

The activities you can use to develop general aerobic endurance include running, swimming, and cycling. In fact, any rhythmic exercise that involves many different muscle groups is suitable. The main goal of training for general aerobic endurance is to improve the efficiency of the cardiovascular system. Besides this effect, general aerobic training improves mental fitness. Because the methods involve prolonged, continuous activity, they promote concentration and the willpower to endure. In addition, these methods instill confidence. For example, youths who can run 16 kilometers (10 miles) in training without struggling will be confident in their ability to race shorter distances such as a 5K cross-country race.

Continuous Aerobic Running

Traditionally, coaches and runners have used the term "long slow distance," or LSD, to describe the main method for developing general aerobic endurance. We will replace this outdated term with "continuous aerobic running," or CAR. For one reason, it fits in nicely with our analogy of training as a journey and methods as vehicles, don't you think? Certainly, the "slow" in LSD may give the faulty impression that runners can improve their aerobic fitness simply by jogging. The pace required to reach the threshold for improvement of aerobic fitness will not necessarily feel fast, but neither will it feel like a jog.

CAR is probably the simplest method of training in terms of how it is carried out. All you need are the right clothes for the conditions, a good pair of shoes, a stopwatch, and a running course. Nevertheless, you should choose the setting and surface for CAR carefully. If possible, courses should avoid city areas and heavy traffic. Country roads and trails in parks are ideal settings. As often as possible, training runs should be on soft surfaces, rather than asphalt or concrete, to avoid excessive jarring. Finally, it's important to have some variety in training courses to make this method more enjoyable. It's fun to be out running with teammates on courses over grassy rolling hills, flat beaches, winding dirt roads, and the like.

Training Dose for Continuous Aerobic Running

The sample sessions below show CAR workouts that we have designed for the preparation period of training for athletes of different developmental levels and event specialties. Depending on these two factors and the phase of preparation for competition, the duration of CAR will vary from 20 to 70 minutes, or approximately 3 to 10 miles (5 to 16 kilometers). For convenience, we have expressed the duration of training in minutes, rather than miles or kilometers. If you run for time rather than distance, you don't have to measure all your running courses. You are also free to venture and explore new areas without having to worry about running too short or too long. Just don't forget your stopwatch!

The low end of the range, 20 minutes, is suitable for beginners at the start of the season. The high end of the range, 70 minutes, is appropriate for advanced runners who specialize in 3,000- and 5,000-meter races and have gradually built up to this volume over the season. To develop general aerobic fitness, the intensity of the run should elevate heart rate to roughly 65 to 75 percent of maximum (see page 43 in chapter 3 for instructions on measuring pulse). The pace should be fast enough to make runners feel as if they are not

SAMPLE SESSION: GENERAL AEROBIC ENDURANCE TRAINING

Duration: 20 to 70 minutes
Frequency: 1 repetition
Intensity: 65 to 75% of HRmax
Recovery: None

Sample Sessions for the Preparation Period

Event specialty	Duration of Run		
	Beginner CA^a = 12-14 TA^b = 0-2	Intermediate CA = 14-16 TA = 2-4	Advanced CA = 16-18 TA = 4-6
800 meters	20 minutes	25 minutes	30 minutes
1,500 meters 1,600 meters	20 minutes	30 minutes	40 minutes
3,000 meters 3,200 meters	20 minutes	35 minutes	45 minutes
5,000 meters Cross-country	20 minutes	35 minutes	45 minutes

[a]CA = chronological age in years.

[b]TA = training age in years.

simply jogging, but slow enough that they can converse with training partners. To ensure that they are within the target intensity range, runners should stop to take their heart rate 10 to 15 minutes into the run. If heart rates are outside of the target range, runners should adjust their paces accordingly. For runs over 40 minutes, it's a good idea to check the heart rate again at the halfway point.

Keep the principle of individual differences in mind when planning CAR sessions. For example, beginners who have been training for less than one year may need to run at an 8:00- to 8:30-mile pace (5:00 to 5:20 per kilometer) to be in the range of 65 to 75 percent of maximal heart rate. In contrast, advanced runners (training age of four years) may need to run at 6:30- to 7:00-mile pace (around 4:00 to 4:20 per kilometer) to attain the target heart rate. If beginners try to keep up with advanced runners, their effort may *exceed* the threshold for aerobic conditioning. If so, anaerobic metabolism will kick in and fatigue will follow rapidly. If runners have to slow down or stop, they won't achieve the beneficial cardiovascular and psychological effects of this training method. Thus, following the principle of individual differences, runners should work at an intensity suited to their own level of fitness. Coaches can apply this principle by grouping teammates of similar developmental levels.

Progression of Continuous Aerobic Running

On a year-to-year basis, increase the duration, or volume, of CAR. The sample sessions on page 102 illustrate this progression. For example, the advanced cross-country runner's session (45 minutes) is over twice as long as the beginner's (20 minutes). Even though the 13-year-old with one year of training experience might be able to run for 50 minutes, doing so could eventually lead to problems. If this 13-year-old has the potential and desire to excel several years down the road, training volume would have to increase over those years for continued improvement. So by age 16 or 17, this youth might need to run for 90 or 100 minutes to enhance aerobic fitness. Such extensive training, which is more suitable for elite adult runners, exposes the young runner to the risk of injury and burnout.

The volume of CAR should also increase gradually over the course of a single training season. For example, over the first two months of the preparation period, beginning cross-country runners might increase the duration of a run from 20 to 35 minutes. At the same time, beginners will have to quicken the pace of the run because their general aerobic conditioning will improve. Over a single training season, the pace required to keep heart rate within the range of 65 to 75 percent of maximum might be lowered by as much as 30 seconds per mile, or 18 seconds per kilometer.

Running Isn't Everything: Other Methods for Developing General Aerobic Endurance

Runners don't necessarily need to run to develop general aerobic endurance. Cardiovascular fitness can be improved by cycling, swimming, and performing other rhythmical activities that involve major muscle groups. Like CAR, these supplementary methods improve cardiovascular efficiency by stimulating the heart to deliver large amounts of oxygen-rich blood to the working muscles.

It's a good idea to include supplementary methods for developing general aerobic endurance in young runners. Too much continuous running can be boring. Nonrunning methods add variety to the training program, making training fun and enhancing motivation. In addition, by performing supplementary activities that stress many different muscle groups, young runners can develop fitness in a well-rounded way. This "whole-body" fitness reduces the risk of injury that can occur from the repetitive stress of running. Finally, in the unfortunate event of injury, runners' experiences with supplementary methods will pay dividends. Injured runners who are familiar with training on the cycle or in the pool are able to use these methods immediately to maintain aerobic fitness while their injuries heal.

THE COMPLETE FUNDAMENTAL TRAINING METHOD: HILL RUNNING

Many of the fundamental training methods described in this chapter and the previous one have crossover effects. That is, they develop more than one element of fitness. For example, circuit training builds both strength endurance and general

Nadia Prasad

Boulder, CO

Personal Bests:

5,000 meters   15:12
10,000 meters   31:38
Marathon   2:29:48

When she was three years old, Nadia Prasad and her family moved from France to New Caledonia, a French territory in the South Pacific. In terms of her future as a world-class distance runner, the move was a mixed blessing. Nadia began running at age 15, and she had very little competition because the sport wasn't very popular in New Caledonia. But because she was never really challenged by other runners, Nadia's thirst for competition grew strong over the years, and it continues to motivate her today.

At age 28, Nadia is one of the world's top road racers. Her recent accomplishments include a victory at the 1995 Los Angeles Marathon, where she ran 2:29:48. And she has won many prestigious road races including the Revco Cleveland 10K and the Bolder Boulder 10K.

Talking about how she started running, Nadia explains, "From age 12 to 15, I was a swimmer. Instead of relaxing during off-seasons, I would run to stay fit. A coach who saw me running asked me to do a six-kilometer cross-country race in my town. I made a deal with myself that if I won the race, I would start training for running." Nadia won the race by two minutes. So she traded swimming for running, and was immediately successful. At age 15, Nadia ran 4:45 for 1,500 meters and 10:21 for 3,000 meters.

Despite some frustration and disappointment in her early running experiences, Nadia attributes the lack of competition in New Caledonia and the low volume of her training to keeping her from burning out as a young runner. Being so much faster than the other girls on the island, however, Nadia felt she would not develop to her greatest potential without stiffer competition. And she wasn't sure that she was doing the right kind of training. "From age 15 to 21 I was training on the track and running short, fast sprints almost every day," she explains. "I almost never ran for endurance. Looking back, I realize that the coaches didn't really know what they were doing."

To improve through having stiffer competition, Nadia moved to the U.S. when she was 21. At first, concentrating on road racing, she was shocked by all the good runners on the U.S. road racing circuit. But she realized that racing against the top road racers in the world would help her. "I like the competition, because it helps you push yourself more and learn to run tactically," she says.

Nadia's advice to young runners is to study their competitors and know their capabilities. "If you go to a race and see no other runners who are as good as you, it's a matter of running against yourself," she says. "But, if there are runners as good or faster than you, it may be better to run together at the start. If the pace feels slow, take off—there's nothing to be afraid of. If somebody beats you, so what? What matters is that you give it your best shot every time."

aerobic endurance. This is because the prolonged, continuous nature of circuit training stresses the muscles as well as the cardiovascular system. Another crossover effect is that general aerobic endurance training develops concentration and other aspects of mental fitness.

One of the most complete crossover methods is hill running. This form of training develops technique, strength endurance, general aerobic endurance, and mental fitness. Therefore, hill

running is a key fundamental method for preparing runners for cross-country and track racing. The key to gaining the crossover effect is to keep the intensity of hill running at a moderate level. That is, when coaches use hill running to develop fundamental fitness, runners need not sprint like mad up and down every hill.

Fast, but controlled, uphill running over distances between 200 and 600 meters will improve technique because the hill forces the athlete to lift the knees, powerfully extend the driving leg during push-off, and pump the arms vigorously. Furthermore, uphill and downhill running are excellent means for developing strength endurance because they add extra loads to the muscles. Finally, if hills are included in continuous aerobic running, they help develop general aerobic endurance. During hill running workouts, practice maintaining your pace after you've crested the top of an uphill section. Inexperienced runners often ease up when they get to the top of an uphill. If you practice holding the pace you'll gain an advantage in cross-country racing.

Interval Hill Running

We recommend using two types of hill training to develop fundamental fitness. The first is interval hill running. A sample training session using this method might be 4-8 × 300 meters uphill with a recovery interval of walking or jogging down the hill. Because the main objectives of hill running are to develop technique and strength endurance, the slope of the hill should not be very steep. As a general guideline, the slope should be steep enough to force runners to alter their technique by using more vigorous actions than would be used when running on level ground. But the hill should not be so steep that it causes runners to strain, lose proper form, and have to stop before gaining an endurance effect.

Continuous Hill Running

The second method of hill training involves uphill and downhill running in a continuous man-ner. For this method, include a series of rolling hills on courses you choose for continuous running. Uphill sections will challenge runners to adapt their technique in order to maintain the rhythm and pace they set on the flat section of the course. Again, runners don't need to sprint up the hills. On downhill sections, runners can relax and recover. Good form, however, is essential during downhill running to avoid excessive jarring. To refresh your memory about the proper technique for uphill and downhill running, refer to tech tip #10 in chapter 5 (see page 70).

SUMMARY

The fundamental training methods we have discussed in this chapter provide a base of muscular and cardiovascular endurance that is essential for distance runners. After all, the capacity to endure is the cornerstone to distance running performance. Furthermore, the foundation of endurance involves the skeletal muscles, which transport the runner's body, and the heart and vasculature that deliver energy and oxygen to those muscles. Circuit and weight training, continuous aerobic running, and hill running all develop the capacity to endure. They further contribute to the base of fitness, reducing the risk of injury as well. But while the cornerstone of distance running may be endurance, the way for young runners to reach milestones and set new PRs is through the capacity to run fast over distances between 800 and 5,000 meters. We'll introduce and describe training methods to develop this capacity in the next chapter.

Advanced Training for Competition

The fundamental methods we have introduced so far are often described as methods that "train the runner to train." They provide a base of fitness upon which you can add more specific or advanced methods. In this chapter, we'll describe the advanced methods of training that can be thought of as methods that "train the runner to race." Coaches use advanced training methods to develop the specific energy pathways, muscle fibers, motor patterns, and psychological skills involved in competition.

The principle of specificity—changes that training causes match the training methods that the runner uses—underscores the physiological reasons for using advanced training methods. These methods condition the fast-twitch (FT) muscle fibers recruited during high-intensity work, as when you race 800 to 1,500 meters. Fundamental training, such as continuous aerobic running, simply won't recruit the FT fibers used in racing. The fast running that characterizes advanced training, however, will recruit and condition FT fibers. Moreover, fast running in training will develop psychological strength and pacing skill for competition. In other words, to race fast, runners have to train fast.

In this chapter, we'll divide the advanced methods into the following four categories of fitness and skill:

- Lactate/ventilatory threshold
- Specialized aerobic-anaerobic endurance
- Anaerobic endurance
- Pacing skill

These methods are used to develop a combination of speed *and* endurance, rather than only speed. This combination is critical because most young runners are not limited by a lack of speed itself; instead, they have not developed the ability to endure or maintain fast speeds. To illustrate this lack of "speed endurance," consider that teenage boys who can run 100 meters in under 15 seconds—a time that most can easily manage—are technically fast enough to run under four minutes for the mile! To run a sub-4:00 mile requires stringing together approximately 16 100-meter runs at just under 15 seconds. But only a handful of teenage runners have ever broken the four-minute barrier. Thus, in this chapter we won't talk about developing speed itself. Instead, we'll emphasize building speed

along with endurance. You can accomplish this goal by training at paces that vary from those slightly slower than race pace (to develop endurance) to those slightly faster than race pace (to develop speed).

As you read about the advanced methods in this chapter, remember that high-intensity training can greatly improve fitness for racing, but it can also lead to injury and burnout. Therefore, when using these methods, you must keep the principle of progression in mind. This means that you must increase the training dose gradually over time. Beginners, especially those who have not yet reached puberty, should start out with very low amounts of high-intensity work and slowly increase its contribution. Remember, as we stressed in the last two chapters, to progress and avoid injury, runners must first develop a solid base of conditioning with the fundamental methods like general aerobic endurance and strength endurance training.

Coaches use the fundamental methods primarily in the early phases of training. Then, as the competition period nears, they gradually add the advanced methods to the training program. You should not, however, eliminate advanced methods completely from early phases of preparation. In fact, you should include some form of fast running in the training program or in supplementary sports and games on a year-round basis. It's critical for young runners to keep their ability to recruit FT muscle fibers and to experience the vigorous movements in fast running. This will ensure a smooth transition from fundamental to advanced methods, reducing the risk of injuries that can occur with sudden changes in training.

INCREASING THE LACTATE/ VENTILATORY THRESHOLD

As running speed and anaerobic energy demands increase, the muscle tissue accumulates more lactic acid than it can remove (see chapter 3). The point at which this excess of lactic acid occurs is called the lactate/ventilatory threshold. It imposes a strong physiological and psychological barrier to performance because lactic acid accumulation leads to fatigue. Therefore, one key objective of advanced training is to be able to run at faster and faster speeds *before* reaching the lactate/

ventilatory threshold. In other words, the goal is to increase the threshold, like raising the ceiling of a room. Accomplish this objective with fast, controlled running, stressing the energy-making systems at the point of the lactate/ventilatory threshold. To meet this training objective, young runners must train at paces that are faster than the pace for continuous aerobic running but slower than race pace for 3,000/3,200 meters.

Here are some more specific guidelines for determining the optimal effort and pace for increasing the lactate/ventilatory threshold:

- The pace should elicit a heart rate of 75 to 85 percent of maximum because this is the range at which most youths reach the threshold. So, if the athlete's maximum heart rate is 200, she would run at a pace that elevates training heart rate to between 150 and 170 bpm ($200 \times .75 = 150$; $200 \times .85 = 170$).

- The pace should stimulate noticeable, but not labored, breathing because lactic acid accumulation triggers an increase in ventilation.

© Terry Wild Studio

- The pace should be fast enough that runners find it difficult to converse with training partners.

- The pace should feel mentally and physically challenging; however, runners should be able to sustain it for at least 15 minutes before having to slow down.

The total duration of a lactate/ventilatory threshold workout should range between 6 to 35 minutes depending on the athlete's level of development. Ten minutes of running at the proper intensity is suitable for beginners whose training age is about one year. At the end of the 10 minutes, athletes should feel fatigued, but also feel as if they could continue at the same pace for another five minutes or more. For mature runners who have been training for four to six years, 30 minutes of running might be appropriate. Again, at the end of the session, runners should feel as if they could continue for another five minutes without having to slow down.

During a workout that targets the lactate/ventilatory threshold, coaches should stress the importance of training at a pace that keeps the heart rate in the critical range of 75 to 85 percent of maximum. Because the methods used for this purpose involve fast, but not all-out, running, it's tempting to push the pace and compete with teammates. If runners get caught up in competing and exceeding the threshold, fatigue will set in quickly, and they may not be able to sustain the necessary pace. Two ways to keep teammates from racing during training are to group runners of common ability or to have them start at staged intervals and run alone.

To increase the lactate/ventilatory threshold, consider the following two training methods: interval tempo running and continuous tempo running.

Dose and Progression of Interval Tempo Running

Many coaches refer to the method for increasing the lactate/ventilatory threshold as "tempo" running because it requires maintaining a fast and rhythmical pace for a fairly long time. But tempo running does not have to be continuous in order to increase the lactate/ventilatory threshold. In fact, interval tempo running is an excellent method for developing this element of fitness. It's a great method for runners at the start of the training season when they may lack the physical and mental fitness needed to maintain a fast pace for more than a few minutes without a break. Interval tempo training is also especially effective for beginners, who might not have the concentration needed for long, continuous tempo running. As shown in the sample sessions below, the duration of repetitions ranges from two to eight minutes. Athletes can do 2 to 10 repetitions a session. Short rest periods of 30 to 90 seconds of jogging or walking separate the repetitions. The rest gives athletes a physical and mental break to prepare for the next repetition.

The sample sessions present interval tempo workouts for runners at three different developmental levels classified by chronological and training age. These sessions are appropriate for the early phases of preparation for an upcoming racing season. The key to progression is to increase the duration, or volume, of training over time. For example, the beginner may run for a total of 8 minutes (4 × 2 minutes @ 80 to 85 percent of HRmax with 90 seconds recovery), while the advanced runner may run for 24 minutes (4 × 6 minutes @ 80 to 85 percent of HRmax with 30 seconds recovery).[1] Notice that two other features highlight the proper progression of interval tempo training. First, the duration of each repetition increases with age. Second, the recovery period between repetitions decreases over time. For reasons we'll consider shortly, these two adaptations are important because they make the session more continuous, while still allowing short rest periods to refresh the athlete physically and mentally.

Using heart rate to determine the right intensity and a stopwatch to time repetitions and intervals, you can do this type of training anywhere. The venue can vary from dirt roads with flat, soft surfaces to rolling, grassy hills. You can also do tempo running on the track. In fact, track running is a great way to practice maintaining a constant tempo because pace can be accurately monitored every 400 meters.

---

1. Most of our examples of interval training sessions throughout the book will have repetitions of a single duration or distance such as 4 × 2 minutes or 6 × 300 meters. We use a common repeated distance for the sake of simplicity. But to add variety to your workouts, you can alter the duration and distance covered in repetitions. For example, the interval tempo session of 4 × 2 minutes might be changed to 1 × 3 minutes, 1 × 2 minutes, and 1 × 3 minutes. The runner would cover the same total duration (8 minutes) and the physiological effect should essentially be the same.

SAMPLE SESSION: LACTATE/VENTILATORY THRESHOLD TRAINING
(Interval Tempo Method)

Duration: 2 to 8 minutes per repetition
Frequency: 2 to 10 repetitions
Intensity: 80 to 85% of HRmax
Recovery: 30 to 90 seconds

Sample Sessions for the Preparation Period

Beginner CA[a] = 12-14 TA[b] = 0-2	Intermediate CA = 14-16 TA = 2-4	Advanced CA = 16-18 TA = 4-6
4 × 2 minutes with 90 seconds recovery	4 × 4 minutes with 60 seconds recovery	4 × 6 minutes with 30 seconds recovery

[a]CA = chronological age in years.

[b]TA = training age in years.

Dose and Progression of Continuous Tempo Running

As athletes gain fitness and experience with interval tempo running, the recovery periods can be shortened until the session becomes continuous. Continuous tempo running increases the lactate/ventilatory threshold and, importantly, improves mental fitness. By running without breaks, runners develop better concentration because they must focus on sustaining a fast, even pace for a prolonged period. To maintain the continuous effort, runners must also focus on relaxation. Ultimately, this type of training builds runners' confidence in their ability to successfully hold a fast pace over a long distance. As you know, these aspects of mental fitness are critical to successful racing.

Our recommendations for the duration of continuous tempo running range from 6 to 35 minutes (see below). Without rest periods, the intensity of continuous tempo running needs to be somewhat lower than for the interval method—about 75 to 80 percent of maximum heart rate. But it's okay if heart rate drifts up to 85 percent of maximum toward the end of the run. To make sure that heart rate is in the target range, runners can stop to check their pulses about one-fourth of the way through the run. With experience, however, runners should be able to judge the right pace for continuous tempo running without having to stop for a pulse check. Heart rate monitors come in handy for continuous tempo runs because athletes can look at their watches for pulse readouts without having to stop.

The sample workouts illustrate the principle of progression for continuous tempo running. As in the interval method, the duration of the continuous method should increase as the runner develops fitness and experience over the years. The duration of tempo running should also increase within a single training season. For example, the intermediate runner might start with 12 minutes during the early part of preparation and progressively increase to 18 minutes by the end of the preparation period; the advanced runner might build up from 18 to 30 minutes or more.

As a result of lactate/ventilatory threshold training, target pace for tempo running will get faster over time. For example, at a training age of two years, runners may require a pace between 7:00 to 7:30 per mile (around 4:20 to 4:40 per kilometer) to elevate their heart rate to 75 to 85 percent of maximum. After three or four years of training, however, the required pace may decrease to 6:00 to 6:30 per mile (around 3:45 to 4:00 per kilometer). In other words, more experienced athletes will need to run at a faster pace both to reach the lactate/ventilatory threshold and to further increase it.

SAMPLE SESSION: LACTATE/VENTILATORY THRESHOLD TRAINING
(Continuous Tempo Method)

Duration:	6 to 35 minutes
Frequency:	1 repetition
Intensity:	75 to 80% of HRmax
Recovery:	None

Sample Sessions for the Preparation Period

Beginner CA[a] = 12-14 TA[b] = 0-2	Intermediate CA = 14-16 TA = 2-4	Advanced CA = 16-18 TA = 4-6
6 minutes	12 minutes	18 minutes

[a]CA = chronological age in years.

[b]TA = training age in years.

Over the season, coaches should frequently change the venue for continuous tempo running to make the sessions more interesting and stimulating. This type of training can mentally tax young runners. As in interval tempo training, the setting can vary from flat to hilly terrain; however, we recommend that beginners start on flat surfaces and gradually progress to hilly courses over time.

DEVELOPING SPECIALIZED AEROBIC-ANAEROBIC ENDURANCE

To compete to their fullest potential from 800 to 5,000 meters, youths must race at an intensity of effort that goes *beyond* the lactate/ventilatory threshold. In fact, the physiological demands of racing these distances can exceed $\dot{V}O_2$max, or the body's maximal oxygen transport/utilization capacity. So it is important for young runners to train at paces that fully tax the aerobic system and require a substantial amount of anaerobic energy. These paces should be "specialized," or designed to match the demands of racing. That is, they should stress the specific energy pathways, motor patterns, and psychological skills that will be used in competition.

Specialized interval training "builds" the race from pieces, almost like putting together a jigsaw puzzle. It breeds confidence in runners because they experience the feeling and success of running at race pace in training. Remembering the principle of specificity, you might come to the conclusion that you should use methods for developing specialized endurance frequently. Ideally, you should. After all, no more better means of training than running at race pace over race distances exists. However, because the physical and psychological demands of specialized training can lead to injury and burnout, you should use methods for developing specialized fitness no more than two times a week during preparation for competition.

Next, we'll introduce three methods of specialized aerobic-anaerobic endurance training: intervals, time trials, and racing. The venue for these training methods should be similar to the racing venue. Thus, when training for cross-country, you should do specialized endurance sessions on courses that pose demands (e.g., hills, turns, and footing) similar to race courses. During track season, coaches should hold specialized endurance sessions either on a track or on a flat, soft surface like a dirt road or golf course fairway. For variety, you can alternate between running on the track and on grass or dirt roads.

Interval Method for Developing Specialized Endurance

Runners can develop specialized aerobic-anaerobic endurance with interval training at goal race pace over total distances that are close to their event specialty. For example, using this method, a boy who has a goal of breaking 5:00 for 1,600 meters should run 400-meter repetitions in around 75 seconds, 600-meter repetitions in 1:52.5, and 800-meter repetitions in 2:30.

The sample sessions on page 113 show workouts for the interval method of specialized endurance training. The duration for each repetition ranges from 100 to 1,600 meters, depending on runners' levels of development and event specialties. The number of repetitions in a session varies from two to eight. Rest periods should last roughly the same length of time as the repetition. So runners should alternate 800-meter repetitions in 2:40 with 2:40 recovery intervals of light jogging or walking. This is called a 1:1 recovery pattern. Athletes should take longer rest periods if they are too fatigued to achieve their goal times in the next one or more repetitions. In other words, it is more important to reach the goal times than to rest a set length of time. The total distance covered in a session should be close to runners' racing distances, plus or minus up to about 50 percent. For example, a 3,000-meter specialist should cover between 1,500 and 4,500 meters in a session ($3,000 \times .50 = 1,500$; $3,000 \times 1.5 = 4,500$).

The sample specialized endurance sessions are geared for runners of different developmental levels and event specialties. Because they run repetitions at race pace, the intensity is relatively equal for both beginners and advanced athletes. With development, however, runners should cover more distance per session. In our example, advanced 1,500/1,600-meter runners cover a to-

SAMPLE SESSION: SPECIALIZED ENDURANCE TRAINING (Interval Method)

Duration: 100 to 1,600 meters
Frequency: 2 to 8 repetitions
Intensity: Race pace
Recovery: 1:1 (duration of recovery = duration of repetition)

	Beginner CA[a] = 12-14 TA[b] = 0-2	Intermediate CA = 14-16 TA = 2-4	Advanced CA = 16-18 TA = 4-6
Sample Sessions for 800-meter Runners During the Preparation Period	3 × 150 meters	3 × 200 meters	4 × 200 meters or 1 × 400 meters and 2 × 200 meters
Sample Sessions for 1,500/1,600-meter Runners During the Preparation Period	3 × 300 meters	3 × 400 meters	4 × 400 meters or 2 × 600 meters and 1 × 400 meters
Sample Sessions for 3,000/3,200-meter Runners During the Preparation Period[c]		3 × 800 meters or 1 × 1,000 meters, 1 × 800 meters, and 1 × 600 meters	3 × 1,000 meters or 1 × 1,200 meters, 1 × 1,000 meters, and 1 × 800 meters

[a]CA = chronological age in years.

[b]TA = training age in years.

[c]No sample workout is given because we recommend that youngsters wait until a training age of 2 years before specializing at 3,000 meters or longer (see table 1.4, page 13).

tal of 1,600 meters (4 × 400 meters), while beginners cover only 900 meters (3 × 300 meters). In this progression, you add distance, or volume, to a base of speed. The following is the appropriate progression for specialized endurance training: Athletes should begin with short distances at fast speeds and increase the volume from year to year.

Follow this principle of adding volume to speed to increase the training load within a single season as well. For example, the intermediate 1,500-meter runner who covers 1,200 meters per session (e.g., 3 × 400 meters) during the early phases of preparation might cover up to 1,800 meters per session (e.g., 1 × 800 meters, 1 × 600 meters, and 1 × 400 meters) as the competitive period approaches. Remember, the key to progression of this advanced method is to build the race up from pieces so that you can cover longer and longer distances (for each repetition and for the total session) at race pace (see chapter 11).

Controlled Time Trials and Racing to Develop Specialized Endurance

In addition to interval training, two great ways to develop specialized endurance are to perform controlled time trials and to race. These methods allow runners to test their fitness and practice different racing tactics before the main competitive season starts. Runners use them primarily at the very end of the preparation period and in the early part of the competition period.

Controlled time trials are training sessions that simulate racing. The term "controlled" means that the runner should try to keep the pace close to race pace without struggling. The duration or distance of the time trial can be between 50 and 75 percent of the runner's event specialty (see page 114). So several weeks before the start of the competitive season, a 3,000-meter runner might do a 1,500-meter to 2,000-meter time trial. Or the runner could do a series of time trials, held once

SAMPLE SESSION: SPECIALIZED ENDURANCE TRAINING
(Controlled Time Trials and Racing)

Duration: 50 to 75% of event specialty (time trials)
                50 to 200% of event specialty (races)
Frequency: 1 to 2 repetitions
Intensity: Race pace
Recovery: Complete

	Beginner CA[a] = 12-14 TA[b] = 0-2	Intermediate CA = 14-16 TA = 2-4	Advanced CA = 16-18 TA = 4-6
Sample Sessions for 800-meter Runners During the Late-Preparation or Early-Competition Periods	1 × 400 meters	1 × 400 to 600 meters	1 × 400 to 600 meters
Sample Sessions for 1,500/1,600-meter Runners During the Late-Preparation or Early-Competition Periods	1 × 800 meters	1 × 800 to 1,200 meters	1 × 800 to 1,200 meters or 1 × 800 meters and 1 × 400 meters
Sample Sessions for 3,000/3,200-meter Runners During the Late-Preparation or Early-Competition Periods[c]		1 × 1,500 to 2,000 meters	1 × 1,500 to 2,000 meters or 1 × 800 meters and 1 × 800 meters

[a]CA = chronological age in years.

[b]TA = training age in years.

[c]No sample workout is given because we recommend that youngsters wait until a training age of 2 years before specializing at 3,000 meters or longer (see table 1.4, page 13).

every week or two, in the weeks leading up to the competitive season.

The objective of these sessions is to run as close to goal race pace as possible. Therefore, you should prepare for the workout as if it were a race by using recovery methods, such as easy jogging, in the few days leading up to it. Then, before the session, you should warm up with jogging, flexibility exercises, and technique strides.

Time trials are a great way to develop mental fitness as well. If athletes run their goal times, they will gain considerable confidence that will come in handy as the racing season approaches. Runners who fall short of their goal times may be disappointed for a short while, but the results may boost their motivation to train harder and perform better in the next time trial. In addition, the experiences of easing up on training before the time trial and simulating a race warm-up is

great practice for actual, upcoming races. The simulated race preparation will make runners feel more comfortable and less nervous in early competitions.

Even more so than time trials, racing itself prepares runners for future competitions. It offers a complete challenge to the body and mind. And with recovery in the days following a race, runners can improve their fitness considerably. So how can a race be a training session? In the early part of the competitive season, you can designate a few races as sessions in which runners practice certain pacing and tactical strategies. Practice races fit nicely into the schedules of high school runners in the United States, who typically have two track and field meets a week. You can designate the first meet, often a dual meet in the middle of the week, as a training session for developing specialized endurance

Martin Keino

Beaverton, OR

Personal Bests:

1,500 meters   3:39.97
3,000 meters   7:56.84
5,000 meters   13:38.53

Martin Keino's running life is a tale of two cultures. Growing up in Kenya, he learned a lot about running from his father, Kip, who was an Olympic champion at the 1,500 meters and steeplechase and a world record holder at several distances, including 3,000 and 5,000 meters. "I was surrounded by running as I was growing up; good runners were always coming around the house to visit. But the only running that I actually did as a boy was in physical education class." The sport Martin liked best in those days was soccer.

When he was 14, Martin came to the United States to attend Fork Union Military School in Virginia. "I wanted to be on the soccer team there, but the only sports that were open were cross-country and track," he reminisces. "When I started running, I was at the back of the pack, and I remember getting lapped in track. I thought a lot about getting back into soccer." But physical maturity, good coaching, and learning about training and racing from books and his father led to a very successful high school career, in which Martin eventually ran the mile in 4:09.

After finishing high school in Virginia, Martin accepted a scholarship to study and run at the University of Arizona. At Arizona from 1991 to 1995, he won two NCAA titles and recorded PRs of 1:48.91 for 800 meters and 3:58.74 for the mile. Now 23 years old, Martin is poised for a bright future among the world's elite distance runners.

Martin attributes his development to good coaching in high school. "My coach at Fork Union, Fred Hardy, Jr., brought me along slowly," he says. "The most running I ever did in high school was about 35 miles a week. I did a lot of faster interval running rather than slow miles. I was fortunate to have good coaching at an age when it's easy to overtrain by doing a lot of miles."

The development principle Martin describes is gradually building the volume of fast running. In his first few years of college, for example, he averaged 30 to 45 miles weekly, focusing on developing anaerobic endurance. During his buildup for track seasons, Martin did long repetitions, ranging from 800 to 3,000 meters, in interval sessions. "During January and February, my hard sessions were something like two or three 2,000s or six to eight 800s on the grass," he explains. "Over the years, I've increased my volume. Now, during my buildup for track racing, I'm doing around 90 miles per week."

This philosophy of progressive increases in volume also applies to racing. Although Martin won the NCAA Cross-Country Championships (10,000 meters) in college and shows great promise at 5,000 meters, he chooses to focus on the 1,500 to develop his speed and racing sharpness. "Down the road, I'm looking at 5,000, but in my mind I'm not ready for world-class 5,000-meter racing yet. I'd rather build up slowly, focusing on the 1,500 for now, and then move up."

His recommendation for young endurance athletes is to balance enjoyment with structured training that focuses on fast running. "I've seen so many runners who ran a lot of miles in high school, did really well, but never developed properly," he says. He also advises young runners to race as often as possible: "Racing is the best way for a young runner to train. In races you develop fitness and learn competitive skills. And competitions are fun. You get to travel and meet different runners."

and racing skill. Then, the second meet, usually a big multiteam competition on a Friday or Saturday, is for "real" racing.

We like this approach because practice races give distance runners the opportunity to experiment with different distances and strategies without any pressure and without having to "scrape the bottom of the barrel" of physical and mental energy. So when the big race of the week comes, runners will be fresh and focused on challenging themselves completely. For this approach to work, however, the coach has to emphasize that it's only practice and that it doesn't matter whether runners score points for the team. In some competitions, coaches can't sacrifice team scoring for the individual development of distance runners because athletes in other event areas will be unfairly denied the opportunity to be on a winning team. So coaches might choose to use practice racing only when the team is far superior to the competition.

The distance of the practice race should be 50 to 200 percent of the runner's event specialty (see the sample session on page 114). Racing at distances less than the specialty event is called "underracing." For example, a 3,200-meter specialist whose goal is to break 12:00 at the end of the competitive season might try to run under 6:00 for 1,600 meters early in the season. For variety and to develop endurance and increase the lactate/ventilatory threshold, it's also a good idea to "overrace" in some early-season meets. For example, a 1,500-meter specialist might run one or two 3,000-meter races before specializing in his main event.

The strategy of using a few early-season meets to practice racing at distances shorter than their event specialties allows runners to develop their racing skills progressively. If they can demonstrate skill in controlling effort and pace for a short distance, they'll feel confident when "moving up" to their specialty. In addition, this approach is fun because most young runners enjoy the variety created by competing in different events throughout the season. Intermediate and advanced runners might even "double" in a track meet. For example, after racing 1,600 meters, 3,200-meter specialists could race the 800 later in the meet. In this way, the volume of fast running is progressively increased. When these runners eventually race their specialty—3,200 meters—they will be prepared to cover the distance at goal pace.

DEVELOPING ANAEROBIC ENDURANCE

During races, the aerobic system sometimes becomes completely "maxed out," and a substantial supply of energy must come from anaerobic energy pathways. For example, the finishing sprint in all distance races requires anaerobic energy. Midrace surges and uphill running in cross-country also tap into the anaerobic supply. And for 800-meter runners, the entire race demands a high anaerobic output. Under these conditions, lactic acid builds up rapidly and fatigue follows. Anaerobic, or speed, endurance training develops the conditioning to withstand anaerobic fatigue. Anaerobic endurance is the ability to maintain a very fast running speed even when you're exhausted.

Anaerobic endurance sessions should be held on a track where level ground and smooth footing is ensured. Given the high speed required during this type of training, it's too risky to perform workouts on cross-country courses that have uneven surfaces. Moreover, as we have cautioned several times, because prepubescent youths are limited in anaerobic capacity, they should start out with extremely low volumes of anaerobic endurance training.

Dose of Anaerobic Endurance Training

The main method for developing anaerobic endurance is interval running at speeds 10 to 15 percent faster than race pace for each repetition. Our recommendation for the duration for each repetition ranges from 100 to 600 meters, depending on the athlete's event specialty and level of development (see the sample sessions on page 117). The number of repetitions ranges from two to eight. The combination of duration and frequency should result in a total volume that is close to the runner's racing distance, plus or minus about 30 percent.

Between repetitions, you should spend as much time recovering as needed to run the next repetition at the prescribed pace. A physiological guideline for recovery in anaerobic training is to rest until the heart rate falls below 120 bpm. During the interval, runners can walk or jog. We recommend jogging at least the last part of the interval, however, because jogging keeps the muscles loose and helps to "push" blood out of the muscles and back to the heart and lungs where the blood can unload carbon dioxide and load up with oxygen. For example, if runners need four minutes to recover between 400-meter repetitions in a session of 4 × 400 meters, they might walk the first two minutes of the interval and jog the last two minutes.

Our guideline for intensity is to run each repetition at a speed that is 10 to 15 percent faster than goal race pace. For example, if Tasha's goal for 1,600 meters is 5:28, she should run her 400-meter repetitions in 70 to 74 seconds.[2] By running faster than race pace, Tasha will develop "reserve speed" that will make race pace feel relatively easy and that she can draw from for sprint finishes.

2. To run 1,600 meters in 5:28, Tasha has to average 82 seconds per 400 meters. To determine her speed for 400-meter repetitions in anaerobic endurance sessions, we subtracted 10 and 15 percent, respectively, from 82 seconds: $[82 - (82 \times .10) = 73.8]$ and $[82 - (82 \times .15) = 69.7]$.

Another intensity guideline for this type of training is to run each repetition as fast as possible, knowing that it has to be repeated a designated number of times. While runners should be fatigued by the last repetition, they should have enough energy left to run it at least as fast, if not faster, than previous repetitions. Finally, the intensity should not be so high that form falls completely apart: Coaches should stop the session if the loss of technique could result in an injury.

Progression of Anaerobic Endurance Training

The sample sessions below show anaerobic endurance workouts for runners of different developmental levels and event specialties. As in specialized endurance training, runners doing anaerobic endurance training should begin with fast speeds over short distances and then increase the distance progressively over the years. The most important element of year-to-year

---

SAMPLE SESSION: ANAEROBIC ENDURANCE TRAINING

Duration: 100 to 600 meters
Frequency: 2 to 8 repetitions
Intensity: 10 to 15% faster than race pace
Recovery: Time needed to run next repetition at prescribed pace
(Use <120 bpm heart rate as a rough guideline.)

	Beginner CA[a] = 12-14 TA[b] = 0-2	Intermediate CA = 14-16 TA = 2-4	Advanced CA = 16-18 TA = 4-6
Sample Sessions for 800-meter Runners During the Preparation Period	3 × 100 meters	2 × 200 meters	3 × 200 meters
Sample Sessions for 1,500/1,600-meter Runners During the Preparation Period	4 × 200 meters	3 × 300 meters	3 × 400 meters
Sample Sessions for 3,000/3,200-meter Runners During the Preparation Period[c]		3 × 400 meters	5 × 400 meters

[a]CA = chronological age in years.

[b]TA = training age in years.

[c]No sample workout is given because we recommend that youngsters wait until a training age of 2 years before specializing at 3,000 meters or longer (see table 1.4, page 13).

progression for anaerobic endurance, however, is to run the repetitions at faster speeds. For example, at a training age of three years, a 15-year-old boy might be able to run 3 × 400 meters with five minutes recovery in an average of 68 seconds. At age 17, the same athlete might improve his average to 61 seconds.

Within a season, progression of anaerobic endurance training occurs by increasing the distance of repetitions and total volume. For example, intermediate-level 3,000/3,200-meter runners might start out the preparation period with a session of 3 × 400 meters. As the competition period approaches, they might be able to handle 5 or 6 × 400 meters or 3 or 4 × 600 meters. Again, the key is to add volume to a base of speed.

ADVANCED METHODS FOR DEVELOPING PACING SKILL

We've described how the advanced training methods develop physiological fitness. Now, let's focus on how you can use these methods to develop a key element of psychological fitness—pacing skill. As you know, the ability to judge effort and pace is critical for success in competition. We'll discuss how you can use the advanced training methods to develop even-pacing and varied-pacing skills.

Even-Paced Running

At the same time a runner is building physiological fitness with the advanced training methods, he can improve his pacing skill as well. The key is to design training in a way that encourages the athlete to focus on maintaining the target pace and effort for the session. Success in training for pacing skill means reducing the difference between the target pace and actual pace. For example, if the objective of a specialized endurance session is to run 4 × 600 meters in 2:00, the runner should strive to run each repetition within a few seconds of this goal time. If he averages 2:00, but runs 1:50 on the first two 600-meter repetitions and then fades to 2:10 on the last two 600-meter repetitions, the workout has not been successful in terms of controlling pace and effort. If, however, the athlete comes closer to hitting the target pace for each 600, he will be improving pacing skill.

During track sessions, coaches can help a runner develop pacing skill by providing feedback in the form of split times for each 200-meter seg-

ment of a repetition. For example, the runner whose target is 2:00 for 600 meters should cover each 200 in about 40 seconds. If the runner hears a split time of 43 seconds for the first 200, she can quicken the pace to get back on target. Pacing skill is improved as the runner adjusts the pace after comparing how a given pace "feels" with feedback from the coach.

Note this important paradox about pacing skill: Young runners need to concentrate on it in training so that eventually they won't have to think about it at all! With practice and experience in adjusting pace according to "feeling" and feedback from the coach, runners won't need the feedback or splits from the coach. They will be able to set the right pace automatically, without having to think about it. At this level of skill, which takes years to develop, runners can focus on other aspects of strategy and let pacing take care of itself.

Varied-Paced Running

Practicing a target pace over and over again is a good way to learn that pace. By repeating the same effort and movement patterns, runners will be able to reproduce the effort from "motor memory." You can, however, also develop pacing skill by using a "varied-pacing" technique. In varied-paced training, runners purposefully change the speed of repetitions in an interval workout. Using this technique, they learn how to set different paces by comparing the effort required to run at different speeds. This type of training challenges the nervous system to work hard at controlling and adjusting the force of muscle contractions from repetition to repetition.

It's a good idea to practice varied-paced running to prepare for both midrace surges and sprint finishes. This type of training is fun because it's challenging and it breaks up the monotony of running long distances at even paces.

The objective is to run at different preplanned speeds for each repetition. You can accomplish this objective with "ladder" workouts. In this type of training, the distances and speeds for successive repetitions either systematically increase, decrease, increase *and* decrease, or decrease *and* increase. Here is a sample ladder workout that increases and then decreases distance and speed. This session might be appropriate for an intermediate or advanced 1,600-meter runner. Let's say the goal time for 1,600 meters is 5:00.

- 1 × 200 meters
- 1 × 400 meters
- 1 × 800 meters
- 1 × 400 meters
- 1 × 200 meters

In this session, which can be done with a 1:1 recovery, the runner covers a total of 2,000 meters. The pace for each repetition is varied systematically. For example, this runner might try to run the 200-meter repetitions at the top and bottom of the ladder in 33 to 35 seconds. He might try to run the 400-meter repetitions in 73 to 76 seconds and the 800 at the top of the ladder in 2:35 to 2:40. This workout, which combines elements of specialized and anaerobic endurance, simulates the way that pace varies in many races: The runner starts out fast to establish position, settles in during the middle part of the race, then sprints to the finish.

You can also vary pace *within* a repetition. For example, in the sample session of 4 × 600 meters with a target time of 2:00, the athlete might run the first 400 in 84 seconds by covering each 200 in around 42 seconds; then, after the 400, the runner might pick up the pace to cover the last 200 in under 36 seconds. The total time is still around 2:00, but the runner has practiced controlled sprinting at the end of each repetition. This type of workout is a great way to learn pacing control and the tactic of sprint finishing in racing. It helps the runner concentrate on maintaining an even tempo and saving energy throughout the early and middle parts of a race. Then, having practiced changing gears at the end of training repetitions, the runner will be able to finish races with a strong kick.

As you can imagine, an infinite number of ways exist to set up training sessions to help runners develop pacing and tactical skill. But you should concentrate on designing such sessions to develop specific racing skills, such as the ability to surge during the middle of a race or kick at the end.

Fartlek or "Speed-Play" Training

A final training method that you can use to develop pacing and tactical skill is *fartlek* running. Fartlek is a Scandinavian term that means "speed play." In this type of training, you run in a natural setting for a given time period, say 30 minutes, but you change the pace playfully and at will. If you feel like sprinting from one tree to the next, that's what you do! If, after the sprint, you're in the mood for a long, controlled effort covering one mile, so be it. This unstructured form of training has its benefits and drawbacks. Fartlek can be very positive for young runners because it's fun to run playfully and by "feeling." In addition, it helps develop varied-pacing skills. But because it is unstructured, fartlek can lead to injury and other negative outcomes. For example, beginners may injure themselves trying to keep up with the surges of fitter, more experienced runners. In addition, the coach can't control the dose of training during a fartlek session either, so it's difficult to know how hard each athlete worked.

You can gain the benefits of fartlek using the version recommended by David Martin and Peter Coe in their book *Training Distance Runners*. In this "controlled fartlek" method, athletes are instructed to change pace when the coach blows a whistle. For example, during a continuous run of 20 to 30 minutes, one sharp blast of the whistle cues the runners to step up their pace. In addition, they maintain the faster pace until the coach blows the whistle again. Then the runners jog until the next whistle. The coach can control both the duration and the intensity of each effort. The coach controls the duration simply by timing the interval between each whistle blast and the intensity by varying the number of whistle blasts. One sharp blast might signal the runners to quicken the pace to 70 percent of maximum; two and three sharp blasts might signal a pace of 80 and 90 percent, respectively. Besides the benefits of improving fitness and pacing control, this type of training is fun, especially when it's done in natural surroundings such as in a park or on a golf course.

SUMMARY

Advanced training methods help runners develop specialized elements of fitness and skill for racing. Because they simulate the physical and psychological demands of competition, these methods are essential to successful performance. However, because these high-intensity methods place particular stress on the runner's body, coaches must apply them with caution. Let's review the keys for using the advanced methods:

- Interval and continuous tempo running are methods for increasing the lactate/ventilatory threshold and developing the mental fitness needed to withstand fatigue over long distances. For these methods, the duration of running ranges between 6 and 35 minutes, and the intensity elicits a heart rate of around 75 to 85 percent of maximum.

- What better way exists to prepare for racing than to run at your goal race pace? Specialized endurance training involves running at race pace over total distances that approximate your event specialty. Interval training, time trials, and practice races are the main methods. Keep in mind that for you to improve over time using this method, you must increase the volume of repetitions during interval training so that you can build to the race duration progressively.

- Anaerobic or speed endurance training involves running at paces that are 10 to 15 percent faster than race pace. This type of short, high-intensity work builds a speed reserve and conditions the body to defy the fatigue associated with lactic acid accumulation.

- Both even-paced and varied-paced running develop pacing skill. These methods, along with fartlek training, help you learn to adjust running speed according to how the movement feels and based on feedback from the coach.

PART III

DESIGNING AN EFFECTIVE TRAINING PROGRAM

So far, we've laid a foundation of scientific knowledge and information on training methods for young distance runners. Now let's apply this background to designing effective training programs. This is the most important part of the book because it covers the *process* of planning progressive training and racing experiences to help runners reach their goals. We'll guide you through this process in a series of five steps:

1. Developmental assessment
2. Goal setting
3. Periodization of, or mapping out, the macrocycle
4. Planning daily training sessions
5. Evaluating and revising the training program

In keeping with our analogy of training as a journey, we'll compare our five-step process for designing training programs to the steps involved in planning an extended trip. Developmental assessment and goal setting (chapter 9) will help you to establish the starting point and destinations of your journey. The process of periodization (chapter 10) will help you chart your course and identify the vehicles you'll use to travel each segment of the way. Designing daily training sessions (chapter 11) will help you decide on the details of your travel over the days and weeks of a long trip. Finally, we'll help you with the process of evaluating and revising training to keep you on course toward your destinations, or goals (chapter 12).

As you read part III, keep three key points in mind. First, although we present the process of designing training in five distinct steps, training is not always a linear process. That is, you don't have to finish one step completely before going on to the next. For example, if necessary, you can always evaluate and change racing goals that you have set before training began. Flexibility and revisions are key ingredients in an effective program.

Second, our guidelines for planning training and examples of training sessions are purposefully general. We didn't want to present the exact details of a particular training journey, or a list of daily workouts, because every young runner is different and has individual needs. Each runner starts from a different place, or developmental level, needs individualized vehicles or methods, and has unique end destinations or goals. Thus, we've tried to provide you with general guidelines to help you design progressive training programs that meet individual needs. To this end, we'll suggest ways to be creative and flexible in adapting the guidelines.

Third, another key to planning effective training is record keeping. Like a travel log from a long trip, written records of training and racing allow you to see the high and low points of the journey. A travel log reminds you of places you'd like to revisit and the roads to which you'd like to return. It can remind you of places you never want to see again as well! Likewise, records of training and racing are reminders of the methods and strategies that worked best and worst for runners pursuing their competitive goals. And when you look at records of a runner's progress, like looking at photos from a great vacation, you get excited about what you've accomplished and where you want to go next!

In part III, we'll help you develop a system for keeping detailed written records. These records will include a formal assessment of the runner's developmental status, fitness levels, and training and racing background. In addition, we'll provide guidelines for recording goals and training objectives. Finally, we'll show you how to record training backgrounds so that you can use this information to evaluate the effectiveness of your program. To provide you with as much help as possible, we'll present many examples of forms, charts, and calculations that you can use for designing training and record keeping.

CHAPTER 9

The Starting Point

If training for distance running is like a journey, then the first steps to planning a successful venture are to define your starting point and set your sights on your destinations. In other words, designing an effective, individualized training program begins with assessing the runner's developmental level—the starting point, and setting training and racing goals—the destinations. In this chapter, we'll guide you through these first two steps. First, we'll present a strategy to help coaches assess each athlete's developmental level based on measures of growth, current fitness, and training and racing experience. Second, we'll discuss how to set training and racing goals for the upcoming season. The product of these first two steps is a general overview of the beginning and end of each young runner's journey. With this overview, the coach will be able to chart a more detailed course and select the best training methods to help young runners reach their goals.

STEP 1: ASSESSING THE STARTING POINT

Development is the product of growth, maturation, fitness, and experience. As the first step in designing training programs, coaches should formally assess these developmental factors for each athlete. The assessment process is essential to setting appropriate goals, choosing the best training methods, and determining the proper doses of training. The "athlete assessment" form presented on pages 135 and 136 is a tool to facilitate this process.

The coach should complete runners' developmental assessments several weeks before the training period begins. The sooner the assessments are completed, the more time will be available to actually plan training programs. Most of the information needed to complete the assessments will come from interviewing the runners and reviewing records of their previous training and racing results. To get measures of current fitness levels, we'll provide guidelines for administering standard tests of key elements of fitness, such as flexibility, strength endurance, and anaerobic endurance. As you read about the assessment process, keep in mind that it is the basis for deciding on the best types and doses of training for different runners.

Recording General Information

Section I of the athlete assessment form is used to record general information, including the athlete's name, the current date, the date of the last assessment, and chronological and training ages. It's important to record the date of the last assessment to account for any developmental changes that have occurred since that time. Unless the athlete is a true beginner and has never been evaluated, her last assessment should have been completed just before the previous season. Typically, for runners who compete in both cross-country and track during the year, this interval will be about four to six months. By considering the length of time since the last assessment, coaches can determine whether developmental changes warrant special training objectives and methods. For example, if a boy has grown six inches in the previous five months, he may need extra technique and strength endurance training to better control his longer limbs.

To design programs that are developmentally sound, remember to carefully consider training age—the number of months or years since the individual began training regularly. For example, coaches can use training age to set restrictions on the racing distances at which individuals can compete. Furthermore, training age helps coaches decide which training methods to use and avoid. For example, we recommend that runners whose training age is less than one year use circuit training before participating in weight training. An awareness of training age helps to make the program progressive, increasing the likelihood that a runner will improve from season to season.

Recording Size and Growth

Section II of the athlete assessment form is used to record measurements of body size and changes in these measurements over time. The example of the boy who has grown six inches in five months illustrates the importance of measuring height before each season. Large increases in height reflect pubertal changes that coaches must consider when planning training programs. Remember, athletes who are experiencing growth spurts are susceptible to musculoskeletal injuries. Therefore, during periods of rapid growth, individuals should avoid high volumes of running in order to reduce stress on their growing bones and unstable joints. Instead, to prevent injury during growth spurts, they should focus on improving technique and strength endurance. Once growth in height stabilizes, athletes can begin to increase running volume.

The assessment of height can also help with event selection in track. Although both short and tall individuals can be successful distance runners, tall individuals with long strides tend to perform better at middle distances, such as 800 meters. And, although it's certainly not always true, shorter runners tend to perform better at long distances, such as 3,000 to 5,000 meters. So coaches may want to take height into consideration when selecting runners for event specialties.

In addition to measuring height, coaches should weigh runners and record any changes since the last assessments. This information will help the coach determine whether athletes need to alter their diets for better health and performance. It's especially important to determine whether changes in body weight are due to changes in fat content; we've included a space for recording percent body fat on the assessment form. The "ideal" body weight for distance runners depends on their makeup of muscle and fat tissue. If percent body fat is within average ranges for teenage distance runners—about 6 to 12 percent for boys and 12 to 16 percent for girls, they don't need to alter their diets. However, if the values are well outside of this range (less than 6 percent or greater than 20 percent for boys and less than 12 percent or greater than 25 percent for girls), we recommend that such athletes and their parents consult with a physician or certified nutritionist for a program to help gain or lose weight. Keep in mind that assessment of body composition requires training and extensive practice. Therefore, coaches who are not experienced in these techniques should ask a qualified athletic trainer or local fitness specialist to take the measurements.

Perhaps you've noticed that we do not have spaces for recording measurements of maturation on the athlete assessment form. Like body fat composition, an accurate assessment of maturation level, or biological age, requires expertise in techniques that go beyond the scope of this book. For example, the best measurement of maturation level—skeletal age, involves x-raying the bones to determine how much they have hardened, or ossified. Still, coaches can get a general overview of each individual's maturation level by observing some of the hallmarks of pubertal change (see table 1.3 on page 7). For example, obvious changes in secondary sex characteristics, such as lowering of the voice in males and breast development in females, indicate that puberty has begun. Coaches can also roughly assess maturation level by using age-based norms for height and weight, such as the ones we presented in tables 1.1a and 1.1b on page 5 (see our example of how to use these tables on page 4). When combined with training age, the informal assessment of maturation level can help coaches prescribe training doses that are developmentally appropriate.

Assessing Fitness Level

Before designing training programs, coaches should assess each runner's current fitness level. This assessment is important for two primary reasons. First, the information can be used to get a general idea of how much work the individual will be able to handle when training begins. Second, the assessment can be used to identify each individual's strengths and weaknesses in different areas of fitness so that the coach can design individualized programs that are specifically geared toward capitalizing on strengths and building fitness in weak areas.

Section III of the athlete assessment form is used to record scores on the key elements of fitness tests for distance running: flexibility, strength endurance, specialized aerobic-anaerobic endurance, and anaerobic endurance. Ideally, exercise physiologists would make the fitness assessment in the laboratory. This would include measures of $\dot{V}O_2$max, running economy, and lactic acid production. Most coaches, however, do not have access to this type of testing. So in this section we'll present standard "field" tests that exercise physiologists have recommended for fitness assessment in youths.

Assessing Flexibility

Figure 9.1 illustrates a sit-and-reach test that measures hamstring flexibility. A group of leading exercise physiologists developed this test for the *Prudential Fitnessgram*, a battery of state-of-the-art field tests of fitness in youths (Cooper Institute for Aerobics Research 1994). The test requires a

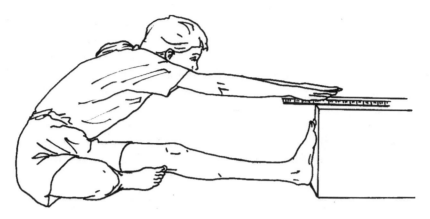

Figure 9.1 Sit-and-reach flexibility test.

sturdy box, about 12 inches high, to which an 18-inch ruler is attached, as shown in the figure. The 9-inch mark of the ruler should be positioned over the edge of the box on the side where the feet are placed.

This test differs from traditional sit-and-reach tests because the individual performs it on one leg at a time. This method prevents hyperextension of the knees. The instructions for the test are as follows:

- With shoes removed, sit on the floor and extend the left leg completely so that the foot is flat against the side of the box. Bend the right leg.

- With the palms facing down, and one hand on top of the other, extend the arms and reach forward, bending at the waist. When reaching forward, the hands should be directly over the ruler.

- Stretch as far as possible, without straining, and hold the position for at least one second. The coach records the distance reached by the fingertips.

- After three practice trials, perform a test trial.

- Repeat the routine on the right side.

The exercise physiologists who designed this test have established standards for good flexibility in youths in different age groups. These standards were developed for normally active youths—not only for young runners. Still, because runners don't train specifically for flexibility, we think the standards are applicable. In fact, many young runners are less flexible than nonathletes because the range of motion in the running stride can be very limited. To meet the standard, boys should be able to reach at least 8 inches. The standards for girls are 10 inches for 12- to 14-year-olds and 12 inches for 15- to 18-year-olds. For runners who do not meet these standards, training should emphasize more stretching.

One word of caution about assessing developmental changes in flexibility with the sit-and-reach test: The results can be flawed if the individual's arms and legs grow at a different rate! For example, a higher score over the last assessment could be due to an increase in arm length without a proportional increase in leg length. Finally, the importance of flexibility for the runner is not limited to the hamstrings. Coaches may choose to design flexibility tests for other muscle groups such as the calves and quadriceps. You can find more techniques for assessing flexibility of different muscle groups in *Physiological Assessment of Human Fitness* (Maud and Foster 1995).

Assessing Strength Endurance

Coaches can assess strength endurance using several of the circuit training exercises we presented in chapter 7. As shown on the athlete assessment form, we recommend using curl-ups for the abdomen (see page 92) and unassisted chin-ups for the arms. The objective of the test is to perform as many repetitions as possible at a steady, controlled rate. The coach records the number of repetitions performed up to the point when athletes are unable to continue or when they lose correct form.

Coaches might also choose to assess strength endurance in leg muscles. Unfortunately, though, no one has developed a standard test for the lower body. One option is squats (see page 92).

Because this is a relatively easy exercise to perform with only body weight resistance, a weighted barbell or sand bag can be placed on the athlete's shoulders. Other options for testing leg strength endurance are knee extensions and knee curls (see pages 99 and 100).

Coaches can use the results of these tests to determine whether an athlete has a particular weak area of the body and whether she is developing strength endurance over time. For example, if an athlete can do only 15 curl-ups in the assessment before cross-country season, she will benefit from extra circuit training to develop the abdominal muscles. If this same athlete improves to 35 curl-ups during the assessment prior to the following track season, the coach can be confident that the extra training paid off.

Assessing Specialized Aerobic-Anaerobic Endurance

A great way to assess specialized aerobic-anaerobic fitness (that is, fitness specifically for running) is to hold a time trial at a distance that approximates race distance. The time trial could be held a few weeks prior to starting the actual training program. Coaches will find this sort of test particularly useful for beginners who have limited training and racing experience. The time can be used as a basis for planning training sessions and setting goals for the upcoming season.

A preseason time trial may not be as necessary or useful for intermediate and advanced runners. Coaches will have a good sense of the specialized fitness in these older, more experienced athletes based on their performance in races at the end of the previous season. In addition, these runners may not feel comfortable running a preseason time trial without having trained for it.

Assessing Anaerobic Endurance

Assessment of anaerobic endurance is useful for the following objectives:

1. Determining whether runners would benefit from more emphasis on anaerobic training
2. Placing runners in their best track events

We recommend a 400-meter time trial for these purposes. For runners who are relatively slow (based on comparisons with others at the same developmental level), the coach should design progressive training to help develop speed. Such

training will help slower runners even if they specialize in the longer events, such as 3,000 and 5,000 meters. Training for runners who are relatively fast may need to focus on developing the endurance to maintain speed. Runners with very fast 400-meter times have the potential to excel at 800- and 1,500-meter races. Because a 400-meter time trial is extremely demanding, coaches should conduct this test when athletes are well-rested, making sure that they have completed a good stretching and jogging warm-up.

In addition to the anaerobic endurance assessment, coaches might want to test strictly for speed—especially for 800-meter specialists. For this purpose, we recommend adding a 60-meter time trial.

Recording Training Background

Section IV of the athlete assessment form is for recording information on the runner's training background. This section of the form summarizes the volume and intensity of training methods undertaken in the previous "macrocycle." A macrocycle covers the period of a single cross-country or track season from the first training session to the last competition. On the athlete assessment form, we have divided the macrocycle into four phases of preparation and competition:

- General preparation
- Specific preparation
- Precompetition
- Main competition

This process of dividing up a season of training and racing into phases is called periodization (see chapter 10).

Coaches can use information from the previous macrocycle to make safe and progressive increases in training for the upcoming macrocycle. For example, consider the first item in section IV of the assessment form: "average number of training units per week." (A training unit is simply the use of a particular method in a daily session. If a runner stretched and performed technique drills in a session, she completed two units—one for flexibility and one for technique.) Let's say that Keiko, whose training age is one year, completed an average of six units a week during the general preparation phase of the previous macrocycle.

For Keiko, an increase to eight or nine units might be suitable for the upcoming macrocycle, but an increase to 15 units would be overdoing it.

Particularly useful for planning upcoming training is information on the "average weekly running volume" for each phase of the previous macrocycle. For example, let's say that Bryce averaged 15 miles a week of general aerobic endurance running during the specific preparation phase of the last cross-country season. For the upcoming season, Bryce might increase his average weekly volume of this method to around 20 miles. He would also have to increase the volume for lactate/ventilatory threshold training, specialized endurance training, and so forth. To plan progressive workouts you must carefully consider the athlete's training background during the assessment process.

The following are guidelines for using each item in section IV of the assessment form to record information about training background:

- Average number of training units per week: For each phase of training, simply add up the number of units completed and divide by the number of weeks in that phase.

- Average running volume and intensity per week: For each of the running methods (general aerobic endurance, lactate/ventilatory threshold, and so on), average the volume of running by adding up the minutes, miles, or kilometers covered in each phase and divide this total by the number of weeks. Then, use the same method to get an average of running intensity based on the pace per mile or kilometer.

- Average duration of circuit training sessions per week: Over each phase of training, add up the time taken to complete each circuit training session and divide by the number of weeks.

- Average load lifted in weight training sessions per week: First, calculate the load lifted in single weight training sessions by multiplying the number of repetitions of an exercise by the load lifted. For example, if the athlete performed 12 repetitions of the bench press with a 50-pound load, the total for that exercise would be 600 pounds ($12 \times 50 = 600$). After figuring the load lifted for each exercise, find the sum of the loads. To reduce this sum to a more manageable number, you can divide it by 2,000 pounds, giving you a measure of tonnage, or the number of tons lifted. Then, average the loads for all sessions over the number of weeks in the training phase.

- Average volume of technique drills and strides per week: First, add up the total distance (in meters or yards) that the athlete covered in drills and strides during each technique session of each phase. Then, divide this total by the number of weeks in the phase.

As you can see, this assessment of training background requires keeping detailed training records on a daily basis. On pages 137 and 138, we present sample forms that coaches can use to quickly summarize daily and weekly training sessions. The form for recording daily sessions shows the volume and intensity of a continuous tempo run for a runner named Kelsey. The planned dose for the day was 1×20 minutes at 80 percent of Kelsey's maximum heart rate (206 bpm), which is around 165 bpm. Kelsey covered 2.7 miles in the 20 minutes at an average pace of 7:20 per mile. The coach's comments at the bottom of the form show that the session went well.

In the weekly training summary on page 138, Kelsey's tempo run (done on a Monday) is recorded in the column for "lactate/ventilatory threshold." Coaches can calculate weekly totals for each training method at the bottom of this form. Then, during the assessment process, these weekly totals can be used to determine the average training loads to record on the athlete assessment form. As we'll discuss shortly, this process of recording training outcomes can become very efficient if it's done on a computer with a standard spreadsheet program.

At the end of the section on training background, we've included space to record information on injuries. Coaches can use this information to detect patterns in a runner's injuries and even to discover their potential causes and solutions. For example, David is a runner who has suffered

Meredith Rainey

Silver Spring, MD

Personal Bests:

400 meters	51.56
800 meters	1:57.63

Meredith Rainey knows that many roads lead to excellence in running and other pursuits in life. She started in track and field when she was 8 years old. As a member of the renowned Atoms Track Club in Brooklyn, NY, she trained regularly and competed in the sprint races at national Junior Olympic meets. But four years later Meredith wanted to try other activities, so she stopped running and pursued basketball, volleyball, singing, drama, and her studies. Throughout high school Meredith never ran track. "Everyone gets to their goals differently," asserts the 27-year-old Rainey. "Look at me—I skipped high school track and then became an Olympian."

Meredith's road to the Olympics and to her place among the world's best 800-meter runners started at Harvard University. During her freshman year at Harvard, Meredith began to miss being an athlete and team member. "When I first went out for the college track team, I was motivated to get in good shape, have fun, and contribute to the team by scoring a few points in meets," she says.

It didn't take long for Meredith to accomplish these goals and reach the highest levels of college competition. Moving from the 400 to the 800, Meredith won the 1989 NCAA Championships as a junior with a time of 2:03. Her postcollegiate achievements include a pair of fifth-place finishes at the 1993 and 1995 World Track and Field Championships. And she was a member of the U.S. Olympic team in 1992.

Meredith credits much of her success to having a strong sense of direction. "You have to know what you want down the road, and you have to focus on what you need to do in training to achieve your goals in running." Meredith's strong sense of direction comes from setting clearly defined and challenging goals. "I post my goals in my bathroom so that I can look at them every morning. I know of other athletes who write their goals down and carry them wherever they go."

The main goals Meredith has set are running 1:55 for 800 meters and winning a medal in the Olympic Games. Her advice to young runners is to shoot for the stars. "Young runners should set specific goals beyond just wanting to do well. And, while young athletes should be realistic, they should set goals that are high. You have to have something to dream about."

A goal-oriented approach to racing begins with having clear objectives and targets to shoot for in training. In her workouts, Meredith focuses on developing her racing fitness and skill to make the most of her strengths and overcome any weaknesses. To hone her skill as a front-runner, for example, Meredith does short repetitions in interval sessions, which condition her to start races at a very fast pace. To build the endurance to maintain that fast start, Meredith does long repetitions of 1,000 meters. "In the past, I had trouble with the 1,000-meter repetitions, but now I have definite time goals for these longer sessions," she says. "And I go into these sessions with an aggressive attitude. I refuse to submit to or be intimidated by them."

To reach their goals, Meredith asserts, young runners will need a strong mental approach. "Read about techniques in sport psychology," she says. "Use these techniques to help you overcome mental barriers. And, with your coach, analyze what training you need to make up for any weaknesses."

strained calf muscles during the first few cross-country races of the season over the last two years. After detecting this pattern, David's coach hypothesized that the injury was linked to his low-heeled cross-country spikes. Because David trained in flats with a high, supportive heel that did not stretch the calf muscles much, the sudden change in shoes and in stress on the calf muscles in the first few races probably caused the muscle strains. To help David avoid this recurring calf injury, the coach had him wear low-heeled racing spikes in one training session per week leading up to the competitive season.

Racing Experience

Section V of the athlete assessment form is used to record racing results from the previous cross-country or track season. Two main reasons for assessing racing experience exist. First, the coach and athlete can use this information to set performance goals for the upcoming season. For example, consider an athlete who ran 16:36 on his school's cross-country course last year. When setting goals for the upcoming cross-country season, the coach and this athlete should use last year's result as a guide. Perhaps a year of training and experience has prepared this runner to break 16:00 on the same course. (We'll discuss the goal setting process in more detail later in the chapter.)

The second reason for assessing racing experience is to track patterns in performance and uncover factors that explain both successful and disappointing outcomes in the past. For example, by examining a runner's times from the previous track season, the coach can determine whether a desired peak was reached at the end of the season when championship meets were held. If the runner's 1,500-meter times dropped consistently (4:48, 4:42, 4:37, and 4:34) the coach should feel confident that training produced a peaking effect. In contrast, if the times reveal a plateau or a trend of poorer performances as the season progressed (4:48, 4:45, 4:46, and 4:50) the coach should question whether the athlete's training was truly progressive. Questioning the effectiveness of training in the runner's racing history should guide plans for the current season.

Strategies for Efficient Record Keeping

As you were reading about the assessment process and going through all the forms we've presented, perhaps you felt a little overwhelmed! Maybe you asked, "Is all this necessary?" As we discussed earlier, detailed records of the runner's training and racing will help coaches make good decisions in choosing the types and amounts of training for each individual. We want coaches to have a complete system with plenty of tools for assessing athletes' developmental levels. But we don't want to bog coaches down with record keeping because it may limit their creativity and take time away from working with their athletes. So you be the judge of how much record keeping you need to do and how much time you have for this process.

But if you want to do it all, we know of a great helper who can keep records and perform calculations for you—a computer! All of the forms that we've presented can be reproduced in word processing programs for easy access, input, and storage. You can record daily training in a standard spreadsheet program as well. You can set up the spreadsheet to calculate, and even graph, training volumes and loads on a weekly basis as well as across phases of the macrocycle.

Another strategy to help coaches manage the assessment process is to have runners on the team record their own training results. Runners can submit these results to the coach on a regular basis for evaluation and calculation of total training volumes and loads. By keeping their own training logs, runners can help the coach out as well as benefit themselves in many ways. Daily training logs can be great sources of motivation because they reflect all the hard work completed and the progress made by the athletes. It's inspiring and fun to look back at challenging workouts conquered. For more inspiration and guidance, runners can fill their training logs with motivational sayings and tips from running magazines and books such as this one. The log also allows athletes and coaches alike to see patterns in training and racing that reveal optimal methods and strategies. By reading over their logs on a regular basis, athletes may find that certain workouts made them feel fit and confident, leading to their best racing performances.

STEP 2: SETTING RACING AND TRAINING GOALS

After the assessment process is complete, the next step is to formally set racing and training goals for the upcoming macrocycle and beyond. In our analogy of training as a journey, racing goals are like end destinations and training goals are key stopping points along the way. When you know where you're going on your journey, it's easier to choose the right vehicles for getting there. It's the same with training: When you have goals, you can choose the best methods for achieving them. In addition, goals boost motivation and focus your mind on positive outcomes.

Formulating Racing Goals

Goal setting should begin with long-term performance or racing goals. Like the end destination of a fantastic journey, long-term goals are powerful motivators. They fill athletes' dreams with the desire to reach great heights. And because long-term goals cannot be achieved immediately, they help athletes focus on the steps, that is, the training, that they must undertake to achieve them in the future. Keep in mind that for goals to have this powerful influence, coaches

and athletes must work together to set them. If runners feel as if they are a part of the goal-setting process, they will be more focused and motivated.

To illustrate the process of setting long-term goals, let's consider the case of Carla, a talented and highly motivated 14-year-old whose training age is two years. Carla's best mile time as a 13-year-old was 5:47—excellent for someone that age. Having completed a developmental assessment, Carla's coach sees the potential for her to break 5:00 in the mile by age 17 when she'll be a high school senior. It's a goal that Carla is excited about and willing to work hard for because she knows that a sub-5:00 mile will earn her a college scholarship. So before planning and starting training for the upcoming track season, Carla and her coach set the long-term goal of breaking 5:00 in four years. Over this period, she will need to lower her time by 48 seconds to run 4:59. The stepping stones to this ultimate goal will be short-term goals for each year.

What strategy should Carla and her coach use to set yearly goals? They could simply divide the total improvement desired by the number of years: 48 seconds ÷ 4 years = 12 seconds per year. Thus, Carla would shoot for 5:35 at age 14 (5:47 - :12 = 5:35), 5:23 at age 15 (5:35 - :12 = 5:23), and so forth. While this strategy is simple, it may not be very effective because it's unlikely that Carla will

improve at a constant rate over the years. Her rate of improvement will be influenced by the four developmental factors: growth, maturation, training, and experience.

Because Carla had already experienced puberty, her coach figured that growth and maturation would not be a strong factor as long as Carla could maintain a low percent body fat. But because Carla had been training for only two years, her coach predicted large early improvements just due to the effects of training and racing experience. Finally, Carla's coach figured that a "ceiling effect" would likely make it harder for her to cut seconds off when she's 16 or 17 versus when she's 14 or 15. Considering all these factors, Carla and her coach set goals to lower her mile time by a relatively large amount at age 14 (18 seconds), and by progressively smaller amounts each year thereafter (14, 10, and 6 seconds). The goal times are listed below:

Age	Goal	Improvement
14	5:29	18 seconds
15	5:15	14 seconds
16	5:05	10 seconds
17	4:59	6 seconds

In all likelihood, Carla won't improve by exactly 18 seconds and run 5:29 at age 14. She might run a little or considerably faster. If she runs 5:20, she'll be nine seconds ahead of schedule. When setting goals and planning training for the following year when Carla is 15, how should her coach respond to this extra improvement? We think that the best response is to keep the age-15 goal at 5:15 and increase the training load for that year by a *small* amount only. The focus of training during the year might be on improving technique and racing strategy. If Carla can run 5:15 at age 15 without putting a lot of extra stress on her body, she'll be leaving more room for improvement as she develops. Or, to quote experts Dr. David Martin and Peter Coe (1991), "Goals are best achieved by doing the least amount of work necessary, not the most, because we want injury freedom as well as continued improvement . . ." (page 120). Because Carla has the talent and motivation to become an elite adult runner, she and her coach must design her training so that improvement will continue over many years—through her college career and beyond.

It's also possible that Carla might not reach her goal of 5:29 at age 14. What if, for example, she is healthy and has a good year, but runs only 5:36? When setting goals and planning training for the next year, Carla and her coach must decide whether a 5:15 is within reach. If reaching the goal means increasing training loads to levels that might cause injury, then it's best to make the goal a bit slower, perhaps 5:20. If Carla can run 5:20 at age 15, she'll still be in reach of her overall goal and, importantly, she will have taken steps to avoid injury.

You can use the same principles for setting time goals to set place goals. For example, a 14-year-old who placed 64th in the district cross-country championships might have dreams of placing in the top five by age 18. Before each season, the coach and athlete should work out the progression for reaching this goal. As in the case of setting time goals, they should consider how developmental factors will influence the individual's potential for improving his place finish in different meets. Finally, if a runner failed to attain his place goal in the previous season, the coach should not increase training loads to levels that might result in injury. It's better to be flexible and simply adapt the place goal so that the athlete improves but doesn't risk injury.

Establishing Training Goals

After racing goals have been set, the coach must develop a plan for how the athlete will achieve those goals. This next step in the process involves establishing general training goals that lead to selecting specific training methods and designing individual workouts. Once established, these general goals also help to ensure that runners will develop progressively.

Table 9.1 presents a list of general training goals for runners of different training ages. Up to a training age of two years, we emphasize introducing athletes to small amounts of all the different training methods used by distance runners. This should even include limited participation in high-intensity running. The main reasons for including all methods are to familiarize beginners with what training for distance running is all about and to instill an appreciation for the athleticism and skill that peak performance requires. Furthermore, by participating in many different kinds of training, beginners will de-

Table 9.1   General Training Objectives for Runners of Different Training Ages

Training Age	General Objectives
0 to 2 years	Introduce the youngster to all methods of training for distance runners.
	Acquire good technique.
	Build a base of strength endurance and general aerobic endurance.
	Develop the ability to race at an even pace.
2 to 4 years	Refine technique.
	Reinforce the base of strength endurance and general aerobic endurance.
	Begin to develop specialized fitness using the advanced methods: Lactate/ventilatory threshold, specialized endurance, and anaerobic endurance.
	Improve even-pacing skill and begin to acquire varied-pacing skill.
	Develop the ability to use various racing strategies.
4 to 6 years	Continue using the fundamental methods to develop the fitness base.
	Develop specialized fitness for racing by increasing the volume of advanced training.
	Refine racing strategies which work best for the individual.

velop a broad base of fitness and skill. For those whose training age is less than two years, we also emphasize the importance of developing fundamental fitness with technique, strength endurance, and general aerobic endurance training. Finally, athletes should devote their early years of training to developing pacing skill. Specifically, beginners should work on the ability to run at even paces by learning target split times and concentrating on effort and "feeling" during training.

For intermediate-level runners (training ages two to four years), the training emphases should be on refining technique and reinforcing their fitness base with strength endurance and general aerobic endurance training. At this stage, runners can also begin to increase their volume of advanced training, including methods for developing the lactate/ventilatory threshold, specialized endurance, and anaerobic endurance. Two other objectives for intermediate-level runners are to improve even-pacing skill and to develop the ability to run at varied paces. They can then apply these skills to developing the ability to race using different strategies.

When runners reach a training age of four to six years, their main objective should be to develop specialized fitness with progressive increases of advanced training, such as specialized endur-

ance and anaerobic endurance. To benefit from advanced training, however, it's essential for runners of this training age to continue building their base of fitness using the fundamental methods. Finally, to round out their programs, advanced young runners should refine their racing skill by selecting the strategies that work best for them.

The training goals outlined in table 9.1 provide general guidelines for goal setting. In addition, coaches and runners should set more specific training goals before planning the program. Specific training goals for the upcoming macrocycle might be set as follows:

- Total number of miles or kilometers per week that a runner wants to build up to

- Average weekly miles or kilometers for each of the different running methods, such as general aerobic endurance, tempo running, specialized endurance, and anaerobic endurance

- Paces (minutes per mile or kilometer) for running methods

- Longest continuous aerobic run and tempo run to be attempted

- Average weekly loads of fundamental training such as circuit, weight, and technique training

Runners who have favorite interval sessions that they've done regularly in the past could also set time goals for the repetitions that would improve times from previous macrocycles. For example, if Manny averaged 2:28 for 4 × 800 meters (with a 2:30 recovery) last season, he might shoot for averaging under 2:20 (with a 2:20 recovery) in the upcoming season.

No formula for how high to set training goals exists. We can't tell you *exactly* how much farther runners should run this coming year. After carefully reviewing runners' training backgrounds, coaches must use common sense and reasoning to consider how much room they have to improve and how much greater training loads they can handle. Most importantly, coaches must be flexible and change goals that become obviously too hard or easy for runners to achieve.

SUMMARY

In this chapter, we explained the first two steps to planning an effective training program. Let's retrace those steps:

- First, in order to set the course for the runner's training journey, the coach has to know where she is starting. The starting point is the runner's developmental status—a product of body size, maturation level, fitness, and training and racing background. Coaches should formally assess these factors to help them choose the best types and amounts of training for each individual. The form on pages 135 and 136 will help with this assessment process.

- Second, a strong motivation and a sense of direction on the runner's journey both depend on establishing end destinations, or goals. With the coach's help, each runner should set yearly racing goals, having considered developmental factors and the principle that no one should risk overtraining or injury to achieve heights that may be out of reach. In addition to racing goals, the coach and the runner should establish training objectives. These include the general developmental objectives on page 133 and more specific training goals for volumes, loads, and intensities.

By assessing each runner's developmental level and establishing racing and training goals, we get a general overview of how to shape the upcoming program. We know the athlete's starting point and destinations along the training journey. Then we can begin to get a sense of the vehicles or methods we'll use to bridge the gap between these points. The following chapters will help you map out the specific steps in your journey to your goals.

ATHLETE ASSESSMENT FORM

I. General information

Name_____

Date_____   Date of last assessment_____

Chronological age: _____years   _____months

Training age: _____years   _____months

II. Size and growth

Current measures:

Height:_____   Weight:_____   % Body fat:_____

Change since last assessment:

Height:_____   Weight:_____   % Body fat:_____

III. Fitness

Flexibility: Sit-and-reach test

Current score: _____

Score on last assessment: _____

Strength endurance: Number of repetitions

	Current score	Score on last assessment
Curl-ups	_____	_____
Chin-ups (unassisted)	_____	_____

Specialized aerobic/anaerobic endurance: Time trial (race distance)

Current time: _____

Time on last assessment: _____

Anaerobic endurance: 400-meter time trial

Current time: _____

Time on last assessment: _____

IV. Training background: Summary of previous macrocycle

Dates of previous macrocycle: _____to_____

	General Preparation	Specific Preparation	Pre-Competition	Main Competition
Average number of training units per week	_____	_____	_____	_____

Average running volume and intensity per week:

General aerobic endurance

Volume	_____	_____	_____	_____
Intensity	_____	_____	_____	_____

Lactate/ventilatory threshold (tempo running)

Volume	_____	_____	_____	_____
Intensity	_____	_____	_____	_____

Specialized endurance

Volume	_____	_____	_____	_____
Intensity	_____	_____	_____	_____

Anaerobic endurance

Volume	_____	_____	_____	_____
Intensity	_____	_____	_____	_____

Strength endurance training:

Average duration of circuit training sessions per week	_____	_____	_____	_____
Average load lifted in weight training sessions per week	_____	_____	_____	_____

Technique training:

Average volume of technique drills and strides per week	_____	_____	_____	_____

Training-related injuries

Type of injury	Period of injury	Comments
_____	_____	_____
_____	_____	_____
_____	_____	_____

Section V. Racing background

Date	Meet	Distance	Time/Place	Comments
_____	_____	_____	_____	_____
_____	_____	_____	_____	_____
_____	_____	_____	_____	_____
_____	_____	_____	_____	_____
_____	_____	_____	_____	_____

SAMPLE LOG FOR RECORDING DAILY TRAINING

Athlete's name: _Kelsey_

Date: _Monday, March 21_

Method: _Lactate/ventilatory threshold: Continuous tempo_

Planned dose (repetitions/duration/intensity/recovery): _1 x 20 minutes @ 165 HR_

Total volume:

Distance: _2.7 miles_

Duration: _20 minutes_

Intensity:

Average pace per mile: _7:20_

Comments: _Handled the session easily and in good form. Pretty even pace the whole way. Heart rate was 168 at end of run._

Weekly Training Summary

Athlete's name: _Kelsey_

Week of: _____

Day	Technique (distance)	Circuit (duration)	Weights (tonnage)	General aerobic endurance (volume/intensity)	Lactate/ventilatory (volume/intensity)	Specialized endurance (volume/intensity)	Anaerobic endurance (volume/intensity)
Monday					_20 mins./7:20 per mile_		
Tuesday							
Wednesday							
Thursday							
Friday							
Saturday							
Sunday							
Week Totals							

CHAPTER 10

Periodization

The first two steps of planning training gave you a general overview of the runner's journey by determining the starting point and helping you set destinations along the way. The next step in the process, called "periodization," gives more specific details about the journey. This step is like drafting a travel map that charts your course from its departure point to its end destination, while identifying the vehicles you'll need to traverse each segment of the journey. Periodization involves the following four components:

1. Dividing up the season, or macrocycle, into smaller and smaller units called periods, phases, microcycles, sessions, and units

2. Setting the main objectives for each phase of training

3. Selecting the key training methods to achieve the main objectives

4. Determining the relative loads or contributions of each method to the training program

Take these steps *before* planning daily training sessions (a process that we'll discuss in chapter 11).

All of the top coaches around the world use periodization to plan training for elite adult runners. Youth coaches will find this systematic approach extremely valuable because it helps answer the most essential questions about training young runners. What types of training are best for each individual? At what point in the season should you use key methods? What amounts of each training method should you prescribe? How can you help runners peak, or reach their highest level of performance, in the most important competitions?

As you read about periodization in this chapter, it may seem a little complex at first. By reading carefully and studying the process, however, you'll find that it greatly *reduces* the complexity of designing training. You won't have to wrack your brain every day thinking about what to do in training because you'll have a "periodized" plan. In addition, periodization instills confidence because it gives coaches and runners a strong sense of purpose and direction. When you have a road map to follow, it's easy to see your destination and work your way toward it!

MAPPING OUT THE MACROCYCLE

Periodization simply means dividing a season into smaller units of time during which training is geared toward meeting objectives for developing fitness and racing skill. In the language of periodization, a season is called a "macrocycle." To be progressive, training must occur in cycles, or repeated rounds of stress and adaptation. Remember the overload-regeneration principle? You're already familiar with a small cycle of training (you may want to refer back to figure 6.1 on page 75). If sufficient recovery follows a single training session, the runner's body will regenerate and become fitter. When repeated over time, this small cycle of overload and regeneration is the basis of progressive training. To guide you through the components of periodization, we'll begin with the largest cycle—the macrocycle, or season, and work our way down to smaller cycles, called microcycles.

Periods of the Macrocycle

A macrocycle consists of the time between the beginning of a season to the beginning of the following season. Figure 10.1 presents a periodization chart that illustrates a sample macrocycle for an intermediate or advanced cross-country runner (training age two to six years) in the United States. This sample macrocycle spans six months from the first day of training for cross-country on July 1 to the first day of training for track on December 30. For most young runners, the calendar year includes two macrocycles with two competitive peaks: one for cross-country and one for outdoor track. This case is called a "double-periodized" year. If you include a macrocycle for indoor track, you would have a "triple-periodized" year. For most distance runners, particularly those in warmer climates, we recommend using a double-periodized year in which you treat the indoor season as part of the training buildup for outdoor track.

A macrocycle consists of three periods: preparation, competition, and transition (see figure 10.1). In the preparation period, runners

Athlete: _____

Season	Cross-country						Track
	July	August	September	October	November	December	January
Periods	Preparation			Competition		Transition	Preparation
Phases	General preparation	Specific preparation		Precompetition	Main competition	Transition	General preparation
Mesocycles	1	2	3	4	5	6		1
Microcycles	7/1 7/8	7/15 7/22 7/29 8/5	8/12 8/19 8/26 9/2	9/9 Lower Richland: Dual 9/16 Sumter: Dual 9/23 Francis Marion Invtl.	9/30 Coaches' Classic Invtl. 10/7 Rock Hill Invtl. 10/14	10/21 District 10/28 Regional 11/4 State	11/11 11/18 11/25 12/2 12/9 12/16 12/23	12/30

Figure 10.1 Periodization chart for intermediate and advanced cross-country runners.

begin training with an emphasis on fundamental methods and progress to advanced methods as competitions approach. The competition period is the racing season. The transition period is the recovery time, or "off-season," between the last race and the next preparation period.

Two factors usually determine the total length of a macrocycle:

1. Standard rules established by administrative bodies, such as high school athletic associations

2. The athlete's developmental level

In the United States, rules limit the time during which runners can train as a team with their coach. For example, in South Carolina, high school cross-country runners cannot begin training as a team until August 1 of each year. Therefore, the preparation period officially begins on that date. The length of the competition period in South Carolina is set by the racing schedule, which runs from early September to early November when the state championship is held. The competitive period is longer for elite runners who compete in postseason regional and national competitions.

Notice that the sample macrocycle in figure 10.1 begins on July 1, earlier than many states in the United States permit runners to train as a team. Intermediate and advanced runners may need a few extra weeks to prepare properly for the racing season. So coaches can provide these runners with summer sessions to do on their own, prior to the first day the team gathers. For beginners, coaches may elect to wait until the standard starting date before assigning any training. Or coaches might give beginners early sessions to do on their own that don't involve much distance running yet start to develop fundamental elements of fitness, such as strength endurance and mobility. Games such as soccer, basketball, and ultimate Frisbee are especially good for preparing beginners for endurance training.

Together, the preparation and competition periods in the sample macrocycle last 19 weeks, or a little over four months. This time gives the coach a general framework for the training and racing program. As you'll learn, the coach can use this framework to answer specific questions about which training methods to use and how much time to devote to accomplishing different training and racing objectives.

Phases of the Preparation Period

The preparation period is divided into two phases: general preparation and specific preparation (see figure 10.1). The general preparation phase is used primarily to develop fundamental elements of fitness, such as technique, strength endurance, and general aerobic endurance. Then, in the specific preparation phase, the fundamental methods are phased out and the advanced methods, such as specialized endurance, are phased in.

In our sample periodization chart, the total preparation period lasts 10 weeks. The general preparation phase covers six weeks, or roughly one-third of the preparation and competition periods of 19 weeks. Devoting about one-third of the macrocycle (excluding the transition phase) to general preparation will help to ensure that runners establish a strong fitness base before beginning to increase the volume of specialized training later in the macrocycle. Remember, the stronger the base, the more potential for developing specialized fitness. So for beginners who haven't done much base training, coaches may choose to lengthen the duration of the general preparation phase to up to one-half of the macrocycle.

In our sample macrocycle, the specific preparation phase lasts four weeks. As a general rule, at least three to four weeks of specific preparation are necessary to introduce advanced training methods and prepare runners for the competition period. In contrast, for advanced runners who have a strong base of fitness, requiring a short general preparation phase, specific preparation might last as long as 8 to 10 weeks.

Phases of the Competition Period

We have also broken down the competitive period of the macrocycle into two phases: precompetition and main competition. In the sample macrocycle in figure 10.1, these phases last six and three weeks, respectively. Why is the main competition phase so short? It's hard to maintain a physical and mental peak over the whole competition period. In fact, many experts believe that peak fitness for distance racing can be held only for about three to six weeks. This is because the intensity of training for competition

Kevin Sullivan

Brantford, ON

Personal Bests:

800 meters	1:47.06
1,500 meters	3:35.77
Mile	3:52.25*

*Canadian record

© Bob Kalmbach/
University of Michigan

Kevin Sullivan started training seriously for distance running when he was 12 years old. In terms of both physical maturity and performance, he developed rather quickly. By the age of 14 Kevin was 5 feet 11 inches and weighed 130 pounds. He was also the world age-group record holder for 800 meters, with a PR of 1:53. Now 21 years old, Kevin still tops the world of middle-distance running, as evidenced by his fifth-place finish in the 1,500 meters at the 1995 World Track and Field Championships in Göteborg, Sweden. Kevin ran 3:52.25 in the mile that same year to set a Canadian record.

Now a junior at the University of Michigan, Kevin trains and races year-round. He competes in cross-country and in both indoor and outdoor track. He began this pattern as a young runner in the Canadian club system. "By racing for the school team during the school year and for the club team during the summer, I had a lot of opportunities to challenge myself and improve," he says. "I benefited on the club team by getting to train with elite, older athletes and their coaches." Over the years Kevin has not only maintained an intense training program but also avoided setbacks due to injuries. The keys to staying injury free, Kevin says, are sound biomechanics and physical strength honed by weight-lifting.

Since he was a teenager, Kevin's coaches have gradually increased his training load. At age 13, Kevin's highest weekly volume during the cross-country season was about 30 miles. Now Kevin covers as much as 85 miles weekly during the cross-country season. During track season he reduces his volume and emphasizes high-intensity running with two key interval sessions weekly.

Kevin's approach to year-round training and racing involves careful planning to gradually increase training loads and reach peak levels of fitness for the most important races of the season. "Every few weeks I sit down with my coach and plan the upcoming weeks of training and racing," Kevin says. "We plan training according to the time of year and how I'm feeling."

Several months in advance of the competitive season, Kevin and his coach choose races to accomplish specific purposes. "We plan certain key races to run fast times," he explains. "In those races, I sometimes go to the front and race by myself. In other races, I might run strategically by varying the point at which I start my kick. But the main focus is on the championship races. I view competitions as stepping stones leading to the championship races."

After the racing season Kevin rests, running very little for a period. Currently, these rest periods last about a week. But as a teenage runner, Kevin's rest periods lasted a month or so. During this time he relaxed and played other sports, like hockey, soccer, and golf. Kevin cites these rest periods as basic to maintaining his health and motivation throughout the demanding training year.

Kevin's advice for coaches of young runners is to take it slow. "If you see athletes with a lot of talent, don't push them into high-mileage and high-intensity training right away," he says. And to young runners, he offers this advice: "Approach every race as a competition against yourself, in which you test your limits. But don't get frustrated if you don't see a lot of improvement right away. Young athletes progress at different rates." Above all, Kevin says, "The biggest secret to improving is enjoyment. For me, having fun with running has been a key to my success."

and the stress of racing itself can drain the runner of physical and mental energy. So the precompetition phase is used to "practice race" and work on technique and strategy without being concerned with top performances. Then, in the main competition phase, runners focus on achieving their racing goals in the key meets of the season. Of course, sometimes important races will occur in the precompetition period. It's okay to shoot for a high-level performance in these races as long as runners can sustain the energy and desire to keep improving over the season.

Mesocycles

We can further divide each phase of preparation and competition into smaller units called mesocycles. Mesocycles are three- to four-week periods during which coaches focus training on specific objectives such as improving technique and strength endurance or refining racing tactics. This length of time is important for two reasons. First, it takes about three to four weeks of concentrated training to improve fitness. For example, runners can't simply do one isolated circuit training workout and experience a significant increase in strength endurance. They have to repeat the method several times with proper recovery over at least a three-week period before significant improvement occurs.

The second reason for organizing training in three- to four-week mesocycles is that after two to three weeks of concentrated training, athletes will need a little extra recovery for both the bodies and minds. This is why coaches typically organize mesocycles in a pattern in which the training load increases over the first two to three weeks and then decreases over the last week to allow for extra recovery and regeneration (see chapter 11 for more details on mesocycles).

Microcycles, Sessions, and Units

We can further divide mesocycles into microcycles, which last from one to two weeks. Our sample plan illustrates one-week microcycles as vertical bars and shows the starting date for each week. For the microcycles during the competition period, we've filled in the cross-country races the athlete will run (see page 141). Coaches divide the microcycles into daily sessions and units. As you

know, a session is a workout on a given day. And a unit of training simply refers to the use of a particular method during the session. (For more information on planning individual microcycles, sessions, and units, see chapter 11.) For the remainder of this chapter, we'll focus on the larger cycles of training—the periods and phases of the macrocycle.

TERMINOLOGY OF PERIODIZATION

- Macrocycle—a span of time lasting from the beginning of a season to the beginning of the following season.
- Periods—each macrocycle has three periods, or phases:
  - Preparation—begins with fundamental training (general preparation phase) and progresses to advanced methods (specific preparation phase).
  - Competition—the racing season, consisting of precompetition and main competition phases.
  - Transition—recovery period between the end of a racing season and the start of the next preparation period. During the transition period, the athlete stops training for running and rests and does other activities.
- Mesocycles—three- to four-week spans during which training is focused on achieving specific objectives. Training load increases over the first two-thirds to three-quarters of the mesocycle and then decreases to allow the runner extra recovery before beginning a new mesocycle.
- Microcycles—one- to two-week spans that are divided up into daily sessions (workouts) and units (particular methods that make up a workout).

SELECTING METHODS AND AMOUNTS OF TRAINING FOR THE PREPARATION AND COMPETITION PERIODS

Now that you've mapped out the macrocycle and created a periodization chart, let's look at the next steps in the planning process. They involve determining both the methods and the amounts of training needed to accomplish your objectives for each phase of preparation and competition. Tables 10.1 and 10.2 give you guidelines for this process, showing the following:

1. Main objectives for each phase

2. Key methods used to accomplish those objectives

3. Recommended relative contributions of each method to the total training amount or load

4. Recommended numbers of units per microcycle devoted to each training method

Table 10.1   Training Objectives, Methods, and Loads for the Preparation Period

Main objectives	Key methods	Range (%)	Relative training load Average (%)	Units per Microcycle
General preparation				
Improve mobility	Games (e.g., Ultimate Frisbee, keep-away, flag football)	8-12	10	2-4
Improve flexibility	Warm-up with stretching	8-12	10	3-6
Detect and correct technical flaws	Technique drills and strides	8-12	10	2-4
Develop strength endurance	Circuit and weight training	23-27	25	2-4
Develop general aerobic endurance	Continuous aerobic running, cycling, swimming	28-32	30	2-4
Introduce advanced training	Tempo running, specialized and anaerobic endurance running	3-7	5	1-2
Recovery between training sessions (or complete rest)	Easy jogging, cycling, swimming	8-12	10	2-4
Specific preparation				
Improve mobility	Games	8-12	10	2-4
Improve flexibility	Warm-up with stretching	8-12	10	3-6
Refine technique	Technique drills and strides	8-12	10	2-4
Develop strength endurance	Circuit and weight training, hill running	18-22	20	2-4
Develop aerobic endurance	Continuous aerobic running	18-22	20	2-4
Increase lactate/ ventilatory threshold	Interval or continuous tempo running	5-9	7	1-2
Develop specialized endurance and pacing skill	Interval running at race pace	3-7	5	1-2
Develop anaerobic endurance	Interval running at faster than race pace	1-5	3	1-2
Recovery between training sessions (or complete rest)	Easy jogging, cycling, swimming	13-17	15	3-6

Table 10.2 Training Objectives, Methods, and Loads for the Competition Period

Main objectives	Key methods	Range (%)	Relative training load average (%)	Units per microcycle
Precompetition				
Maintain flexibility	Warm-up with stretching	18-22	20	4-8
Refine technique	Technique drills and strides	8-12	10	1-2
Maintain strength endurance	Circuit and weight training, hill running	8-12	10	1-2
Maintain aerobic endurance	Continuous aerobic running	13-17	15	1-2
Increase/maintain lactate/ventilatory threshold	Interval tempo running	3-7	5	1-2
Develop specialized endurance and pacing skill	Interval running at race pace, time trials, or racing	8-12	10	2-4
Develop anaerobic endurance	Interval running at faster than race pace	3-7	5	1-2
Recovery between training sessions (or complete rest)	Easy jogging, cycling, swimming	23-27	25	3-6
Main competition				
Maintain flexibility	Warm-up with stretching	18-22	20	4-8
Refine technique	Technique strides	8-12	10	1-2
Maintain strength endurance	Circuit/weight training	8-12	10	1-2
Maintain aerobic endurance	Continuous aerobic running	8-12	10	1-2
Maintain lactate/ventilatory threshold	Interval tempo running	8-12	10	1-2
Tease out specialized endurance and pacing skill	Racing	8-12	10	1-2
Tease out anaerobic endurance	Interval running at faster than race pace	3-7	5	1-2
Recovery between training sessions (or complete rest)	Easy jogging, cycling, swimming	23-27	25	3-6

We have based our recommendations for relative training loads on the percentage of training time that runners spend on a particular method. For example, let's say that a runner trains for five hours (300 minutes) a week. Considering the time spent studying in school, doing homework, and hanging out with friends, we think that this is a reasonable number of hours for young runners to commit to training. In a given phase, we might recommend that an average of 10 percent of those five hours be devoted to lactate/ventilatory threshold training. Thus, the runner would spend about 30 minutes per week on interval or continuous tempo running (300 minutes ×.10 = 30 minutes). Looking at the tables, you'll see that, in addition to the average relative load for each method, we present recommended ranges that allow for variation based on individual needs.

We want to give coaches a sound developmental framework for deciding on how much training to assign; however, you must recognize that individual differences and needs ultimately determine the right loads for each runner. For example, physically mature track runners who specialize in the middle distances, 800 and 1,500/1,600 meters, may need a greater contribution of high-intensity interval training than we recommend in tables 10.1 and 10.2. Nevertheless, the guidelines in these tables are based on scientific and developmental principles of training, and they will give coaches a good, safe starting point from which they can make changes if necessary.

In the following sections, we'll discuss the guidelines for determining key methods and relative loads of training for the different phases of the macrocycle. These steps are still somewhat general because they don't create actual day-to-day workouts. Still, as you'll see here and in chapter 11 (where we'll show you how to design daily sessions), this process is an essential stepping stone to planning effective training programs.

A REMINDER: DON'T FORGET ABOUT FUN

While you are reading the detailed training guidelines in this chapter, don't forget about one of the most important parts of training—fun! You can have a well-designed program, that, on paper, offers great potential to condition runners' bodies and minds. But if training isn't fun, your program simply won't work because the athletes will lose interest and motivation. To train hard and keep at it, runners need a program that offers creativity, variety, camaraderie among team members, and friendly interaction with the coach. We'll focus on strategies for cultivating these in chapter 12.

General Preparation Phase Objectives: Improving Fitness Fundamentals

The overall goal of the general preparation phase is to build a base of fitness that serves as a foundation for specialized training. The main training objectives during this phase emphasize fundamental elements of fitness (see table 10.1). These objectives include improving mobility, flexibility, and technique. We recommend that training for these three elements of fitness should make up an average of 30 percent of the total training time in a microcycle (i.e., a one- to two-week period): 10 percent for mobility, 10 percent for flexibility, and 10 percent for technique. So in the case of an intermediate-level runner who trains six hours (360 minutes) in a one-week microcycle, about 36 minutes of that time would be spent on playing mobility games, 36 minutes on stretching, and 36 minutes doing technique work.[1] As shown in the last column of table 10.1, a typical microcycle might include two to four units of mobility, three to six units of flexibility, and two to four units of technique.

We recommend that an average of 55 percent of training time during general preparation be spent on developing strength endurance (25 percent) and general aerobic endurance (30 percent). As you know, the methods for developing strength endurance include circuit training, weight training, and hill running. For at least the first mesocycle of this phase (three to four weeks), it's best to use circuit training to build a base for weight training. The key methods for developing general aerobic endurance are continuous running, swimming, and cycling. For the runner who trains six hours a week, about 90 and 108 minutes would be devoted to strength endurance and general aerobic endurance, respectively. Each of these methods can be covered in two to four units per microcycle.

Let's say that for our hypothetical, intermediate-level runner, 30 percent of his weekly workload of 360 minutes was general aerobic endurance running, which he did in two or three separate units. If he averaged 7:15 per mile, he would cover about 15 miles (108 minutes ÷ 7.25 minutes per mile = 14.90 miles). That may not seem like much weekly mileage for someone who has been training for two to four years. When you add the volume from other methods including tempo

---

1. Again, we've calculated these durations by multiplying the total training time in the microcycle by the recommended averages for relative loads, as presented in table 10.1. So in the general preparation phase, mobility training (10 percent) would account for 36 minutes of the total because 360 × .10 = 36.

running and recovery running, however, his weekly total is much higher—closer to 30 or 35 miles.

It's important to note that although fundamental methods dominate the training load during the general preparation phase, advanced methods should still be a part of the program for runners of all developmental levels. We recommend that about 5 percent of general preparation training time be devoted to advanced methods, or running at paces that are close to race pace. For runners who train 360 minutes a week, then, methods such as tempo running and specialized endurance will account for 18 minutes of training time in one or two units per microcycle. Coaches should stress hitting target paces and provide plenty of feedback on split times to help runners develop pacing skills.

Small doses of fast running will also come from technique strides and mobility games. As we've stressed throughout the book, fast running should always be a part of training. Besides its role in developing specialized fitness for racing, fast running during this early phase of preparation will help prevent injuries. When athletes suddenly add fast running to their programs after weeks of nothing but relatively long, slow running, they are at risk for muscle strains and other injuries.

The general preparation phase also features recovery methods to speed regeneration after demanding workouts. But because the intensity of training is quite low during this early phase,

recovery methods account for only a small part of the training load. We recommend that about 10 percent of training time be devoted to easy jogging, cycling, or swimming. As you will see, the contribution of recovery methods increases as training becomes more intense in the specific preparation, precompetition, and main competition phases.

Specific Preparation Phase Objectives: Preparing for Racing Demands

During the general preparation phase, you build a base of fitness by gradually increasing the volume of fundamental training. For example, over the weeks in this phase, athletes will increase their volume of continuous aerobic running and add circuits to strength endurance workouts. In contrast, the overall goal during the specific preparation is to gradually increase the volume of advanced training while maintaining a fairly high level of fundamental fitness. As the name implies, specific preparation is intended to prepare runners for the specific physical and mental demands of racing.

In our sample macrocycle (figure 10.1), the specific preparation phase lasts four weeks, or one mesocycle. This may not seem like a long enough time to develop a high level of specialized fitness for racing. It doesn't take as long, however, to build specialized fitness as it does fundamental

fitness. In addition, the type of training you do during specific preparation will carry over into the precompetition phase. So you can develop specialized fitness gradually, according to the principle of progression.

Coaches should continue fairly high levels of flexibility and technique training during specific preparation to prevent injuries and refine running form. Mobility games are less important, but they should still be included a few times a microcycle for variety and fun. We've kept the relative contribution of these three methods the same as in the general preparation phase.

Because the relative contribution of advanced training increases during specific preparation, the percentage of fundamental training decreases. For example, we've lowered the contribution of strength endurance training from 25 to 20 percent (see table 10.1). You can use hill running and weight training to complement circuit training during this phase. We've also lowered the contribution of general aerobic endurance training from an average of 30 to 20 percent. During this phase, the main method for developing general aerobic endurance should be running, rather than swimming or cycling. This is because specificity of training becomes more important as the competition period approaches.

The key methods during specific preparation are tempo running and interval training to develop specialized and anaerobic endurance. We recommend that you devote an average of 7 percent of training time to developing the lactate/ ventilatory threshold. So an intermediate-level runner who trains 360 minutes in a seven-day microcycle might do one unit of tempo running for about 25 minutes.

You should allot an average of another 5 percent of training time to develop specialized endurance and pacing skill and 3 percent to develop anaerobic endurance. Our hypothetical, intermediate-level runner who trains 360 minutes a week would do about 18 and 11 minutes of specialized and anaerobic endurance running, respectively. When you think about it, these are fairly long durations to be running at fast speeds. For example, in 18 minutes, a runner could do a 5,000-meter time trial or an interval session of 6 × 800 meters.

Remember that you should increase the volume of high-intensity training very gradually. So for the advanced methods, we recommend starting out at the low end of the recommended ranges and progressively increasing their contribution. Given this increase in high-intensity training, combined with relatively high loads of fundamental training, it's important to devote more time to recovery methods during specific preparation. Therefore, we've increased our recommendation for recovery training from 10 to 15 percent from the general to the specific preparation phases. Be sure, however, to make individual adjustments of the contribution of recovery methods for athletes—particularly beginners, who may need extra rest.

Precompetition Phase Objectives: Simulating Competition

After the many weeks of preparation, runners begin the competition period of the macrocycle. During the precompetition phase of this period, the overall goal is to build racing fitness and skills for peak performance in races during the main competition phase. Precompetition allows runners to test and fine-tune their fitness in low-key races before major competitions.

Training during precompetition should emphasize methods that simulate the physical and mental demands of competition. The main objectives during this phase are to maintain fundamental fitness while developing specialized fitness for racing (see table 10.2). Compared to the specific preparation phase, precompetition increases the contribution of advanced methods and decreases that of the fundamental methods. For example, we recommend lowering the percentage of strength endurance training from about 20 percent during specific preparation to 10 percent during precompetition. Lower the percentage of general aerobic endurance training as well, from 20 percent to 15 percent. We've also reduced the number of units of these methods per microcycle from two to four during specific preparation to one to two during precompetition.

Given the reduction of fundamental methods such as circuit training and continuous aerobic running, both of which take a long time to do, you will cut back the total training time per week in the precompetition phase. In addition, the shorter high-intensity sessions and the need for more recovery days will reduce training time during the precompetition phase. So the intermediate-level cross-country runner who trained six hours per week in the preparation period might train only four or five hours per week in the precompetition phase.

We recommend devoting an average of 20 percent of training time to the advanced methods during this phase. Gear about 10 percent, or half of this time, toward developing specialized endurance. Thus, the runner who trains four hours per week (240 minutes) will spend roughly 24 minutes on methods such as interval running at race pace, time trials, and low-key races. You can do this training in two units during the week or four units during a two-week microcycle. Spend another 5 percent, or one-quarter of the advanced methods training time, on developing the lactate/ventilatory threshold and 5 percent on anaerobic endurance.

With the increase in high-intensity training, runners will need to spend more time warming up and stretching before workouts; therefore, we've increased the contribution of flexibility to 20 percent. In addition, because these sessions will be very demanding and energy-draining, we've increased the time for recovery methods, such as easy jogging or swimming, to an average of 25 percent. It may seem like too much time to be warming up and recovering, but during the precompetition phase these methods are critical for helping runners prepare for demanding sessions and recover from them quickly.

View the races in the precompetition phase as "stepping stones" to the ultimate challenges of key races in the main competition phase. The overall objective of racing during this phase is to gain experience, skill, and comfort in competition. One key to gaining experience and skill in racing is experimenting with different tactics. In each early-season meet, runners can practice a different racing plan. It could be even pacing, negative-split pacing, or front running. Two purposes for practicing different tactics during precompetition exist. First, the practice will prepare runners for the many tactical scenarios that could arise in later, more important competitions. Second, it will help runners find the racing strategies that work best for them.

Low-key races during the precompetition phase allow runners to gain comfort and boost their confidence in racing situations. By getting a few races under their belts, runners can get rid of the nervousness and jitters that come with competition. This phase allows runners to fine-tune their mental fitness so that they have the right level of mental energy. In addition, runners can use the first few meets to make sure that they feel comfortable with the fit of their racing uniforms and shoes. For example, you might try racing in track shoes with spikes to find out if they feel better and make you run faster than flat racing shoes do. You should make adjustments in such gear before the main competition phase so that you are comfortable and confident when it really counts.

Setting new personal records is not necessarily an objective of the precompetition phase. Although some runners, especially beginners, may cut seconds off their best times in early-season races, they should focus primarily on the means of achieving goals—technique and strategy—instead of on the goal itself. The danger of setting PRs early is that runners may not continue to improve as the competition period progresses. Lack of improvement could dampen motivation to excel in major races at the end of the season.

It's quite a challenge for coaches to discourage motivated young athletes from going all-out in races during the early part of the competitive period. To help runners focus on these races as stepping stones, coaches must clearly communicate technical and tactical objectives. Another way to discourage early-season burnout is for runners to underrace or overrace their event specialty. This means competing at distances that are shorter or longer than their best events.

A final word about training and racing in the precompetition phase: We do not recommend "training through," a technique in which runners compete without taking recovery days before and after the competition. Even when runners aren't out to set PRs in early-season races, they should still be physically rested and mentally sharp. In this condition, runners have much to gain in fitness, experience, and confidence from races. If, however, the runners toe the starting line tired from hard training sessions on the previous days, they risk poor performance, injury, and a loss in confidence for future races.

Main Competition Phase Objectives: Running Your Best

By the end of the precompetition phase, runners have done all the hard training and have refined technique and tactics. Recalling our travel analogy, once the main competition phase begins, runners have arrived! Now they can focus on competing, setting new PRs, and enjoying the high level of fitness that they have developed in the earlier phases. If training has gone well up to this point, don't worry about improving fitness through more and harder training. Instead, the races themselves will increase fitness, creating optimal performances.

The main competition phase typically revolves around three to six key races at the end of the season. For beginners who will not qualify for championship meets, the key races might be in the last few dual meets and invitationals of the season. For intermediate and advanced runners, the key races will be city, regional, state, and perhaps, national championships. Coaches should develop this pattern of peaking at the end of the season when championship meets are held, to condition runners to do their best when it counts the most.

The main objectives of training during the main competition phase are to maintain the fundamental fitness and to tease out the advanced fitness runners developed in earlier phases of the macrocycle (see table 10.2). Runners should focus their physical and mental energies on racing—not on trying to improve fitness by continuing to increase training loads. To accomplish these objectives, runners must cut back on the quantity while maintaining the quality, or speed, of training.

One key focus of training during the main competition phase should be on keeping active the neuromuscular pathways used in racing. This involves flexibility training and running at speeds that recruit FT muscle fibers and simulate racing biomechanics. We recommend devoting about 20 percent of training time to stretching and 10 percent to technique strides. The contribution of flexibility is high because you must precede all of the sessions involving fast running with a warm-up with stretching. Much of the training in the days leading up to races should include some form of interval running at close to race pace. To maintain strength and general aerobic endurance, we recommend devoting about 10 percent of training time to each of these methods.

As shown in table 10.2, we have assigned a total average of 25 percent of training time to the advanced methods of interval tempo running (10 percent), and specialized (10 percent) and anaerobic (5 percent) endurance running (the specialized endurance should come mostly from races).

In this phase, when using fast, interval running to increase fitness, it's important to keep the distance of repetitions short and the recovery intervals long so that the athlete is running fast, but not building up too much lactic acid and draining energy. That's why tempo running is a key component of this phase: It's not so fast that it builds up too much lactic acid.

A common mistake during the competitive season is to train at such high intensities that runners are too fatigued to compete at their best. Therefore, during this phase, runners should finish interval training sessions feeling light and energized, as if they could do several more repetitions with little trouble. This type of work—fast running that doesn't drain energy, sharpens mental fitness because it makes you feel fast. When race-week training consists only of easy, slow running, runners often feel sluggish and tired. Feeling this way, they may begin to have doubts and worries about their upcoming races.

Of course, recovery is vital during the main competition phase, particularly in the last few days before the race and a day or two afterwards. We recommend that recovery training contribute an average of 25 percent to the training time during this phase.

Transition: Recovering, Regenerating, and Reflecting

Our discussion of periodization in this chapter has focused on the training objectives, methods, and loads for the preparation and competition periods. But we can't forget the transition period because it is a critical part of the young runner's program and development. As you recall, transition is the rest period between the end of competition and the beginning of preparation for the next macrocycle. The overall objectives for the runner during the transition period are to recover from the stress of training and racing and regenerate physical and mental energy for the upcoming macrocycle.

In our sample macrocycle, the transition period lasts seven weeks, from early November to the end of December (see figure 10.1). The amount of actual training done during this period depends on the level of development. Beginners and some intermediate runners may take this entire period off. They can use this time to participate in other sports and activities just for fun. Advanced runners might take three to four weeks off and then begin to do some very light fundamental training.

For coaches, the transition period is a time for reflecting on each runner's training and racing outcomes over the previous months and for planning the upcoming macrocycle. During the transition break, coaches can begin planning by completing the assessment process that we discussed in chapter 9.

SUMMARY

Periodization, the process of mapping out training and competitive experiences in a season or macrocycle, is one key to designing effective training programs. The guidelines for periodization that we presented in this chapter will help you prepare periodization charts, such as the one in figure 10.1. Our recommendations for methods and loads of training should give you a feel for the types and amounts of training you should assign in each phase of the macrocycle.

Let's review the major training and competitive objectives in each phase of the macrocycle:

- *General preparation:* This phase, which should last at least one-third of the total number of weeks for the preparation and competition periods, is for building a base of fundamental fitness.
  - *Key methods:* Mobility, flexibility, technique, strength endurance, and general aerobic endurance
- *Specific preparation:* This phase, which usually lasts from one to two months, is for developing specialized fitness with advanced training.
  - *Key methods:* Strength endurance, general aerobic endurance, tempo running, specialized endurance, and anaerobic endurance
- *Precompetition:* This phase accounts for the early part of the racing season and is used to develop racing fitness and skill with advanced training and "practice" competitions.
  - *Key methods:* Tempo running, specialized endurance (racing), anaerobic endurance, flexibility, and recovery
- *Main competition:* This phase covers the later part of the racing season during which key meets are held. The focus is on top-level racing and teasing out the fitness and skill developed in previous phases.
  - *Key methods:* Tempo running, specialized endurance (racing), anaerobic endurance, flexibility, and recovery

Before going on, we want to stress again that you should view the recommendations we presented for training methods and loads in tables 10.1 and 10.2 as general guidelines. We don't expect you to plan your program to match exactly the recommended percentages for different methods. You'll most likely need to adapt these guidelines to meet the specific needs of individual athletes. Generally speaking, some beginners may need a greater percentage of fundamental training than we've recommended, while some advanced runners may need a greater percentage of specialized training. In any case, through a process of trial and adjustment, you can use these guidelines, which are based on scientific and developmental principles, to determine what works best for individual athletes.

CHAPTER II

Progression

Once you've charted your course with periodization, the next step in the process is to plan the specific details of daily training. This step is akin to making your travel plans for each day of an extended journey, plans that include the time of departure, the vehicle you'll use, the speed at which you'll travel, and the time of arrival at your next stopping point. In this chapter, we'll be answering the following questions about planning daily and weekly training sessions:

- How should I combine different methods of training on a day-by-day basis?

- Do optimal patterns for implementing training methods over the course of a microcycle (one to two weeks) exist?

- What type of training should I plan for the days leading up to a race?

- How can I make training progressive over the course of several microcycles?

We'll guide you through the process of planning the specific details of training by first presenting guidelines for organizing units, sessions, microcycles, and mesocycles. Then we'll focus in on the sessions and units themselves by providing examples of daily workouts. Finally, we'll address progression of training by illustrating how specific methods should evolve over time to meet the objectives of each phase of preparation and competition.

PLANNING TRAINING SESSIONS, MICROCYCLES, AND MESOCYCLES

At this point in the process of planning training, you should have a good idea of

1. your main objectives,

2. the methods you'll use, and

3. the relative contribution and number of units of each method in a given phase.

For example, let's say that in a seven-day microcycle during the general preparation phase, the coach decides to assign a beginner three units of flexibility, two units of circuit training, two units of technique work, one unit of continuous aerobic

running, one unit of interval tempo running, and two units of recovery. Before actually planning the specific details (i.e., the workouts) for these units, the coach should consider how to arrange them in daily sessions and how to "string together" those sessions in the microcycles and mesocycles of the phase.

A number of questions come up when you think about this organizational challenge. In what order should runners do the different units for a particular training session that has more than one unit? On which days of the week should runners do certain sessions? How many days should separate workouts that involve similar training methods? At what point in the week should runners do the most intense sessions? How should a particular method of training evolve over the microcycles and mesocycles of a macrocycle? In this section, we'll present guidelines for organizing training in each division of the macrocycle to answer these kinds of questions.

Organizing Training Units in a Session

Most of the daily training sessions coaches plan will have more than one unit. For example, on a day when the runners stretch and do technique drills, they complete two units. In such a session, the coach could even add a unit of circuit training without overdoing it. It's the way that the different units are arranged in a particular session that largely determines how effective training will be. The first step to planning the details of daily training is to decide on the units to use in individual training sessions. At this point, it isn't necessary to write down the actual doses (repetitions, intensity, and so on) for each unit. Instead, the coach should arrange the units for the best outcomes, according to the following guidelines.

> ▶ **Combine units of fundamental training in the same session.**

Certain combinations of training units are optimal, while others can lead to negative outcomes. For the general preparation phase, we recommend sessions that combine flexibility, technique, and strength endurance training in that order. Another of our favorite combinations is general aerobic endurance and mobility training. Runners can do several fundamental units in a session without the risk of overtraining because these methods are relatively low in intensity. Generally, a unit of advanced training should not be combined with a fundamental unit, except for flexibility, on the same day. For example, it would be inappropriate to have an intense, anaerobic interval workout in the same session with a continuous aerobic run.

> ▶ **A warm-up unit of jogging and stretching should precede units of advanced training.**

Flexibility exercises prepare the muscles for intense work and prevent injuries during fast running. Therefore, any session that involves advanced training methods should be preceded by a thorough warm-up that consists of 10 to 15 minutes of jogging and a complete stretching routine. It's a good practice to do some light stretching *after* all running sessions as well.

> ▶ **Athletes should not do technique units when fatigued.**

Do technique units involving drills or strides following a warm-up with stretching. Technique training should not follow a unit, such as circuit training or anaerobic endurance, that fatigues runners and prevents them from learning and practicing good form.

> ▶ **Units of continuous aerobic running should precede units of strength endurance training.**

In a session that includes running and strength endurance training, run first. For example, a continuous aerobic run should precede circuit or weight training. The local muscular fatigue caused by the strength endurance unit could lead to injury if it is followed by a run.

Organizing Training Sessions in a Microcycle

Let's say you're planning an upcoming microcycle, and you've decided to combine a continuous aerobic run with mobility games on one day and stretching with an interval tempo session on another day. On what days of the microcycle will you place these two sessions? What about the other days of the microcycle?

Follow these important guidelines to arrange sessions in a microcycle in a way that helps runners successfully and safely accomplish their training objectives.

> ▶ **Avoid using the same training method two days in a row.**

Given the principle of overload-regeneration, it's essential to allow the body to recover following training, before it is stressed again. At least one day should separate the use of a particular method. For example, if a runner does circuit training on a Monday, he should wait at least until Wednesday before repeating the method. This doesn't mean that Tuesday should necessarily be devoted to complete recovery. If, for example, the circuit session on Monday primarily stressed muscles of the upper body, the runner's legs may be fresh enough to allow for a continuous aerobic run on Tuesday.

A few exceptions to this rule exist. First, recovery methods can be used two days in a row, particularly in the days leading up to a race. Second, elite runners who compete in track meets that feature a semifinal on the day before the finals can do back-to-back days of specialized training to simulate these racing demands.

> ▶ **Low-intensity or recovery days should both precede and follow high-intensity days.**

Again, following the principle of overload-regeneration, the training program should allow for recovery following demanding, high-intensity sessions. It's important to plan for enough recovery so that runners are physically regenerated and mentally fresh for the next challenging workout. Usually, one day of recovery exercise (e.g., easy jogging, cycling, or swimming) is sufficient for this purpose. Coaches must be aware, however, of individual differences in the rate of recovery. Some runners, particularly beginners, may need extra days of recovery or complete rest before they are ready to train hard again. On the day before a demanding session, runners should either use recovery methods or relatively low-intensity methods, such as continuous aerobic running or technique strides.

> ▶ **Assign advanced training methods on the days of the week that competitions are usually held.**

During the specific preparation and precompetition phases, runners will benefit from doing their specialized, advanced training on the same days of the week that they will run key races. For example, if championship cross-country races are going to be on Fridays and Saturdays, the coach should plan the most demanding sessions for the end of each week, during the phases leading up to the main competition phase.

It's a good idea to train at the time of day that key races will be held as well. So if key cross-country races are scheduled for 8:00 A.M., the coach should plan several advanced training sessions for that time. These sessions could be held on successive Saturdays during the specific preparation phase. By performing the most demanding sessions of the microcycle on the days and the time of day that races will be held, runners will condition their bodies and minds for the ultimate challenge of competition.

> ▶ **The race microcycle should include sessions with low volumes of fast running and sessions of recovery.**

In microcycles leading up to races, the main objective is to rest and refresh the body and mind without losing fitness. This objective can be met by planning interval running over short distances at close to race pace. Remember, however, that these sessions should not be so intense that they drain energy. We'll present a sample race microcycle shortly.

Organizing Microcycles in a Mesocycle

After arranging units in sessions and sessions in microcycles, the next step is to organize the microcycles in a mesocycle, stringing together individual weeks of training into a block of three to four weeks. The following steps should guide this process.

> ▶ **Repeat key training methods throughout the mesocycle.**

Let's say that, for the specific preparation period, you've set up a three-week mesocycle made up of three one-week microcycles. You've planned a tempo run for the first Monday of the first microcycle. You should repeat tempo running, developing the lactate/ventilatory threshold and several aspects of mental fitness, several times throughout the mesocycle. If you've planned one unit of tempo running for each week, we recommend assigning it for the next two Mondays in the mesocycle. So for three Mondays in a row, runners will do a tempo run. Every Tuesday, they should do a recovery unit because tempo running is an advanced method.

This cyclical pattern ensures that runners stress particular elements of fitness, adapting for improvement, on a regular basis. Of course, the training dose for each method has to increase each time for this improvement to occur. We'll discuss the pattern for increasing training doses shortly.

If your microcycles are longer than one week, simply repeat key training methods at the same point in successive microcycles. For example, let's say you've decided to have one unit of continuous tempo running in a 10-day microcycle, placing it on the first day of the microcycle, a Monday. When that microcycle ends 10 days later on a Wednesday, you should start the next microcycle with a continuous tempo run on the next day, a Thursday.

> ▶ **Arrange training loads in a mesocycle to peak and then taper off.**

In general, set up mesocycles in a pattern that increases the training load over the first two to three weeks and decreases it in the last week. Figure 11.1 illustrates this pattern by showing an increase in running volume, or miles per week, over the first two weeks of two successive mesocycles, each lasting three weeks.

In the first mesocycle, we've scheduled 25 and 32 miles of running in successive seven-day microcycles. Then, after a week of reduced volume, the runner starts the second mesocycle at 32 miles and increases to 37 miles across the two weeks. This progression will result from increasing the volume for all the running methods (e.g., continuous aerobic running, tempo running, and specialized endurance). The intensity will also increase as the pace gets faster each time the runner performs the unit from week to week.

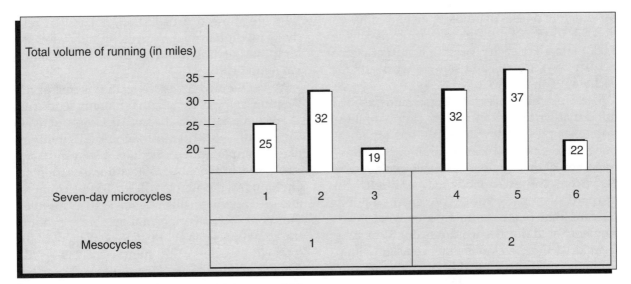

Figure 11.1 Two mesocycles structured in pyramid form.

Notice that the volume drops during the third week of both mesocycles. In this pattern, the third week is called an "unloading" microcycle because the training load decreases. In the unloading microcycle, we recommend cutting training volume by 25 to 50 percent of the highest volume in the mesocycle. For example, we've lowered the mileage by about 40 percent from the second (32 miles) to the third (19 miles) week of the first mesocycle. The unloading microcycle gives runners a little extra recovery from training and refreshes their mental outlook for the next mesocycle. This pattern is based on the principle of overload-regeneration. Considerable improvement in performance can occur during unloading microcycles as the body and mind regenerate and fitness levels rise.

During the precompetition and main competition phases of the season, it's ideal to plan mesocycles so that the unloading microcycles lead up to races. This way, the reduction in training load will result in a timely regeneration for the ultimate physical and mental demands of competition.

PLANNING INDIVIDUAL TRAINING SESSIONS: SAMPLE MICROCYCLES

Now we get to the culmination of the process of designing training: planning the individual training sessions that make up the microcycle. Before we take this critical step, let's briefly review our path to this point. First, having completed a developmental assessment of your runners, you have a sense of the training methods and loads that each will need to improve. Remember, the assessment of training in previous macrocycles can be used to progressively increase loads in the upcoming macrocycle.

The second step in the process, goal setting, provides key information that will help you design individual training sessions as well. For example, if the runner's goal for the 1,500-meter run is 4:40, you should plan specialized endurance interval sessions to simulate that pace (i.e., just under 75 seconds per 400). If one of the runner's training goals is to build up to an eight-mile continuous aerobic run, you might start out with a five- or six-mile session.

The third step, periodization of preparation and competition, gives you a framework for choosing the methods and amounts of training you'll devote to accomplishing different objectives in each phase of the macrocycle. Tables 10.1 and 10.2 (pages 145 and 146) presented guidelines for setting up this framework and determining the relative training loads and number of units for each method.

Now we're ready to plan the actual training sessions of the macrocycle. In taking this fourth step, we'll use the guidelines we've presented in this chapter for organizing units, sessions, microcycles, and mesocycles. We'll describe sample microcycles designed for a hypothetical intermediate-level cross-country runner during the different phases of preparation and competition. We'll say that this athlete's racing distance is 5,000 meters. For each phase, we'll present a table that shows the units and sample workouts for each day of the microcycle.

As you examine these training sessions, keep in mind that we've designed them simply to illustrate examples of how to apply our organizational guidelines to planning training. We'll remind you of these guidelines as we explain why we've chosen given methods and organized them in a particular way. We do not present the training sessions that follow as models of what every runner should do. The workouts don't consider individual and developmental needs and different event specialties. In addition, they don't include creative elements like variety in the venue of training or in the types of exercises used for flexibility and circuit training. The workouts are, however, based on sound general principles for designing training. We encourage you to design your program by considering each runner's special needs and by applying the organizational guidelines that we have presented in this chapter and the previous one.

A Sample Microcycle for the General Preparation Phase

On page 159, we present a sample seven-day microcycle for an intermediate-level cross-country runner during the general preparation phase. We've designed the sample workouts for the first mesocycle of this phase, so the runner is just starting to train for the upcoming racing season. These sessions are much like the ones in chapters 6 through 8, in which we presented sample workouts for each training method during the general preparation phase.

The microcycle features units of general aerobic endurance and mobility training on Monday and Thursday, flexibility, technique, and strength endurance on Tuesday and Friday, lactate/ventilatory threshold training on Wednesday, and recovery and complete rest on the weekend. Notice that we've repeated the sessions for developing fundamental fitness throughout the microcycle, but that we've avoided repeating the same method (with the exception of flexibility) two days in a row. This cyclical pattern allows specific muscles and energy systems to regenerate after

they are stressed. In addition, notice that relatively low-intensity days precede and follow the high-intensity session on Wednesday—the interval tempo run.

We've planned the sessions in this microcycle keeping in mind the relative training loads that we recommended in chapter 10. For example, in the roughly 4 1/2 hours of training (270 minutes) of this sample, we've scheduled between 70 and 80 minutes of general aerobic endurance training. On Monday, the athlete will run 35 to 40 minutes and on Thursday will cycle for 35 to 40 minutes. This contribution of general aerobic endurance training represents about 26 to 30 percent of the total (70 minutes ÷ 270 minutes = .259 or 25.9 percent; 80 minutes ÷ 270 minutes = .296 or 29.6 percent). These values are close to our recommended range of 28 to 32 percent for general aerobic endurance during the general preparation phase (see table 10.1 on page 145).

To illustrate the pattern of training during the general preparation phase, we chose a seven-day microcycle for simplicity: it's convenient to think about training on a weekly basis. Still, coaches may need to adapt the sample microcycle if the training sessions do not allow runners to recover sufficiently. Beginners may need an extra day or two of recovery during the middle of the week, particularly before the interval tempo session on Wednesday. If so, add these recovery days, lengthening the microcycle, perhaps to 9 or 10 days.

On the other hand, some intermediate and advanced runners may be able to handle more units of training than we've prescribed. One way to increase the training load for these fit and experienced runners is to schedule additional units on two or three mornings of each microcycle before school. Coaches can use morning sessions for recovery or even general aerobic endurance training. These extra units will help young runners who have the desire and potential to continue beyond high school prepare for the two-a-day sessions that are a part of the training program for many college and international-level runners.

Coaches must plan for variety in training during the general preparation phase because its length may make the racing season seem far away. When two continuous aerobic runs are scheduled in a microcycle, for example, it's a good idea to plan them for different courses. On the first day, runners might train on a flat dirt road in the country. On the second, they might run on

GENERAL PREPARATION PHASE SEVEN-DAY MICROCYCLE
(Intermediate Level, Cross-Country)

Monday	Unit #1:	**General aerobic endurance** Continuous running, cycling, or swimming 35 to 40 mins. of running @ 65 to 75% of HRmax
	Unit #2:	**Mobility** Flag football, ultimate Frisbee, keep-away, etc. 10 to 20 mins.
Tuesday	Unit #1:	**Warm-up/flexibility** 10 mins. of jogging and complete stretching routine
	Unit #2:	**Technique** Drills or strides
	Unit #3:	**Strength endurance** Circuit training 1 × 3-station circuit
Wednesday	Unit #1:	**Warm-up/flexibility** 10 mins. of jogging and complete stretching routine
	Unit #2:	**Lactate/ventilatory threshold** Interval tempo running 4 × 3 mins. @ 80 to 85% of HRmax w/60 secs. recovery
Thursday	Unit #1:	**General aerobic endurance** Continuous running, cycling, or swimming 35 to 40 mins. of cycling @ 65 to 75% of HRmax
	Unit #2:	**Mobility** Flag football, ultimate Frisbee, keep-away, etc. 10 to 20 mins.
Friday	Unit #1:	**Warm-up/flexibility** 10 mins. of jogging and complete stretching routine
	Unit #2:	**Technique** Drills or strides
	Unit #3:	**Strength endurance** Circuit training 1 × 3-station circuit
Saturday	Unit #1:	**Recovery** 20 to 30 mins. of easy jogging, swimming, or cycling
Sunday	Rest	

Note: For complete sample sessions for the technique and circuit training units, see pages 85 and 91, respectively.

© Terry Wild Studio

a hilly golf course. If you live anywhere near parks, beaches, mountains, or other interesting natural settings, you might consider driving the team to these places for continuous runs. Similarly, if two or three circuit training sessions are planned in the microcycle, coaches can vary the exercises in the circuit or even change the venue of the workout each time.

Furthermore, it's vital for coaches to set a tone of camaraderie and fun during this first phase of training. Many of the sessions, such as technique and circuit training, allow for plenty of group interaction, helping team members get to know one another. You can talk and joke around because the workouts are not yet so intense that they take your breath away! The mobility games are also vital to establishing the philosophy that training is fun. We encourage coaches to use other training games, fartleks, and supplementary methods such as cycling and swimming to make this phase interesting, motivating, and fun.

A Sample Microcycle for the Specific Preparation Phase

On pages 161 and 162, we present a sample 12-day microcycle during the specific preparation phase of cross-country for an intermediate-level runner. We've designed this microcycle for the start of the phase; thus, it begins after the last week of general preparation. As you can see, training is very diverse during the specific preparation phase,

with every method contributing to the total load. Indeed, we've planned this 12-day cycle to fit in all the key methods, still allowing for sufficient recovery between training sessions.

Once again, we've designed the sample sessions so that the relative contribution of each training method is consistent with our guidelines in table 10.1 (page 145). For example, this runner will do 35 minutes of tempo running in the two units of the microcycle. We've scheduled these units for the first Tuesday (15 minutes continuous) and the second Thursday (4 × 5 minutes). The total training time over the 12 days is roughly 500 minutes, or just over eight hours. This means that the tempo running contributes 7 percent to the total ($3 \div 500 = .07$), within our recommended range of 5 to 9 percent.

If you compare the sample microcycles on pages 159 and 161-162, you'll notice several features of progression from the general to specific preparation phases. For example, we've increased the volume of continuous aerobic and tempo running. Note that the tempo run on the first Tuesday is continuous. The interval method of tempo running is ideal for the start of the preparation period (see chapter 8). To simulate the demands of racing, however, runners should do at least one session of continuous tempo running per microcycle during the specific preparation phase.

Another change across the two preparation phases is the addition of weight training in one of the strength endurance units (the first Thursday of the specific preparation phase microcycle). In

SPECIFIC PREPARATION PHASE 12-DAY MICROCYCLE
(Intermediate Level, Cross-Country)

Monday	Unit #1:	**General aerobic endurance** Continuous aerobic running 45 to 50 mins. @ 65 to 75% of HRmax
	Unit #2:	**Mobility** Flag football, ultimate Frisbee, keep-away, etc. 10 to 20 mins.
Tuesday	Unit #1:	**Warm-up/flexibility** 10 mins. of jogging and complete stretching routine
	Unit #2:	**Lactate/ventilatory threshold** Interval or continuous tempo running 15 mins. of continuous running @ 80 to 85% of HRmax
Wednesday	Unit #1:	**Recovery** 20 to 30 mins. of easy jogging, swimming, or cycling
Thursday	Unit #1:	**Warm-up/flexibility** 10 mins. of jogging and complete stretching routine
	Unit #2:	**Technique** Drills or strides 5×30 meters of high knees 5×60 meters of skipping 5×30 meters of butt kicks 5×20 meters of fast feet
	Unit #3:	**Strength endurance** Circuit training, weight training, or hills 2 sets of weight training routine
Friday	Unit #1:	**Recovery** 20 to 30 mins. of easy jogging, swimming, or cycling; or complete rest
Saturday	Unit #1:	**Warm-up/flexibility** 10 mins. of jogging and complete stretching routine
	Unit #2:	**Specialized and anaerobic endurance** Interval running at race pace and faster 3×800 meters @ race pace w/ 1:1 recovery[a]; 3×200 meters @ 10 to 15% faster than race pace w/ 2 mins. recovery
Sunday	Unit #1:	**Recovery** 20 to 30 mins. of easy jogging, swimming, or cycling; or complete rest

Monday	Unit #1:	**General aerobic endurance** Continuous aerobic running 45 to 50 mins. @ 65 to 75% of HRmax
	Unit #2:	**Mobility** Flag football, ultimate Frisbee, keep-away, etc. 10 to 15 mins.
Tuesday	Unit #1:	**Warm-up/flexibility** 10 mins. of jogging and complete stretching routine
	Unit #2:	**Technique** Drills or strides 8 × 150 meters (strides)
	Unit #3:	**Strength endurance** Circuit training, weight training, or hills 2 × 3-station circuit
Wednesday	Unit #1:	**Recovery** 20 to 30 mins. of easy jogging, swimming, or cycling; or complete rest
Thursday	Unit #1:	**Warm-up/flexibility** 10 mins. of jogging and complete stretching routine
	Unit #2:	**Lactate/ventilatory threshold** Interval or continuous tempo running 4 × 5 mins. @ 80 to 85% of HRmax w/60 secs. recovery
Friday	Unit #1:	**Recovery** 20 to 30 mins. of easy jogging, swimming, or cycling

Note: For a sample weight training routine, see page 97.

[a]1:1 recovery means that the interval between repetitions should last as long as the repetition itself.

addition, we've increased the number of circuits in the circuit training unit (on the second Tuesday of the specific preparation phase microcycle) from one to two, thereby increasing the volume of strength endurance training. For variety in strength endurance work, coaches can substitute hill running for circuit and weight sessions.

Finally, the specialized and anaerobic endurance unit (on the first Saturday of the specific preparation phase microcycle) increases the contribution of advanced training in the specific preparation phase. Note, however, that the volume of running in this session, a total of 3,000 meters, is fairly low compared to the 5,000 meters this athlete will cover in cross-country races. Following the principle of progression, the volume

of advanced training should increase gradually over the weeks in this phase. By the start of the next phase, precompetition, the runner should be able to handle volumes of specialized endurance that are closer to 5,000 meters.

The total volume of all running methods should be greater in the specific versus general preparation phase, particularly because methods such as swimming and cycling will be replaced by running. From the general and specific preparation phase sample microcycles, we've calculated the running volume to be approximately 15 miles (24 kilometers) a week in the general preparation phase and 25 miles (40 kilometers) a week in the specific preparation phase. Over the course of the specific preparation phase, the running volume should continue to increase so that the athlete might approach 35 miles (56 kilometers) or more a week. Of course, the exact amount that training increases over the course of a phase depends on the capacities and needs of the individual.

Keep in mind that the sample microcycles are for a cross-country runner who will race 5,000 meters. During specific preparation for track racing, coaches should design training units to meet the needs of runners in their event specialties. So, while 800-meter and 3,000/3,200-meter runners might train together on days featuring strength endurance and technique work, they should do separate workouts that are geared to their events, developing specialized fitness with the advanced methods. To simulate the demands of their races, 800- and 1,500-meter specialists will run faster and cover shorter distances in training sessions (see chapter 8).

Furthermore, it's important to simulate the specific demands of competition in terms of surfaces and terrain. So for cross-country preparation, athletes should run on hills, grass, dirt, or whatever surfaces and terrain simulate your race courses. For track preparation, do most sessions involving specialized, high-intensity running on the track or on flat, soft surfaces such as dirt roads or flat fairways on a golf course. We must emphasize again that coaches can make the basic sessions we've presented more creative and fun by varying the venue of training.

A Sample Precompetition Phase Microcycle

On pages 164 and 165 we present a sample 12-day microcycle for an intermediate-level runner at the start of the precompetition phase of cross-country. Training during this phase is similar to training during the specific preparation phase. However, the precompetition microcycle features a slightly greater contribution of advanced methods. The key method is specialized endurance because it simulates racing. We've scheduled three units of specialized endurance in this sample microcycle for a total of about 40 minutes of running for an athlete whose goal for 5,000 meters is 18 minutes. The sessions on the first Saturday and second Friday total 4,000 and 5,000 meters, respectively. At goal pace (3:36 per kilometer or 5:45 per mile), these sessions should take about 14 and 18 minutes. The session on the second Wed-

nesday totals 2,400 meters and should take about 8 minutes, bringing the total for specialized endurance to approximately 40 minutes. We've calculated the training time for the entire microcycle to be around 400 minutes, or just over 6 1/2 hours. Thus, the contribution of specialized endurance training accounts for about 10 percent of the total ($40 \div 400 = .10$), within our recommended range for this method (see table 10.2 on page 146).

The first specialized endurance unit (on the first Saturday) is the most challenging and demanding workout of the microcycle. Notice that we've scheduled this session for a Saturday because it's the day for major races during the main competition period. It would be ideal to hold this workout at race time and on a surface and terrain that simulates race courses; it's especially important to train on hills if you'll be racing on them. The session begins and ends with a 1,000-meter run; between these longer runs are 4×500-meter repetitions. We intend the first 1,000 repetition to help the runner set and maintain a fast, steady pace at the start of a race. The last 1,000 will physically and mentally challenge the runner to maintain that fast pace when fatigued from the 500-meter repetitions. Note that the total volume for this session is 4,000 meters, approaching this runner's racing distance. It's a fairly long session, but when you consider that the racing distance adds another 1,000 meters, you can see that these long repetitions are necessary to prepare the runner for racing. The key to success in this type of training is to control the pace at race pace and no faster so that the runner can cover the entire distance.

The second specialized endurance unit (on the second Wednesday) is primarily to practice running at race pace and to bring out the fitness gained in the more challenging session earlier in the microcycle. The 300-meter repetitions in this session, run at 5,000-meter race pace, are not fast or long enough to build up very much lactic acid, so the runner should be relatively fresh throughout the workout. Notice that this session comes two days before the last unit of specialized endurance, a 5,000-meter cross-country race or time trial. Leading up to a race, the optimal training methods involve fast running, which does not drain the athlete, and recovery. We've planned one day of recovery before the race or time trial for this intermediate-level runner. Beginners may need a second recovery day.

We've scheduled an anaerobic endurance unit (5×400 meters) for the first Tuesday of the

PRECOMPETITION PHASE 12-DAY MICROCYCLE
(Intermediate Level, Cross-Country)

Monday	Unit #1:	**General aerobic endurance** Continuous aerobic running 35 to 45 mins. @ 65 to 75% of HRmax
	Unit #2:	**Flexibility** Complete stretching routine
	Unit #3:	**Technique** Drills or strides 8 × 150 meters (strides)
Tuesday	Unit #1:	**Warm-up/flexibility** 10 mins. of jogging and complete stretching routine
	Unit #2:	**Anaerobic endurance** Interval running at faster than race pace 5 × 400 @ 10 to 15% faster than race pace w/3 mins. recovery
Wednesday	Unit #1:	**Recovery** 20 to 30 mins. of easy jogging, swimming, or cycling
Thursday	Unit #1:	**Warm-up/flexibility** 10 mins. of jogging and complete stretching routine
	Unit #2:	**Technique** Drills or strides 12 × 150 meters (strides)
	Unit #3:	**Strength endurance** Circuit training or weight training 2 sets of weight training routine
Friday	Unit #1:	**Recovery** 20 to 30 mins. of easy jogging, swimming, or cycling
Saturday	Unit #1:	**Warm-up/flexibility** 10 mins. of jogging and complete stretching routine
	Unit #2:	**Specialized endurance** Interval running at race pace 1 × 1,000 meters w/ 1:1 recovery 4 × 500 meters w/ 1:1 recovery 1 × 1,000 meters
Sunday	Unit #1:	**Recovery** 20 to 30 mins. of easy jogging, swimming, or cycling; or complete rest
Monday	Unit #1:	**Warm-up/flexibility** 10 mins. of jogging and complete stretching routine

	Unit #2:	**Lactate/ventilatory threshold** Interval tempo running 6 × 3 mins. @ 80 to 85% of HRmax w/60 secs. recovery
	Unit #3:	**Strength endurance** Light circuit training or weight training 1 × 3-station circuit
Tuesday	Unit #1:	**Recovery** 20 to 30 mins. of easy jogging, swimming, or cycling; or complete rest
Wednesday	Unit #1:	**Warm-up/flexibility** 10 mins. of jogging and complete stretching routine
	Unit #2:	**Specialized endurance/pacing control** Interval running at race pace 8 × 300 meters w/ 1:1 recovery
Thursday	Unit #1:	**Recovery** 20 to 30 mins. of easy jogging, swimming, or cycling
Friday	Unit #1:	**Warm-up/flexibility** 10 mins. of jogging and complete stretching routine
	Unit #2:	**Specialized endurance** 5,000-meter race or time trial

microcycle. We placed this high-intensity session early in the microcycle because we want the athlete to be well-rested and fresh for it. Thus, the preceding Monday session, which includes a continuous aerobic run at 65 to 75 percent of HRmax, is relatively easy. Notice that on the day after the anaerobic endurance workout as well as after all sessions involving advanced methods, we've scheduled a recovery day.

The interval tempo run on the second Monday should maintain the lactate/ventilatory threshold that the runner developed in the specific preparation phase. We assigned the interval, rather than continuous, method of tempo running to go along with the fast, continuous run of the race or time trial at the end of the week. A continuous tempo run might be too mentally draining for the runner during a race week.

The key features of progression from the specific preparation to precompetition phase are an increase in the volume of advanced training and maintenance (or even a decrease) in the volume of fundamental training. Therefore, continuous

aerobic runs, such as the one scheduled for the first Monday of the precompetition phase sample microcycle, should be shorter than they were in the specific preparation phase. The goal of fundamental training during precompetition is simply to maintain the levels of fitness developed during the preparation period.

As in the specific preparation phase for track, workouts should be assigned according to runners' event specialties during precompetition. This will make the specialized and anaerobic endurance sessions for 800- and 1,500-meter runners shorter and faster than sessions for runners who compete at longer distances.

A Sample Main Competition Phase Microcycle

Now let's discuss a seven-day microcycle during the main competition phase (see page 167). We've reduced the number of days from the last two sample microcycles for the specific preparation and precompetition phases because the training load is much lower. The overall objective of training during this phase is to sharpen racing fitness with fast running that does not drain physical or mental energy. We want the runner to feel fresh, fast, and mentally focused on racing day. So leading up to the 5,000-meter race on Saturday, the sample microcycle includes some form of fast running every day except Thursday. Keep in mind that it's extremely important both to curb the volume of this fast running and to allow for complete recovery between repetitions.

The specialized and anaerobic endurance session on Monday allows the runner to get the feel of running at race pace and a bit faster. The runner does two sets of 1×600 meters followed by 1×200 meters. The runner should perform the 600-meter repetitions at close to race pace; we intend these relatively short runs to stimulate the neuromuscular pathways and specific muscle fibers that the nervous system will recruit in the race later in the week. After each of the 600-meter repetitions, the runner takes a lengthy recovery, maybe four to six minutes, of jogging and walking. Then, the runner does a 200-meter repetition at slightly faster than race pace. The 200-meter repetitions open up the stride and make the runner feel fast and powerful.

Tuesday features an aerobic endurance unit that should be run at a fairly easy pace, perhaps even as slow as a recovery run. The technique strides that follow add more fast running at short distances that will not drain energy. For Wednesday, we've scheduled a short interval tempo unit that further serves our purpose of bringing out racing fitness. The circuit training unit that follows the tempo running should be very light. We've scheduled two days, Thursday and Friday, for recovery. Keep in mind, however, that the time needed for regeneration before a race is highly individualized. Some runners may do better with only one recovery day, while others may need two days or more. Runners should experiment with different periods of recovery to find their optimal one.

For the day after the race, Sunday, we've planned a recovery unit. Because racing demands so much physical and mental energy, runners should not attempt any training that may further drain energy until after they have fully recovered from the race. Finally, you should note that we have not designated the race (scheduled for Saturday) as a unit of specialized endurance training, as it was during the precompetition phase.

Remember that in the main competition phase, runners should be completely focused on racing. If they have had a productive precompetition phase, they don't need to use races to practice tactics or to elevate fitness levels.

FLEXIBILITY AND INTERACTION IN TRAINING PLANS

We must stress again that many of the guidelines presented in this chapter for planning training are general in the sense that they won't work for every runner. For the best outcomes, coaches must consider individual differences and patterns of training that work best for individual athletes (that's why the individual assessment process we discussed in chapter 9 is so important). Coaches should be flexible and change training plans to account for unexpected circumstances. For example, let's say that the coach has planned two recovery days following units of anaerobic endurance running for an individual. If the runner is recovering completely with one easy day, then the coach might adjust the plan and cut out one recovery unit.

We recommend that coaches do not finalize the training program for a weekly microcycle until a few days before it starts. It's good to have a general idea of the workouts that will be performed, but it's also important to be flexible in case a runner gets ill or isn't mentally prepared for the scheduled workout on a given day. In the next chapter, we'll talk more about being flexible when planning training.

It's also vital that the coach discusses upcoming training plans with runners. An open line of communication is essential to finding out which methods of training work best for each individual. A great way to start the conversation is to hand out a weekly workout schedule a few days before it begins. This way, the runners and coach can discuss the plan and make suitable changes. In addition, runners can use their plans to prepare physically and mentally for the challenges of particular sessions. For example, athletes who know that they will be running a time trial on Saturday can prepare by eating a high-carbohydrate meal and getting a good night's sleep on Friday. During the week, runners can

MAIN COMPETITION PHASE SEVEN-DAY MICROCYCLE
(Intermediate Level, Cross-Country)

Monday	Unit #1:	**Warm-up/flexibility** 10 mins. of jogging and complete stretching routine
	Unit #2:	**Specialized and anaerobic endurance** Interval running at race pace and faster $2 \times (1 \times 600$ and $1 \times 200)$ w/complete recovery
Tuesday	Unit #1:	**General aerobic endurance** Continuous aerobic running 30 to 35 mins. @ 65% HRmax
	Unit #2:	**Technique** Drills or strides 6×100 meters (strides)
Wednesday	Unit #1:	**Warm-up/flexibility** 10 mins. of jogging and complete stretching routine
	Unit #2:	**Lactate/ventilatory threshold** Interval tempo running 6×2 mins. @ 85% HRmax w/60 secs. recovery
	Unit #3:	**Strength endurance** Light circuit training or weight training 1×3-station circuit
Thursday	Unit #1:	**Recovery** 20 to 30 mins. of easy jogging, swimming, or cycling
	Unit #2:	**Flexibility** Complete stretching routine
Friday	Unit #1:	**Recovery** 20 to 30 mins. of easy jogging, swimming, or cycling
	Unit #2:	**Flexibility** Complete stretching routine
	Unit #3:	**Technique** 6×100-meter technique strides
Saturday		**5,000-meter cross-country race**
Sunday	Unit #1:	**Recovery** 20 to 30 mins. of easy jogging, swimming, or cycling; or complete rest

plan their strategies for the time trial and perform mental imagery to fine-tune mental fitness.

SUMMARY

In this chapter, we described guidelines for designing units of training and building them into the microcycles to make up phases of preparation and competition. Let's summarize these guidelines and their application.

- Organizing training units into individual sessions

  - Before units of advanced training that require high-intensity work, do a complete warm-up with stretching.
  - Perform technique training early in the session when you're fresh.
  - If you combine units of running with units of strength endurance training, do the running method first.

- Organizing training sessions into microcycles

  - Avoid using the same method two days in a row, unless it's recovery or flexibility.
  - Use low-intensity or recovery methods on days before and after high-intensity training days.
  - Ideally, runners should do their advanced, specialized training on days of the week and at times of the day when they will race.

- Organizing microcycles into mesocycles

  - For an optimal pattern of overload-regeneration, repeat key methods throughout the mesocycle.
  - Arrange training loads to peak and then taper off during the mesocycle. We recommend a pattern of two to three weeks of increasing loads followed by an "unloading" microcycle in which runners cut the volume by 25 to 50 percent.

To show you the application of these guidelines, we presented sample microcycles in this chapter. We based our decisions about the actual doses of training and the combinations of different units and sessions for our hypothetical, intermediate-level cross-country runner on

- developmental factors,
- training and racing goals,
- periodization of the macrocycle, and on
- guidelines for the objectives and loads of training in each phase.

With careful thought and planning, coaches can help young distance runners of different developmental levels and event specialties experience the satisfaction of progressive improvement toward their goals. Before you start planning, however, let's consider one more step in the process, evaluation and revision of the training program, in the next chapter.

CHAPTER 12

Revising the Program

Carefully consider every step when designing a systematic, developmental plan for training, and the program will help runners reach their goals. Like travel plans for a dream vacation, your program may be perfect—on paper, that is; in reality, unexpected events that occur in training and competition can lead you off course, away from your goals. These unexpected events include injury, illness, loss of motivation, stretches of bad weather, and personal problems. All runners have experienced the frustration of such detours on their training journeys. But successful runners and their coaches have strategies for adjusting the course to get back on the road toward their destinations.

This may seem strange, but successful runners and coaches also have strategies for veering off course on purpose! As you know from your experiences in traveling, sometimes it's fun to take the side roads, discovering new places that you didn't plan to see. It's no fun to be constantly pressured to stay on schedule.

In this chapter, we'll address strategies for getting back on course in the event of unexpected detours. In addition, we'll consider strategies for taking purposeful detours to make training more interesting and fun. Compare the coach's role in this process to that of a travel agent who organizes trips that get people to their destinations safely and in an enjoyable way. The coach, however, is a special kind of travel agent who goes along with runners on their journeys, regularly evaluating how they're going. If a journey isn't going according to plans, the coach adjusts the training program on the spot. This coaching skill requires creativity and flexibility. In this chapter, we'll help you add these features as you design and implement your program.

CHECKING YOUR COURSE: EVALUATING TRAINING AND RACING EXPERIENCES

The sure signs of a successful program are that runners are improving, healthy, and highly motivated to continue training and racing at higher levels. Coaches must evaluate runners for these signs to judge the effectiveness of your programs. Earlier, we talked about evaluating runners' development and performances in the assessment process after each season and before planning training for the next season. However, coaches don't have to wait until the season is over to evaluate individuals' programs. The process should occur both on a weekly and a daily basis. Let's discuss strategies for regularly evaluating training and racing experiences to determine whether runners are on target for achieving their goals.

How's the Training Going?

Setbacks in training can occur for many reasons, but most boil down to either accidentally deviating from a well-planned program or to poor planning. Deviations from well-planned training programs occur when, for one reason or another, runners inadvertently don't stick to their daily and weekly plans. Poor planning—using inappropriate training methods and loads for given individuals, usually becomes evident when runners fall far short of their training and racing goals. Inappropriate methods and loads violate developmental guidelines, such as those we presented in chapter 1 (pages 11 to 14), and general training objectives, such as those we presented in table 9.1 (page 133). For example, poor planning is reflected in drastic increases in training loads to levels that runners are not prepared to handle. Programs that don't systematically increase the training load, but instead, keep it constant over time reflect poor planning as well.

To evaluate how training is going, coaches can begin by asking whether their runners are accomplishing the main training objectives that were established in planning. Ask, "Are we following the planned path to our destination?" Sometimes it's easy to take a wrong turn without realizing it. One way to find out whether a program is on course is to calculate the relative contributions of different training methods on a weekly basis to see if they agree with those that were planned before the season started.

Let's say, for example, that a coach planned for 25 percent of the load during the general preparation phase to be strength endurance training. In one week, a runner's training time for this method might have totaled only 10 percent. Maybe the runner had to miss practice to work on a school project on the day of a planned circuit training session. It's no problem to miss one workout. If, however, over several weeks a runner misses out on a particular training method repeatedly, he won't develop the fitness to reach his racing goals. This can happen for any number of reasons, most often when a runner becomes sick or injured. Shortly, we'll discuss strategies for getting back on course when the actual training load deviates from the planned program. But for now, keep in mind that the coach must regularly evaluate whether each runner is actually carrying out the training plan.

Another strategy for evaluating training on a daily basis is to use indicators such as heart rate and running time to make sure that a runner is meeting objectives for intensity, a critical element of the training dose. Consider, for example, that the purpose of a particular workout is to develop general aerobic endurance. If a runner's pace is too fast, as indicated by a heart rate above the intended range of 65 to 75 percent of maximum, she may not be able to maintain it long enough to develop the aerobic system. Sometimes in a situation such as this one, it's tempting to let the runner keep going because she is feeling good and working hard. The workout may even lead to a breakthrough. Remember, though, that if a runner strays too far off course, and doesn't accomplish the planned objectives of training, she could be risking negative outcomes such as injury and illness. By monitoring heart rate, coaches can evaluate whether the runner is meeting training objectives during the workout and then, if necessary, cue the runner to adjust the pace.

Coaches can also use the stopwatch to assess performance in daily training. Consider a runner whose 3,200-meter goal is to break 10:00. In specialized endurance sessions, he would need to run repetitions at close to this pace. So, in a session of 3 × 1,000 meters, the coach might assign repetitions at 3:05 to 3:10 (actual race pace is 3:07 per 1,000 meters). If the runner's times are far outside this range, then the coach should revise future sessions, and perhaps even change the runner's racing goal. It's a good idea for coaches to regularly time sessions that involve running to get a sense of the athlete's progress. For example, you can tell that a runner is on target if he progressively lowers his time for a tempo run over the same course from week to week. Coaches should, however, steer the runner away from competing against the stopwatch and turning training sessions into races against time instead of focusing on the training objectives.

Finally, coaches can evaluate the training by asking their athletes for plenty of feedback about how things are going on a daily basis. The question, "How do you feel?" is a powerful tool for evaluating the effectiveness of the training program. Infinite variations to this question exist, such as the following:

- How are your legs feeling after yesterday's interval workout? Are they sore?

- How is your breathing? Are you working harder than we planned?

- How did your technique feel on that last stride? Can you tell whether your arms are crossing the front of your body or not?

- Do you think you had enough recovery time yesterday to work hard today?

- Are you psyched to run these 200s in under 35?

- Did you like that workout? How would you change it to make it better?

The runners' answers help the coach determine whether the training objectives are being met and whether runners are enjoying the training and think it's having a positive impact. Most importantly, the answers help coaches adapt the program to avoid negative training experiences. For example, sometimes runners just don't feel up to doing hard training—maybe they had to stay up late studying the night before, or maybe they've got a cold coming on. Coaches who take the time to ask runners how they're feeling and to listen carefully to the responses can help steer them away from detours. As another example, runners may express a strong dislike for a certain method of training because they feel it isn't helping. If the coach forces runners to continue using the method, without discussing it, the dislike may lead to burnout. All it takes to get a good sense of whether you're on the right path is a simple question asked regularly: How do you feel?

Evaluating Racing Performance: The Ultimate Test of an Effective Training Program

The ultimate test of an effective training program is whether runners are performing up to their capabilities and improving in races. Racing performances are measures of runners' physical and mental fitness as well as their general health. If runners are performing well, expressing enjoyment and motivation, and experiencing good health, there's no need to make any changes in their programs other than progressively increasing their training loads. As the expression goes, "If it ain't broke, don't fix it!" If, however, the runners' performances and health aren't up to par, the coach must search for reasons and revise their training programs to correct problems.

What should coaches look for in runners who aren't racing up to their potential? Let's first examine runners who shine in training sessions but then flicker out in races. For these runners, psychological factors such as nervousness, lack of confidence, poor concentration, or ineffective tactics are likely limiting competitive performance. To figure out the source of the problem, the coach must become a detective of sorts:

- Is the runner tight and anxious before the race starts? Maybe he's nervous.

- Does the runner truly believe that she can achieve her goal? Maybe she lacks confidence.

- Does the runner fall behind on uphill sections of cross-country courses? Maybe he's not concentrating on the right cues for good uphill running technique.

- Does the runner finish the race with too much energy left? Maybe she isn't pacing herself properly.

Having asked these kinds of questions, the coach can adapt the training program to focus on helping the runner develop specific aspects of mental fitness that need improvement.

Another scenario is one in which a runner has a high level of mental fitness but simply lacks the physical fitness to achieve his goals. This case is evident in competitions where the runner starts out on goal pace and in good position but slows and fades markedly as the races goes on. If the coach's evaluation doesn't indicate low levels of mental fitness, the explanation is likely that the runner is not physically prepared. Assessment of recent training sessions may bear out this conclusion. The coach should carefully examine records of these sessions to see whether the athlete has conditioned his body for the physical demands of racing. Let's say, for example, that Vijay's goal is

to break 2:10 for 800 meters, but he has struggled to run just 2:16. A careful review of Vijay's recent training shows that he has been far from hitting goal times in specialized endurance workouts. For example, the fastest 400-meter repetition he has run in training has been only 67 seconds, a 2:14-pace for an 800-meter race. And he has only done a few workouts with 200-meter repetitions that were faster than race pace. A clear reason for Vijay's disappointing racing performances exists: He simply has not prepared his body for running under 2:10. Remember, it's vital for coaches to keep records of daily training so they can make this type of assessment.

Another source of poor performance is health problems such as injuries and common colds or more severe illnesses. Almost every runner gets injured and has to cut back on training at one time or another. Of course, if the injury is severe and causes the runner to stop training for long periods, her racing performance will suffer. Good coaches carefully evaluate whether the training program itself is responsible for injuries. For example, impact-related injuries such as stress fractures are often linked to running long distances on hard surfaces. Lack of flexibility, resulting from lack of stretching, may cause muscle strains. Furthermore, many injuries can result from increasing advanced, high-intensity training loads sharply when the runner doesn't have a strong fitness base. If coaches systematically and thoroughly ask questions about what might have caused an injury, they may find that some aspect of the training program is responsible. Then they can eliminate the harmful aspect of training or add methods that counteract it. For the runner who gets injured frequently, evaluation of the training program should be made with the help of a physician who specializes in sport injuries.

Several factors can cause illness in runners. Overtraining can weaken the body's immune system, making it susceptible to illness, such as colds and the flu. Nothing is more frustrating than racing when you're recovering from an illness. You've lost valuable training time and it's hard to get motivated, especially if you're still feeling under the weather. In addition to overtraining, several other factors can lead to illness. These include poor nutrition, inadequate sleep, emotional stress, and exposure to people with contagious diseases. To help avoid this setback in the future, the coach should work with runners to determine which factors might cause them to become sick. For example, some individuals get colds when they cut back on their normal sleeping hours. Others get sick with changes in the weather as the seasons turn. Successful coaches look for patterns in runners' repeated illnesses, and cut back on training when susceptibility is high.

A fine line exists between being in top racing shape and being sick or injured. That's because the training required to reach the highest levels of fitness drains the body of energy and challenges its defenses. The first step to preventing these setbacks is to keep tabs on how each runner is feeling in training on a daily basis. A scratchy throat, runny nose, or high resting heart rate are indicators that the runner should take it easy and, if necessary, take a day or more off from training. If these are false alarms, and the runner is feeling better after resting, then get back on the training journey right away. Again, the question, "How do you feel?" is a great tool for evaluating how the journey is progressing.

Personal Setbacks

Some teenage athletes fail to reach their goals because of personal setbacks that many teenagers, whether they are athletes or not, experience. Everyone who has been a teenager knows that it's not an easy time of life. Many pressures are involved in doing well in school, fitting in socially, and conforming to parents' expectations. For some young runners, these pressures make it hard to focus during the hour or so that is set aside for training each day. Some runners bring their personal problems to practice, and they become frustrated when these problems interfere with their training and racing performance.

Coaches and parents must be aware of signs that the young runner is having trouble in school, at home, or with friends. Look for personality changes and behaviors that indicate that the athlete is experiencing problems. Perhaps the athlete has become suddenly withdrawn and gets upset easily during training sessions. Or maybe the athlete is missing training sessions altogether. The best advice that we can offer coaches and parents is to keep the lines of communication open with their young runners, so that personal problems can be revealed and dealt with before they interfere with training, school, and social activities.

In addition, it's essential for coaches and parents to help young athletes deal with their personal problems. However, it's extremely risky to counsel teenagers if you don't have training and skill in this area. Problems that adults might view as insignificant, such as breaking up with a boyfriend or girlfriend after dating for only two weeks, can be sources of great emotional disturbance for some teenagers. In addition, teenagers with problems such as chronic depression and eating disorders need more help than coaches and parents can offer. Counseling young athletes with deep personal problems goes beyond the scope of our own training and experience, so we help these athletes by directing them and their families to professional counselors.

Our advice to young runners who are having personal problems is to talk with your coaches and parents, or to go directly to your school's counselor for help. We know that sometimes it's hard to talk about things that trouble you. But if you really want to do your best in running, you've got to be able to concentrate on your training.

That means dealing with negative distractions and behaviors that make it hard to concentrate. All elite runners know that it takes a team effort—made up of the athlete, coach, family, and health professional, to reach their potentials. Sometimes, however, it's the athlete's responsibility to get the team together by asking for help.

CHANGES FOR THE BETTER: REVISING THE TRAINING PROGRAM

Part of the great challenge and fun of planning training and coaching runners is adjusting the program to account for individual differences and to meet individual needs. This is the art of coaching. It requires creativity and flexibility in the process of steering runners toward their goals. These are essential coaching skills because, as we've been discussing in this chapter, the road to the runner's goals can have many potholes and detours. In this section we'll talk about strategies for avoiding potential setbacks in training and for getting back on course should they occur. We'll also discuss strategies for purposefully taking runners off the planned course to make training interesting and fun.

Getting Back on Course After Detours in Training

Table 12.1 summarizes several reasons for training detours and presents strategies for getting back on course after unfortunate circumstances.

Table 12.1 Strategies for Revising the Program: Detours and Setbacks in Training

Potential detours and setbacks	Ways to get back on course
The program inadvertently violates developmental guidelines and objectives.	• Look for signs of overtraining and undertraining. • Identify inappropriate methods. • Cut back on loads that are excessive; add to loads of developmentally appropriate methods.
The actual training load deviates from planned loads.	• Evaluate training loads on a weekly basis and adjust if necessary; don't move on to advanced training without a solid base.
The runner doesn't meet the objectives for intensity in a given session.	• Use target heart rates and running times to set the right intensity.
The runner has a cold, upset stomach, or other illness.	• Take time off from training until health *completely* returns. • See the family physician for treatment.
The runner is injured.	• Take time off from training until injury *completely* heals. • See the school's athletic trainer or the family physician for treatment. • Use supplemental training methods if possible (swimming, cycling, water running, circuit or weight training).
The runner has an "off day."	• Stop the training session and try again in the next few days. • Be positive and upbeat: "It's only a bad day. We'll make up for it." • Seek the source of problem to eliminate it in the future.

For example, a major setback in training occurs when the program inadvertently violates developmental guidelines and objectives. Even when a coach has thought very carefully about a runner's developmental status, it's sometimes hard to account for the types and amounts of training that will best suit each runner. One runner may not be able to handle much high-intensity interval training, while another runner who is the same chronological and training age might thrive on this type of training.

How can coaches adjust the program when methods and loads aren't helping an individual? First, look for signs of overtraining and undertraining. Overtraining means doing excessive amounts of stressful work that break the body down so that it can't recover normally, that is, within a few days. The signs of overtraining include long-lasting fatigue and muscle soreness, injury, illness, difficulty falling asleep at night and waking in the morning, altered mood states, and loss of motivation. The key signs of undertraining are a lack of progress in workouts that are easy for the runner to complete and failure to improve in races. A runner who is undertraining is simply not challenged physically and mentally by workouts.

If a coach finds out that overtraining or undertraining is the root of a setback in the program, she must identify the inappropriate methods and make adjustments accordingly. For example, consider a runner whose training age is one year and who complains of muscle soreness for several days after doing anaerobic endurance work. To avoid the major detour of a serious injury, the amount of this type of training should be cut back. If the coach has planned for it to account for 5 percent of the total load in a given phase, she might cut back to 1 or 2 percent or eliminate the method altogether if necessary. Then, over the next few seasons and years, this form of high-intensity work can be increased as the runner matures and becomes better conditioned to handle it.

Training programs can also be developmentally inappropriate if they lack sufficient amounts of work with key methods. For example, consider the runner who handles and recovers from high-intensity training easily. This runner might benefit from increasing the contribution of such specialized methods, especially if he isn't improving in races. For another runner, our recommendations in tables 10.1 and 10.2 (pages 145 and 146) for the contribution of fundamental methods, such as strength endurance and technique work, may not be enough. If a coach sees that a runner is not improving in these areas, he might consider progressively increasing the training loads for these methods.

As we've discussed, another setback occurs when the actual training load deviates from planned loads. Let's reconsider the case of the runner who had to skip a circuit training session during the week to work on a school project. At the end of the week, the coach evaluates the contribution of strength endurance to this runner's program and finds that it falls short of the planned load. For just one workout the coach might not make any adjustments to upcoming training. If, however, the runner misses several sessions— especially if the cause is injury or illness, the coach is faced with a dilemma about which road to take when the runner is able to train again. Should the coach skip over the lost training completely and advance the runner to where his teammates are? Should he pick up where he left off and try to catch up? Or should he go back to the start of the training journey and build a base again?

The answers to these questions depend on how much training the runner has missed and how much fitness he has lost. No firm guidelines for determining how to get back on course after missing training exist. Generally speaking, however, the more fitness lost, the closer you must go back to the start of the training journey, using fundamental methods such as general aerobic endurance and strength endurance, to rebuild a base. The danger of advancing a runner to where he would have been had he not missed training is that he won't be able to handle the advanced loads and might suffer an injury or illness in the process. To help the runner who has missed training get back on track, coaches must evaluate progress and plan training on a day-to-day basis. In this case, the coach can't rely on the road map you designed weeks ago. The coach has to plan her journey daily, after finding out whether the athlete is in good enough shape to travel.

We recommend that runners who are ill or injured take time off from training until they're *completely* recovered (see table 12.1). It's simply

Joan Nesbit

Chapel Hill, NC

Personal Bests:

3,000 meters	8:51.14
5,000 meters	15:24.35
10,000 meters	32:04.02

© 1995 Tim De Frisco

When Joan Nesbit was a 16-year-old high school sophomore, she ran 6:04 in the mile and qualified for the Alabama state track and field championships. "But my coach wouldn't let me run in the meet unless I could do 12 laps around the track without stopping," she explains. "I started with 1 lap and added another each day until I did 12. I looked at it as a fun challenge, and when I accomplished my goal I felt like running was my friend for life."

Running has been a good friend to Joan for nearly 20 years now. After moving to North Carolina for her last two years of high school, Joan ran 5:06 in the mile to win the state championship in her senior year. She earned a scholarship to the University of North Carolina at Chapel Hill, where she was a three-time NCAA all-American from 1980 to 1984. Continuing to improve over the years, Joan had her best year in 1995 at age 34, when she finished third in the 3,000 meters at the World Indoor Track Championships and sixth at the World Cross-Country Championships, and won the U.S. Cross-Country Championships.

Added to being a world-class athlete, Joan is a wife and mother. And she's a successful coach of the men's and women's cross-country and track teams at her alma mater, the University of North Carolina.

Joan attributes part of her success to being flexible in her training when a change is necessary. For example, in 1990 she suffered plantar fasciitis, a painful foot injury, which kept her from running for a few months: So Joan swam her workouts. Today, swimming is a regular part of her training. On the days she schedules hard running sessions in the afternoon, Joan swims a hard workout in the morning. Then, the day after demanding running sessions, she swims easily for recovery.

"Some runners don't improve because they are not willing to revise their programs. They just stick with the same system," Joan says. To keep improving, Joan thinks, it's necessary to add variety to daily training sessions. "I don't like repetition, so I never do the same workout in the same way twice. If I run a hill workout once a week for 12 weeks, I'll do it on 12 different hills."

Joan's philosophy about revising her own training also applies to the college runners she coaches. "If an athlete looks tired on the third rep of an interval session, I might have her sit out the fourth rep and then let her run the fifth one. This way, she can finish the workout with her confidence high. But, it takes a lot of honesty and open communication between athlete and coach to make the right adjustments."

When things don't go so well for her athletes or her, Joan focuses on finding the cause of the problems. "A good coach searches for reasons, not excuses," Joan puts it. This is a philosophy she learned from her former adviser, Great Britain's Harry Wilson, one of the top endurance coaches in the world.

Joan advises beginners to enjoy running and never give up on training and racing. These are the two most important lessons she learned as a beginner. Remembering her early achievement of finishing 12 laps without stopping, Joan also urges young runners to see running as a challenge and friend, and not to let anyone pressure them. "Let running be for you" is Joan Nesbit's motto.

too risky for young runners to train when they're not in optimal health because the added stress of training can make the injury or illness worse. In the case of certain injuries, however, it's possible to keep training with methods that supplement running in order to maintain fitness. For example, runners with knee pain will make their injuries worse if they continue to run. But they can maintain a high level of cardiovascular and muscle fitness by swimming and doing upper body circuit training.

In addition, some leg and foot injuries that keep you from running are not at all affected by activities such as cycling and deep water running. For deep water running, the athlete mimics the running action while suspended in deep water by a floatation vest. Cycling and deep water running sessions can elevate the heart rate for prolonged periods, so they're great for maintaining general aerobic fitness. The key to using these supplemental methods is to work at an effort level that keeps heart rate in the range of around 65 to 75 percent of maximum. For injured runners, the best duration of supplemental training depends on their familiarity with the exercise. For example, injured runners who have never done deep water running might start out with only 10 or 15 minutes a day and gradually build up to a duration that approaches their longest continuous aerobic run. Runners who are accustomed to riding bicycles can start cycling at 30 minutes or more.

While recovering from injuries, runners shouldn't be pressured to do much high-intensity supplemental training. They might suffer a new injury from overtraining with unfamiliar activities. If they were in good shape before the running injury occurred, it takes a long time to lose fitness. So to return to training safely, be patient and maintain general aerobic fitness.

Of course, the best advice for getting back on course after an injury is to seek medical treatment as soon as possible. But when the runner returns to training, coaches must revise the program to prevent injuries from reoccurring. This might include more running on soft surfaces, more stretching, more recovery days between demanding sessions, and extra attention to fundamental methods to lay a better foundation for advanced training.

Another troublesome detour in training is failing to meet objectives for intensity. Usually, this means running too fast or too slow, missing out on the intended training effect. Let's reconsider the case of the runner whose 3,200-meter goal is to break 10:00. In a session of 3 × 1,000 meters, he is shooting for 3:05 to 3:10, a range that closely approaches his race pace of 3:07. What should the coach do if the runner struggles to hit 3:10 on the first repetition, and then fades to over 3:20 on the last two repetitions? It might be necessary to change the workout on the spot if the runner has lost form and is overly fatigued. In this case, if the coach senses that the struggling runner can't complete the last two repetitions in 3:05 to 3:10, he could shorten the distance of these repetitions from 1,000 to 800 or 600 meters. Then in future sessions for developing specialized endurance, the coach might either shorten the distance of each repetition or make the runner's goal times slower. This might mean going back to revise his overall goal of breaking 10:00. In contrast, if this same runner is handling 3:05s easily, his future specialized endurance sessions should have faster goal times. And the runner's racing goal to break 10:00 might be lowered to sub-9:45.

Even though changes to the training program are inevitable to keep runners on course, it's important for coaches to understand that they should not make changes hastily and without careful thought. Sometimes runners veer off course from training plans simply because they have bad days. Typically, the younger the runners in terms of training ages, the more bad days they will experience. Many circumstances may cause disappointing results in a training session: a sleepless night, an upset stomach, a side stitch, bad weather, a demanding test in school, or an argument with a friend. When runners are having really bad days in training, the coach should stop the session and, on a very upbeat and positive note, suggest that they try it again on the next day or within the next few days. It's extremely important to try again so that runners can regain confidence. Still, it doesn't make sense to let young runners fail in achieving training objectives and risk losing confidence, if a good reason for the temporary setback exists. On those days when things aren't going very well, the coach should seek the source of the problem, let runners know that it's only a bad day, and try to eliminate that problem in the future.

DEALING WITH SIDE STITCHES

One of the most common reasons for setbacks in training and racing is a side stitch, or a sharp pain just under the ribs, typically on the right side of the body. Exercise scientists are stumped about the cause of side stitches; however, they have found some clues to the mystery.

• First, stitches tend to occur in runners who are just starting to train and are relatively unfit. It's possible that these runners get stitches because their respiratory or breathing muscles (the diaphragm and muscles attached to the ribs) fatigue and cramp due to insufficient blood flow and oxygen delivery. Like the leg muscles, the respiratory muscles work very hard during high-intensity running, and stitches seem to occur when runners breathe vigorously. Because highly fit runners tend to experience fewer stitches, it's possible that they have conditioned their breathing muscles to receive and use more oxygenated blood. Thus, one key to getting rid of stitches is to improve your fitness with progressive increases in training.

• Second, stitches tend to occur in runners who train soon after drinking a lot of water or eating. Food and water in the stomach can cause pressure that triggers pain by pulling on muscle and connective tissue. A solution to this problem is to allow several hours for food to digest before training and racing. However, don't avoid drinking water just to prevent a stitch—you could risk dehydration. In the hours before training and racing, drink several small cups of water rather than one or two large cups.

Experts recommend that runners who get stitches during training stop, bend over at the waist, and massage the area in which they have pain. Another method is to tighten the abdominal muscles and breathe deeply. At first, this method might worsen the pain, but within a minute or so, the stitch might go away. The best approach to getting rid of the pain is to stop running. No runner, however, likes to stop during a race. So during races, runners should try bending over slightly and massaging the affected area while breathing in and out deeply. If the pain gets severe, the runner should slow down and, if necessary, walk until the pain goes away. If the pain from a side stitch persists over several days, the runner should seek medical attention because of the possibility of a strained or torn muscle or connective tissue in the abdomen.

Getting Back on Course After Detours in Racing

The primary reason for setbacks and detours in races is a lack of physical and mental fitness. As we've discussed, some runners who are clearly in great shape physically—as indicated by impressive training sessions—fall short of their racing goals because they lack mental fitness. Table 12.2 lists some general strategies for getting these runners back on course. First, coaches must evaluate each runner for specific weaknesses in mental fitness. Then, the coach can design training and racing experiences to improve mental fitness in those weak areas. Let's consider the case of Julia, a runner who has been getting nervous before races and who has not been performing up to par. Julia's coach notices that she is normally relaxed, talkative, and playful before her everyday training sessions, which have been very successful lately. But, on race days, she isolates herself from teammates and takes on a serious attitude. Sensing that Julia might be putting too much pressure on herself before races, her coach suggests that she hang out, warm up, and joke around with her teammates to help her relax. Julia and her coach agree to try this plan for one race. As it turns out, being around teammates before the race helps Julia relax and forget about being nervous, enabling her to race faster than ever before.

If a lack of confidence is the source of a shortcoming in mental fitness, the coach might tailor training sessions to ensure successful outcomes because, as we discussed in chapter 4, success in training breeds confidence. This might mean making goal times for repetitions in interval sessions easy to reach. Or the coach might prescribe sessions that the runner enjoys and always seems to master. In addition, a coach should bolster the athlete's confidence by reminding him about recent workouts and races that went well. Other training changes for improving mental fitness might include extra attention to relaxation techniques, more work on pacing control, and time set aside for visualization of successful racing outcomes.

Table 12.2 Strategies for Revising the Program: Detours and Setbacks in Racing	
Potential detours and setbacks	**Ways to get back on course**
The runner is physically fit but not mentally fit.	• Evaluate elements of mental fitness: confidence, concentration, pacing or tactical skill, relaxation, anxiety or fear, and motivation. • Design training and racing experiences to improve mental fitness in specific weak areas.
The runner lacks physical fitness.	• Evaluate elements of physical fitness: technique, strength endurance, general and specialized aerobic endurance, and anaerobic endurance. • Evaluate recent training sessions to determine whether they simulate racing demands. • Design training to improve specific weak areas and stress the body to meet racing demands.
The runner is injured or ill.	• Hold off on racing until *completely* recovered and healthy. • Stay on treatment and therapy schedules; use supplemental training methods if possible.
The runner has an "off day."	• Seek the source of problem to eliminate it in the future. • Use poor performance as a source of motivation to do better next time. • Put running in its proper perspective. • Race again as soon as possible. • Try not to drop out of the race.

Evaluation of weaknesses and changes in training to eliminate them are also the keys to getting a runner back on course when she lacks the physical fitness needed to attain her racing goals. In this case, the coach must systematically analyze the racing performances to detect weak areas. Perhaps the runner's form falls apart in the last half of the race. This would indicate that she needs to work on strength endurance and technique. Maybe the runner can't respond to midrace surges and finishing sprints. She probably needs more varied-pace training that stresses the fast-twitch muscle fibers and anaerobic energy pathways. In many cases, a runner falls short of competition goals because she simply has not conditioned her body to handle the specific physiological demands of racing. Previously, we presented the case of Vijay, who is shooting for a sub-2:10 800-meter time, but hasn't been able to go under 2:16. Vijay starts out on 2:10-pace for the first 200 or 300 meters, then fatigues, slowing down over the last half of the race. After reviewing Vijay's recent training sessions, his coach discovers that he hasn't covered much distance at race pace or faster in training. To get back on course, Vijay's coach should increase the volume of training at race pace and faster.

It's important to emphasize, however, that any drastic changes in the training program during the competition period could result in overtraining and injury. Thus, rather than trying to catch up by assigning heavy loads of advanced training during the racing season, the coach should progressively increase advanced loads, perhaps revising performance goals to bring them within safe reach. Again, flexibility is an important key to effective goal setting; it's okay to revise a goal after it has been set in the early steps of planning the program. It's better to change a goal to make it attainable rather than to risk not attaining the goal or overtraining to achieve it. For Vijay, this might mean adjusting his goal for this season from 2:10 to 2:13. Maybe next season he can shoot for 2:08 or 2:09.

Injury and illness are other reasons for setbacks during races. As we advised in our discussion of training setbacks, we strongly urge injured and ill young runners to wait until they are completely recovered and healthy before they compete. It's not worth risking an additional setback due, for example, to reinjuring a strained muscle or making a cold worse. In many cases, for runners who race when they're not at their best, the setback is psychological in nature. Poor performance leads to a loss of confidence and anxiety about upcoming competitions. So the best advice for runners on the "injury-illness detour" is to seek medical attention, stay on treatment and therapy schedules for a speedy recovery, and maintain basic fitness by using supplemental training methods if possible.

Probably the most common reason for disappointing performances in distance running is an "off day." Sometimes, an obvious reason exists when runners have bad races. As in the case of off days in training, the key to preventing them in races is to seek the source of the problem. If you have an upset stomach and a side stitch, perhaps you ate too soon before competing. A painful blister that makes you slow down could be due to wearing a new pair of spikes without first breaking them in. Perhaps you feel tired before the race started because you didn't sleep well the night before due to nervousness. Once you have an idea of what caused an off day, you can devise a plan for eliminating the problem in the future. To avoid the side stitch, you should try eating an hour earlier. To prevent blisters, make sure to wear new shoes a few times in training before you race in them. To be fresh and well-rested on race day, take your mind off racing the night before by watching television or reading a favorite book—preferably one that isn't about running! Or listen to relaxing music before you go to sleep.

Often, you can find no obvious reason for what went wrong in a race. You're healthy, fit, and have been training well. You feel great before the race starts. But during the race, it all falls apart, and you can find no clear explanation for the disappointing result. This is a scenario that all elite adult runners experience many times in their careers. Successful runners and coaches take advantage of these disappointments to get back on course for future races. How can a bad race put

you back on track? If you use poor performance as a source of commitment to do your best in the next race, you can raise your level of motivation and determination to succeed. Coaches: repair the emotional wounds of bad races as quickly as possible and direct the runner's focus to the next race. It's important for the runner to race again as soon as possible after unexplained off days. You don't want to allow doubts about your fitness and ability to build when there's likely no reason for the uncertainty.

Sometimes runners have a few unexplained bad races in a row. From our own experiences as young runners, we know well the disappointment that comes from this sort of a setback. But we also see in this scenario an opportunity for coaches and parents to help young runners put athletics into its proper perspective. When young runners realize that the sun will come up tomorrow and that the coach, family, and friends will be there with encouragement, it's a wonderful lesson about sport and about life. Young runners who love to train and race have many sessions and competitions to look forward to down the road. Bad races are just temporary detours along the way.

One last bit of advice about setbacks in racing: We think it's important to try to finish every race you start *unless* you suffer an injury or experience pain during the event. Some runners get in the habit of dropping out of races because they're fatigued or they've fallen off pace for a PR. These runners may never fully challenge themselves because the thought of quitting is ever-present. So, even if you have to slow down to a jog on off days, you should try to finish the race. Under no circumstances, however, should coaches or parents encourage runners to finish races when they are experiencing pain and extreme discomfort from an injury, a cramp, or health-threatening responses to very hot or cold weather. If runners insist on finishing a race when their health is in danger, it's the coach's responsibility to physically remove such athletes from races.

Going Off-Course on Purpose for Variety and Fun

Sometimes when you're traveling on a long journey, the most effective and fun way to reach your destination is to venture off on side roads and unpaved paths. It's the same with training for distance running. Sometimes it's worthwhile to experiment with different training methods and doses that deviate from the planned program. Occasional detours that add variety and fun to training are essential to good outcomes because they keep young runners motivated, interested, and engaged. If young runners' experiences are limited simply to completing the assigned workouts every day, week after week and month after month, they will very likely become bored with running and seek out other sports and activities.

For coaches, one key to cultivating plenty of interest in training is to make the program as varied as possible. That means using different training methods, exercises, and drills from day to day. Coaches can avoid the monotony and boredom of training that features long, slow running every day by following our recommendations in chapters 10 and 11 for using various methods to develop all aspects of fitness for running. Another way to add variety to training is to change the venue and environment as often as possible. For example, coaches can plan training runs on different courses with varying ter-

rain. Or coaches might hold circuit training sessions in different parks from week to week. To make interval sessions on the track more interesting, coaches can have runners reverse direction, and make right-hand instead of left-hand turns, on certain repetitions. Or coaches can start repetitions in odd places on the track such as in the middle of curves or at the top of the straightaway, instead of at the standard start-finish line.

Every so often, coaches should surprise their athletes with a change in plans that spices up the day's training. For example, instead of announcing ahead of time that the team will do its continuous aerobic run on the beach (a 10-mile drive from school) the coach might just show up at practice that day with a van and pile everyone in. Or, on a day scheduled for an interval tempo session, the coach might change the workout to a controlled fartlek just for variety. Coaches might even surprise the team on one or two days in every macrocycle by canceling practice altogether and taking the team to the movies or to a museum.

Of course, training methods that are inherently fun should be a regular part of the program. Especially in the general preparation phase, coaches should include games, such as basketball, soccer, ultimate Frisbee, and keep-away, several times each week for developing mobility and endurance, but also just for fun. What about training methods that aren't necessarily inherently fun, such as recovery sessions on days following demanding workouts? Coaches can turn potentially boring sessions into exciting ones by adding variety and making them playful. For example, on a recovery day during the spring, runners can go for a swim in a local pond or river, or they can go for a mountain bike ride. In winter, a recovery session might be 20 minutes of cross-country skiing. If the recovery session is an easy 20-minute run, the whole team can run together, talking and joking around along the way. If the course goes through a park, you can play a game that awards points to the runner who first spots a chipmunk, sparrow, deer, or other animal that might appear. If the course goes through an urban neighborhood, you might substitute different makes and colors of cars for different animals.

Sometimes experienced coaches and runners unexpectedly change training and racing plans on a hunch that a detour might lead to a breakthrough. For example, the coach might postpone a key specialized endurance session until the next day if the wind is blowing hard on the day that the session is scheduled. A 1,500-meter runner might abandon a racing plan to sit and kick over the last 300 meters if she feels strong and has energy to surge and break up the field with 800 meters to go. You should act on these hunches every so often because they might be shortcuts on the road to your goals. Then again, they might take you on detours that are miles and miles off course! But you can learn important lessons from such detours if you keep track of how you veered off course and avoid those roads in the future.

Above all, the most important feature of the training program is an atmosphere of fun because, without it, young runners won't be motivated to improve themselves through hard work and dedication. Coaches and parents foster this atmosphere when they adopt the philosophy that youth sport is about doing your best and enjoying the journey on the road to self-improvement. When they're not pressured to win, young athletes are truly motivated by the challenge of this journey. Still, they want to have fun along the way. Successful coaches and parents realize these aspects of motivation and use their creativity to make sure that training and competitive experiences are challenging and fun.

Coaches who follow the guidelines that we have presented for designing and adapting training will surely challenge their young runners with sessions that develop physical and mental fitness. But, as complex as designing training can be, it can sometimes be relatively easy compared to creating an atmosphere of fun and enjoyment. These key elements of the training program require plenty of thought and ingenuity on a daily basis. Our advice to coaches who want to add more fun to daily training is to listen carefully to your athletes to find out what they enjoy most about running and about their lives as teenagers. Maybe they'd like it if you played popular music over the speaker system at the track every once in a while. They'd surely enjoy dressing up in running costumes on special holidays such as Halloween and St. Patrick's Day; they'd like to see you in costume, too! They enjoy team parties and awards banquets where everyone is recognized. Your runners rely on you to build team morale and

camaraderie with these sorts of special experiences and events that add excitement to their training.

SUMMARY

No training program is perfect when it's first planned. To successfully adapt their program to keep runners on course toward their goals, coaches must ask, "How's the training going?" on a daily and weekly basis. Let's review some key strategies for staying on course:

- When evaluating each runner's training process on a daily and weekly basis, identify and eliminate training methods that aren't improving fitness or that are causing injury. In contrast, add methods that are developmentally appropriate and are helping the runner build a strong foundation of fitness and skill.

- If actual training loads deviate from planned loads because the runner misses key workouts, adjust upcoming sessions so that she gains the missing element of fitness. Don't skip over fundamental training methods to get to advanced training.

- Runners who are injured or ill should seek medical attention and wait until they are completely recovered and healthy before training and racing again.

- Every runner experiences off days in training and racing. Examine these experiences to discover the source of the problem and to eliminate it in the future. Remember, don't let disappointments get you down. They can be the source of tremendous motivation to do better next time.

- Every so often, take purposeful detours on the journey to achieving performance goals by adding creativity and fun to the training program.

We congratulate you on your efforts to learn about training for young distance runners and to apply the science of distance running to the artistry of coaching, parenting, and, for you who are young runners—running itself. We leave you with one last bit of advice for ensuring successful and safe training journeys in the future: Keep asking for directions! You can always learn and apply more about training. As sport science and training theory evolve, so too will new ideas and training methods for you to learn about and consider applying to your own program to make it even better.

By reading books and running magazines, attending clinics, and discussing ideas and strategies with others who share your interest, you will be rewarded in many ways. If you are a coach, you'll experience the incredible satisfaction of helping young athletes achieve their goals. In addition, your own experience will be enriched because you'll be engaged in an exciting discourse among other coaches and sport scientists about the best methods for developing young runners. Perhaps you'd like to learn more about exercise physiology. Or maybe you want to set up a computer system for keeping training records and tracking your athletes' progress. To advance your coaching skills, you'll need to keep seeking knowledge about training for young runners.

If you are a parent, you'll do a great service to your child by learning more about nutrition, the effects of training on maturation and growth, and other areas that influence the young runner's health. If your child's experiences in distance running are positive ones, they have tremendous potential for establishing behaviors and values that will contribute to a lifetime of good health. It's your responsibility, along with the coach and family physician, however, to ensure that your child has good experiences in training and competition. To meet this responsibility, you'll need to continue learning about youth distance running.

If you are a young runner, you should realize that learning more about distance running is the key to progressing and developing in future years. To direct beginners, the coach takes the wheel on the training journey. But as you gain experience over the years, you should also gain more control over your own training program. After all, who knows better than you about what's working in training and what's not working at all? As an advanced runner, you can learn about your body and how it responds to training and racing, and you can share some of the responsibility of directing the journey with your coach. When you and your coach work together in this way, you increase your potential for success. Most importantly, if you are committed to learning more about running, you'll gain knowledge and experience that will be the source of a lifetime of good health.

We wish you all success in your journey in youth distance running. Perhaps our paths will cross along the way!

References

Berning, J.R., and S.N. Steen. 1991. *Sports nutrition for the 90s: The health professional's handbook.* Gaithersburg, MD: Aspen.

Brooks, G.A., T.D. Fahey, and T.P. White. 1995. *Exercise Physiology: Human Bioenergetics and Its Applications.* Mountain View, CA: Mayfield.

Burke, E.J., and F.C. Brush. 1979. Physiological and anthropometric assessment of successful teenage female distance runners. *Research Quarterly* 50: 180-187.

Butts, N.K. 1982. Physiological profiles of high school female cross country runners. *Research Quarterly* 53: 8-14.

Clark, N. 1990. *Nancy Clark's sports nutrition guidebook.* Champaign, IL: Leisure Press.

Cooper Institute for Aerobics Research. 1994. *The Prudential Fitnessgram test administration manual.* Dallas: Author.

Cunningham, L.N. 1990. Physiologic comparison of adolescent female and male cross country runners. *Pediatric Exercise Science* 2: 313-321.

Daniels, J.T. 1985. A physiologists's view of running economy. *Medicine and Science in Sports and Exercise* 3: 161-165.

Gatorade Sports Science Institute and U.S. Swimming. *The swimmer's diet: Eating for peak performance.* Chicago: Gatorade Sports Science Institute.

Human Kinetics. 1996. *Practical body composition kit.* Champaign, IL: Author.

Kraemer, W.J., and S.J. Fleck. 1993. *Strength training for young athletes.* Champaign, IL: Human Kinetics.

Leger, D., D. Mercier, and L. Gauvin. 1986. The relationship between % $\dot{V}O_2$max and running performance time. In *Sport and Elite Performers*, edited by D.M. Landers. Champaign, IL: Human Kinetics.

Martin, D.E., and P.N. Coe. 1991. *Training distance runners.* Champaign, IL: Human Kinetics.

Maud, P.J., and C. Foster. 1995. *Physiological assessment of human fitness.* Champaign, IL: Human Kinetics.

Noakes, T. 1991. *Lore of running.* Champaign, IL: Leisure Press.

Pate, R.R. and D.S. Ward. 1990. Endurance exercise and trainability in children and youth. In *Advances in sports medicine and fitness*, edited by W.A. Grana. Chicago: Year Book Medical.

Péronnet, F., and G. Thibault, 1989. Mathematical analysis of running performance and world running records. *Journal of Applied Physiology* 67:453-465.

Sizer, F.S., and E.N. Whitney. 1994. *Hamilton and Whitney's nutrition: Concepts and controversy.* 6th ed. Minneapolis/St. Paul: West.

Sundberg, S., and R. Elovainio. 1982. Cardiorespiratory function in competitive endurance runners aged 12-16 years compared with ordinary boys. *Acta Paediatrica Scandinavica* 71: 987-992.

Tulloh, B. 1995. Running through the years. *Runner's World* (British edition) (November):45-46.

Index

About the Authors

Larry Greene knows all about the challenges facing young runners. During high school, he was the Florida state champion in cross-country in 1977 and in the 2-mile run in 1978. He also finished 10th in the National Junior Olympic Cross-Country Meet as a senior. Greene's high school accomplishments earned him a scholarship to Florida State University, where he set the school record for the indoor 3,000-meter run and qualified for the NCAA Championship Meet three times.

After college, Greene competed and excelled as a distance runner. In 1984 he ran the fastest half-marathon in the world and finished 4th in the 10,000-meter run at the U.S. Track and Field Championships. In 1987 he finished 3rd in the half-marathon at the U.S. Olympic Festival.

Greene is an instructor of scientific writing and motor behavior in the Department of Kinesiology at the University of Colorado at Boulder. He received an MS in movement science from Florida State University in 1988 and a PhD in exercise science from the University of South Carolina in 1993. A former cross-country and track coach, Greene served as the director of the Carolina Marathon Youth Cross-Country Run from 1990 to 1993. His leisure interests include running, hiking, and mountain biking.

Russ Pate has been an exercise physiology instructor and researcher since 1972. He is also a lifelong distance runner. Pate has a personal best time of 2:15:20 in the marathon, plus he has competed in the marathon at three U.S. Olympic Trials. A professor in and chair of the Department of Exercise Science at the University of South Carolina, Pate's research has focused primarily on the relationship between physical activity and health in children and adolescents.

Pate has served as president of the American College of Sports Medicine (ACSM) and as chairman of the Physical Fitness Council of the American Alliance for Health, Physical Education, Recreation and Dance. He has also been recognized with Scholar Awards from both organizations. In addition, he is a member of the North American Society of Pediatric Exercise Medicine.

Pate received a PhD in exercise physiology from the University of Oregon in 1974. He received the T.K. Cureton Award, presented by the National Fitness Leaders Association, in 1995, and in 1996 he received the ACSM's Citation Award. In his free time, Pate enjoys running, traveling, and spending time with his kids.

Joe Henderson

Foreword by Jeff Galloway

1996 • Paperback
264 pp • Item PHEN0866
ISBN 0-87322-866-9
$15.95 ($22.95 Canadian)

Michael Sandrock

Foreword by Kenny Moore

1996 • Paperback
592 pp • Item PSAN0493
ISBN 0-87322-493-0
$19.95 ($29.95 Canadian)

In *Better Runs*, Henderson shares what he and others have learned about running over the past quarter century. Both inspirational and instructional, this book will boost your motivation, performance, and enjoyment as a runner. It's filled with anecdotes and insights on training, racing, and much, much more.

Running with the Legends details the development, training techniques, coaching, competitions, motives, and perspectives of 21 all-time great runners.

This book is full of material to enhance your own running and your appreciation of those who have set the standard for excellence.

**Lyle J. Micheli, MD
with Mark Jenkins**

1996 • Paperback
264 pp • Item PMIC0524
ISBN 0-88011-524-6
$16.95 ($24.95 Canadian)

Timothy D. Noakes, MD

*Foreword by
George Sheehan, MD*

1991 • Hardback • 832 pp
Item PNOA0437
ISBN 0-88011-437-1
$30.00 ($44.95 Canadian)

1991 • Paperback
832 pp • Item PNOA0438
ISBN 0-88011-438-X
$22.95 ($32.95 Canadian)

Healthy Runner's Handbook shows runners how to diagnose, care for, and rehabilitate 31 common overuse injuries, plus it provides useful advice on how to prevent such injuries.

Lore of Running combines personal experience and professional knowledge with important research findings. It covers everything from physiology, training, and history to health and medical considerations. Noakes presents comprehensive information that is firmly based on science, but is written in a down-to-earth way that every reader can understand.

HUMAN KINETICS
The Premier Publisher for Sports & Fitness
www.humankinetics.com

2335